WHY I STAND

FROM FREEDOM TO THE KILLING FIELDS OF SOCIALISM

BURGESS OWENS

AUTHOR OF *LIBERALISM OR HOW TO TURN GOOD MEN INTO WHINERS, WEENIES AND WIMPS*

Post Hill
PRESS

A POST HILL PRESS BOOK
ISBN: 978-1-68261-739-7
ISBN (eBook): 978-1-68261-740-3

Post Hill Press
New York • Nashville
posthillpress.com

Published in the United States of America

TABLE OF CONTENTS

History/Career 7

I Believe 8

Introduction 10

Chapter 1: American Individualism 11

Chapter 2: The Flag and Why I Stand 15

Why I Stand 18

Chapter 3: The Killing Fields of Socialism 20

Chapter 4: Socialism vs. Capitalism: Which is the Moral System?..................... 30

Chapter 5: The NAACP Strategy: The Trojan Horse................................. 36

Chapter 6: Planned Parenthood: The Sophistry of Margaret Sanger 82

Chapter 7: The Chinese Bamboo Tree 99

Chapter 8: America's Promise..104

Chapter 9: It's All About Team 114

Chapter 10: The Royalty Class Black Man...............................122

Chapter 11: For the Record: The Congressional Black Caucus Vote.............135

Chapter 12: The Davis-Bacon Act..141

Chapter 13: The Big Lie 149

Chapter 14: John Lewis: The Man, the Bridge, the Socialist Hero 158

Chapter 15: James Meredith: The Forgotten/Ignored Civil Rights Pioneer.. 168

Chapter 16: The Royalty Class Black Man: Who's Who......................................172

Chapter 17: The State of President Obama's Black America 206

Chapter 18: The NFL, the Flag, and Globalism..211

Chapter 19: Corporate Globalist: Profits over Patriotism..................................222

Chapter 20: The Solution: "We the People"...249

Chapter 21: The Solution: Chivalry..258

Chapter 22: The Solution: Man-Up/Stand-Up..269

Chapter 23: The Solution: Courage..272

Chapter 24: Black American Conservatives: America's Freedom Sentinels.. 281

Conclusion..284

Acknowledgments..287

About the Author..288

HISTORY/CAREER

Burgess spent his childhood growing up in the Deep South during a time when the barriers of segregation were being torn down. He was the third Black American to be offered a football scholarship at the University of Miami. He earned a Bachelor of Science degree in Biology/Chemistry and simultaneously gained national recognition as a First Team All-American.

During his college career, Burgess was named to *Who's Who Among College Students in American Universities and Colleges*. He was inducted to the Hall of Fame of Outstanding College Athletes of America, and later to the University of Miami's Hall of Fame and the Orange Bowl Ring of Honor. Following college, the New York Jets picked Burgess in the NFL 1st round as the draft's first defensive back, and 13th overall pick. Later that year, he was selected as the Jets "Rookie of the Year" and to the NFL's All-Rookie team. He played with the New York Jets for seven years and was selected as the Defensive Team Captain his last three seasons. After being traded to the Oakland Raiders, Burgess led the Raiders defensive squad in tackles during their championship season and in Super Bowl XV in 1981. In 1982, his final season, he led the Raiders in interceptions and was selected as a First Alternate to the NFL All Pro-Bowl. Since retiring from the NFL, Burgess has been involved in the corporate and entrepreneurial arenas. He travels throughout the country speaking about the blessing of freedom that underlies the foundation of our American way of life. He is the Executive Director for the Utah Chapter of The One Heart Project whose mission is: "To rescue, restore, and rehabilitate youthful offenders, and provide them with a true second chance to experience the American Dream."

Facebook: www.facebook.com/officiallyburgessowens

Twitter: @BurgessOwens

Website: www.BurgessOwensTalks.com

One Heart Utah Website: www.OneHeart.com

I BELIEVE

I believe that my worth is not measured by what I do, by the honors bestowed upon me, or by the material wealth I might obtain. Instead, I am measured by the courage I show while standing for my beliefs, by the dedication I exhibit to ensure my word is good, and the resolve I undertake to establish that my actions and deeds are honorable.

I believe that the principles upon which our country was built are founded on the bedrock of eternal truths; that these truths, when applied, build men and women of character and families with purpose and vision.

I believe that men can be inspired by powers from on high as evidenced by the immortal words penned by our country's Founding Fathers: "*We hold these truths to be self-evident that all men are created equal, that they are endowed by their Creator with certain unalienable Rights; that among these are Life, Liberty, and the pursuit of Happiness.*"

I believe in the concept embodied by the words "*We the People.*" That our country stands as the most unique among all the world's societies because it was not founded on We the Blacks, We the Whites, We the Christians, We the Jews, We the Muslims, We the Buddhists, We the Old, We the Young, We the Rich, or We the Poor, but "WE THE PEOPLE.". Though different, we have, through the power of unity and adherence to concrete core beliefs, found the common thread that defines the American Way.

I believe that a country is no better than its people, and its people are no better than its dream; that the ability to dream, to hope, and to envision the possibilities is among the greatest and most precious gifts. Living in the freest country in the world we owe it to our creator to "*Dream Big.*" It is a gift from a big God.

I believe that success is a matter of choice, not chance. As we choose to control our attitude, we begin to control our actions. As we choose to control our actions, we are choosing to form new habits. As we choose to control our habits, we are choosing to define our character. As we choose to define our character, we begin to choose our destiny and our happiness. Success is therefore a matter of choice, not chance. Your choice.

I believe the impact of our lives will be determined by our courage to have a vision, our wisdom to understand and overcome life's obstacles, and our faith to know that we're meant to be.

I believe that we are in life exactly where we see ourselves. If we want to change our station, we'll have to change our vision and expectations.

I believe that to obtain true success we must not look to the past as if it represents the future. The future is a place of opportunity and where our happiness is forged. Live there and learn to enjoy it there.

I believe only through struggle and persistence can we take advantage of the special talents we have hidden within. It is not the Super Bowl Ring that I wear but the character and resolve I exhibit during the downtimes that defines me as a champion.

I believe failure can be our best friend, if we choose not to quit once we've been formally introduced.

I believe that as "the individual" is empowered with the freedom of choice, self-direction, and financial incentives, he will do all within his power to be the very best that he can be. With every effort toward improvement will come, as a by-product, an increased value to our communities and country.

I believe that we're all created in the image of God, who loves us and has designed each of us to win. Life's struggles, from which no one is exempt, are opportunities to find our better selves. In a land explicitly set aside for freedom, we're only asked to do our best, do it honorably, do it with confidence, with power, and with high expectations. Remember, we are not alone.

"Dream Big."

INTRODUCTION

"Black People Don't Have to Be Democrats."

— *Chance the Rapper*

"The first battlefield is the rewriting of history."

— *Karl Marx, Father of Communism,*
  whose theories are known as Marxism

"You can't make Socialists out of individualists. Children who know how to think for themselves spoil the harmony of the collective society which is coming, where everyone is interdependent."

— *John Dewey, Socialist, Humanist, Atheist,*
  NAACP Board Member, and father of the
  progressive public school system

"By 1905 Tuskegee University [the southern Black college founded in 1885 by Booker T. Washington], produced more self-made millionaires than Harvard, Yale, and Princeton combined."

— *Harvard President, Charles W. Elliott*

"If we forget what we did, we don't know who we are."

— *President Ronald Reagan*

CHAPTER 1

AMERICAN INDIVIDUALISM

"The most precious possession of American civilization."

—Herbert Hoover

After losing his bid for a second term to Franklin Roosevelt in 1932, President Herbert Hoover wrote of his concerns as he witnessed Americans' willingness to accept and implement foreign ideologies that were abhorrent to our American culture. It was this culture that has been deemed by millions from other lands as the most exceptional of any around the world. Hoover highlighted this difference in 1934, when he penned the following:

"Every homecoming is an inspiration. In America is found a greater kindliness, a greater neighborliness, a greater sense of individual responsibility, a lesser poverty, a greater comfort and security of our people, a wider spread of education, a wider diffusion of the finer arts and an appreciation for them, a greater freedom of spirit, a wider opportunity for our children, and higher hopes of the future, than in any other country in the world".[1] How inspirational is this vision of American one-hundred years ago? It has been these same thoughts of optimism and hope that have driven generations from our inception to dream bigger, reach higher, and overcome more in their quest to experience the collective opportunities granted only in a free America. During his extensive worldwide travel from 1914–1920, Hoover and his American Relief Administration delivered food to millions, reorganized the transpor-

---

1   Herbert Hoover, *The Challenge to Liberty*, New York: Charles Scribner's Sons, 1934.

tation and communication networks, and helped check the
advance of a Communist revolution from the East at the end
of WWI. Owing in considerable measure to the herculean ef-
forts of Hoover and his associates, perhaps one-third of the
population of post-war Europe was saved from starvation
and death.[2]

After coming home in 1919, Hoover was concerned about the infection of America by diverse and anti-American European philosophies he considered "social diseases." He implored his fellow citizens not to turn their country into a "laboratory for experiments in foreign social diseases."[3] Instead, he contended that a "definite American substitute is needed for these disintegrating theories of Europe," a substitute grounded in "our national instincts," and "the normal development of our national institutions."[4]

In defining this American substitute, Hoover summarized it as the following:

"The foundation of America's distinctive social philosophy was
the principle of equality of opportunity: the idea that no one
should be handicapped in securing that particular niche in the
community to which his abilities and character entitles him."

Unlike Europe, where oppressive class barriers had generated misery and discontent, the American social system was based on "the negation of class." "A society," said Hoover, "in which there is a constant flux of individuals in the community, upon the basis of ability and character, is a moving virile mass."[5] Such a society was the United States of America. In 1921, as Secretary of Commerce, Hoover distilled his experiences of the America experiment into a book called *American Individualism*. It was during a time in which cauldrons of social philosophies were vying for the minds of the American people; among them were Communism, collectivism, Socialism, syndicalism, Capitalism, autocracy, and elitism. It was against this flush of diverse foreign ideologies that Hoover saw a need to define the American alternative, *"American individualism."* Hoover prized *individual initiative* among the most important character trait that should be stimulated and rewarded. "Progress is almost solely dependent on the few creative minds who create or who carry discoveries to widespread application." But with too much individualism, it

---

2   Herbert Hoover, and George H. Nash, *American Individualism*, New York: Double-
     day, Page & Company, 1922.
3   Herbert Hoover, "The Safety of New-born Democracies," *Forum 62*, December 1919.
4   *Ibid.*
5   Herbert Hoover, inaugural address to AIMME, February 17, 1920.

could run riot, leading to injustice and even tyranny in the form of domination of government and business by the powerful.[6]

The "values of individualism" must therefore be tempered by the firm and fixed ideals of American individualism, an equality of opportunity. Equality of opportunity, "the demand for a fair chance as the basis of American life," was "our most precious social ideal." Hoover insisted that equal opportunity and a "fair chance" for individuals to develop their abilities were the fundamental sources of progress and the impulses behind American civilization for three centuries.[7]

Hoover did not believe that equality of opportunity was automatically self-sustaining in a modern, industrial economy. A certain amount of government regulation and legislation (such as anti-trust laws) was necessary to prevent inequality of opportunity, private economy "autocracy," and the throttling of individual initiative. It was imperative to "keep the social solution free from the frozen strata of classes" that the human particles must be able to move freely in the social solution. This was not, however, doctrinal social Darwinism. In American individualism, he explicitly repudiated *laissez-faire*, which he defined as "every man for himself and evil take the hindmost."

The benefits that thrive with the presence of fairness and the promised rewards of meritocracy are key cornerstones of American individualism. Upon this cornerstone, individuals are empowered by such attributes as initiative, desire, discipline, tenacity, dream power, and grit. They are emboldened with the faith to envision, courage to act, and the tenacity to start anew, until their dreams become a reality. It is this American individualism that is at the center of our nation's fight for its very heart and soul. This fight is not of the divisive nature of race, gender, creed, or religion. It is a battle of competing ideologies…one of truth and freedom, and the other, insidious evil, leading to spiritual, mental, and emotional dependency. It is a fight for respect and acknowledgement of the Judeo-Christian values ensconced in our nation's foundational documents— the Mayflower Compact, the Declaration of Independence, the Bill of Rights, and the Emancipation Proclamation. Highlighted within each is the promise of God's gift of freedom and opportunity. It is against this American Way there stands the destructive and deceitful ideologies of Socialism, Marxism, atheism, and their kissing cousin, liberalism.

Unique to this nation has been its historical commitment to God, allowing for the genesis of a special society where American individualism can be defined. It is a special social system of our own making. We have made it ourselves from materials brought in revolt from conditions in Europe. We have lived it, we constantly improve it, though we have seldom tried to define it. It abhors autocracy and does not argue with it but fights it. It is not Capitalism,

---

6   Herbert Hoover, American Individualism.

7   *Ibid.*

Socialism, syndicalism, or a cross breed of them. The social force in which I'm interested is higher and far more precious a thing than all of these. It springs from the one source of human progress, that everyone shall be given the chance and stimulation for development of the best with which he has been endowed in heart and mind. It is the sole source of progress; it is American individualism."[8]

---

8   *Ibid.*

CHAPTER 2

THE FLAG AND WHY I STAND

The Great Experiment, America, has constructed the greatest civilization the world has ever seen. While it took principles and practices from a variety of other civilizations, the configuration is utterly unique. Never before has man put together such a system which has continuously delivered more freedom, liberty, and prosperity. It is unique in history and remains unique in the world today. As John Quincy Adams stated in 1837: "This organization is an anomaly in the history of the world."

Other successful modern civilizations owe their success to America and are themselves modeled after it, though none have *ever* reached its level of success. The key element of the American experiment was the focus on the *individual*, and the individual's relationship with God. "You're individuals, [the Founding Fathers were] saying to the colonists. You're children of God. You're no longer subject to the king."[9] It was this concept of pride in the "individual's" personal efforts to contribute, via work ethic, tenacity, sacrifice, and devout loyalty that had made the NFL "America's Favorite Pastime.". The NFL's earlier generation of players innately connected pride in their accomplishment, the blessings of good health, mentorship/coaching, and disciplined decisions, with a sense of abundant gratitude—a. gratitude to God, who placed them in a nation that allowed them the freedom to pursue far-reaching dreams and visions, and the opportunity to see them come true. As we enter another season of protest of our country's flag by young, wealthy Black NFL athletes, millions of fans will continue to turn off America's favorite past time. The NFL, whose brand was once one of our country's most uniting, is rapidly re-

---

9   Jim Huntzinger. "How The Gospel Led To American Individualism And Prosper-
     ity." Townhall Finance. n.d., Online edition, sec. Columnists. finance.townhall.
     com/columnists/jimhuntzinger/2018/04/24/how-the-gospel-led-to-american-
     individualism-and-prosperity-n2474065.

branding itself as a divisive one. In a sport where a player's lack of decorum deemed detrimental to the game is met with harsh penalties, like celebrating in the end zone, the NFL's corporate leadership has taken a knee as they allow their platform to be used for political anti-America sentiment.

It is possible that by visiting our past, Americans might gain insight as to why successful Black American athletes feel compelled to kneel as we honor our flag, and why White corporate leaders refuse to take a stand to defend it.

In a world where slavery, totalitarianism, and kingdoms were the accepted norm, the young American experiment was indeed a paradox. Though it was America that introduced to the world game-changing concepts like "We the People" and "We hold these truths to be self-evident, that all men are created equal," it would take another eighty-seven years and over 600,000 American lives to atone for slavery and to begin to align ourselves with our Founders' vision.

Meanwhile, there was another reality for millions of African slaves whose experience mirrored that of a young African boy brought to America in 1848. He arrived in the belly of a slave ship and was sold with his mother at a Charleston, South Carolina auction house. Orphaned by age eight, his harsh, abusive, and deprived American experience was just beginning. His name was Silas Burgess.

How can our nation reconcile the depravation of that young eight-year-old slave with inspirational success stories of other Americans during that same century? For an example, it was the American culture that granted opportunity to a middle-aged Texan, a Republican, whose "federally protected" freedom allowed him to pursue his dreams, to work/risk, overcome, and to prosper. Respected as a pillar of his community, he was a successful entrepreneur who owned over one hundred acres of farmland, which he paid off within two years. He also founded the first church and elementary school in his region of the state. He was referred to as fiercely independent and a very proud American. He was also a Republican. His name was Silas Burgess.

Is it possible to embrace a national history today that is such a dichotomy regarding the human experience? The Liberal/Socialist Left says that we shouldn't. They feel that all reference to "successful" Black American history should be hidden and neglected, leaving behind a narrative of a race that has been weak, overpowered, and oppressed for close to two hundred years. They indoctrinate American children at all levels of education that our country should transfer wealth to today's Black American population (reparations) to atone for the deeds of White strangers who died one hundred and fifty years ago. They suggest that slavery is the root cause of the misery found within today's urban community and that there is a "slave owner" gene that has evolved into the DNA of White Conservatives. As per this articulated viewpoint, critical thinking and common sense is not a prerequisite of the Socialist/Marxist Left.

Conservatives, on the other hand, point to the success of the Texas Republican as an example of the possibilities available to all Americans when individuals are granted a choice to adhere to the principles and values of success.

The middle-aged Texan proved the truth of this philosophy as he partook in the fruit of his labor. His gratefulness and unique connection to an eight-year-old South Carolina slave boy gave him an enduring love and respect for his country and his flag. The two, after all, were one and the same; my great, great grandfather Silas Burgess, whose name I'm honored to carry. Millions of other Americans from every other culture share a similar American experience. It is the gratitude of our present generation for our ancestors' grit and tenacity that forges a spiritual connection that gives us pride in our country's flag. It is this connection that has been lost to most Black Americans due to the sanitization of their history.

WHY I STAND

I **Stand**—in gratitude to an eight-year-old boy, my great, great grandfather, who remained hopeful, tenacious, and faithful as he grew to proudly serve his family, community, and country.

I **Stand**—in gratitude to a grandfather who, at the age of fifteen, volunteered to serve in WWI. As a successful farmer, he raised twelve children, all of whom, earned college degrees, were part of the Black middle class, and took part in the mid-1900s American Dream.

I **Stand**—in gratitude to a father who succeeded in the day of institutional racism in the arenas of academia, as a researcher, an entrepreneur, a dedicated father and husband, and a pillar of his community. He once recounted that his greatest life decision was volunteering and returning home as a proud WWII veteran.

I **Stand**—in gratitude for the proud, successful, entrepreneurial, and segregated Tallahassee, Florida community that I grew up in. They were determined that they would never be looked down upon or pitied as a race of victims.

I **Stand**—as an example for the millions of Black youth who have not been taught to love God, country, family, and themselves by the Liberal/Socialist Leftist overseers who have controlled the urban community for the last sixty years.

I **Stand**—against the sanitizing of our history. The Liberal/Socialist Left has already done so effectively within the Black community, resulting in the anger and ingratitude seen within the ranks of wealthy and free Black and White entertainers and NFL athletes. This top one percent income-producing group of Americans, who live the American Dream daily, feel justified to kneel in protest when the American flag is presented to honor.

And finally...

I **Stand**—to acknowledge my respect for the greatest civil experiment in the history of mankind, America. America is God's Dream, a land set aside, hidden and protected for eons as a gift to the rest of the world, a promise called Freedom. It is a nation whose beautiful tapestry is highlighted within its diversity, its geological landscapes, people, ideologies, and religions blended and connected with the ideals of tolerance found uniquely within its borders. It is a country whose perfect distance between the equator and the North Pole grants a traveler the opportunity to experience every worldwide clime within its Northern Continent boundaries. It is a nation protected by two vast oceans on its Eastern and Western borders, and two free nations on its Southern and Northern borders. It was the first nation in history to begin its journey to freedom with a prayer and the signing of a covenant called "The Mayflower Compact."

Before leaving the Mayflower and setting foot in their new land, this fledgling group of forty Christian pilgrims, called Saints, had traveled from Holland, seeking religious freedom. The Mayflower Compact was a foundational document for the Plymouth Colony. The first of its kind, it was a covenant whereby the settlers subordinated their rights to follow laws passed by the government to ensure protection and survival.[10] It was this same nation, America, that held true to its founding mission statement never before formulated, "We the People" (US Constitution) and "All Men Are Created Equal" (Declaration of Independence). Unlike the 3,000 years worldwide of tolerance for slavery and one thousand years of the same on the African continent, America had, within eighty-seven years of its founding, "violently" expelled the evil stain of slavery from its soul. It did so at a cost not matched in all the future wars combined, more than 600,000 American lives. America is indeed a nation built by immigrants from every part of the world seeking their dreams and embracing a love and loyalty, the American way of life. They seek with pride to assimilate and to be called by the rest of the world...Americans. It is a land of hope, opportunity, freedom, and many, many second chances as it challenges its citizens to dream big. In doing so, this effort collectively adds to our country's majesty.

It is within the American culture where intelligence, character, courage, and the divine spark of the human soul are considered the property of the individual, not of the state or of a tyrannical dictator. It is within this collective heart of appreciation, gratitude, and historical acknowledgment where an American can best be summarized as "We the People." For it is indeed what we have dreamed, struggled, and overcome together that stirs within us, as countrymen/women, the desire to stand tall and erect with hand over heart, as we hear our beautiful National Anthem. It is with this simple gesture that we reverently and proudly salute our American flag and the culture of the American Way. It is because of God's precious gift of freedom and a proud history of millions of Americans who have lived, died, dreamed, failed, and with "Dream Big" tenacity fought to start anew, that *with pride and honor...I STAND.*

---

10   Martin Kelly. "The Mayflower Compact of 1620." ThoughtCo.com, February 5, 2018. thoughtco.com/mayflower-compact-104577.

CHAPTER 3

THE KILLING FIELDS OF SOCIALISM

Due to the desired message that is being addressed in this book, there will be the addition of three chapters from my previous book, *Liberalism or How to Turn Good Men into Whiners, Weenies and Wimps.* They are:

- Chapter 4: Socialism vs. Capitalism—Which is the Moral System?
- Chapter 5: The NAACP Strategy—The Trojan Horse
- Chapter 6: Planned Parenthood—The Sophistry of Margaret Sanger

These chapters are imperative for a comprehensive understanding of the historical stealth and destruction of Socialism. The kissing cousin ideologies of Marxism, Liberalism, and atheism have slowly, over this last century, eaten away at the foundation of the once-successful Black community. Unbeknown to most Americans, it was a community that, within the first fifty years after the end of the Civil War, showed its gratitude for its hard fought freedom. By the beginning of the 1900s this community, with deep-seated Christian roots, strong family units, and commitment to education and entrepreneurship, had become our nation's most competitive and prosperous minority.

The history of betrayal of the Black community can serve as a warning beacon for Americans in our new millennium. Though the target today is on a much grander scale, the Transformation of America—the subversive methodology remains the same. With an understanding that America's most dangerous enemy is an ideology found within our own borders, citizens of all colors, creeds, and religions will be better equipped to defeat it. These anti-American ideologies, embraced by Black and White elitists, have undermined Black manhood, Black womanhood, and the Black family for over a century. Through our recommitment to education and our foundational Judeo-

Christian values, the Black community will pull itself back from the dark, evil, and corrupt abyss of Socialism/Marxism. Once accomplished, this same community, recommitted to innate American values and principles, will play a major role in pulling our nation back from that same abyss.

The Left's subversive attack on our society continues today and can be witnessed in *every* urban community throughout our nation. Its targeted message of radicalization has been relentless. Consistent over the decades has been its stealth, deceit, and betrayal from within. Through a seductive blending of entertainment, compliant news media, and an elitist class of Black Americans as willing advocates, there has been a successful indoctrination of millions throughout our country. It has been an indoctrination of acceptance, by both Black and White Americans, of a demeaning caricature of the Black race as weak and hapless, hampered by its history of slavery and abused by a more powerful, oppressive White race ever since. It is this narrative that accepts as the norm within the Black Race academic failure, joblessness, irresponsible manhood, dependency on the welfare state, high criminality, and a "thinking with their Black skin" loyalty to one party. This racist/elitist view of the innate inferiority of the Black population is not new, but consistent for over a century with those who find a home within the Democratic Party. The pre-Civil War Democratic Vice President John C. Calhoun stated that "slavery was good not only for the slaveholder, but also for the slave".[11]

Convinced that the Black race could not survive without the care and largesse of Whites, members of the Democratic Party felt that extinction would be the natural result of granting them freedom. It was also members of the Democratic Party that would display, as scientific proof of evolution and the inferiority of Blacks, an African pigmy. Ota Benga was caged in a NY Bronx monkey cage in 1904 with a chimp as his companion. Black Americans have fought against these demeaning perceptions for generations. Previous generations have fought and won by competing and winning in the arenas of education, by participation in the Capitalistic free market, and with high morality, standards, and expectations within the family unit.

In June 2017, a study was released stating that seventy-five percent of Black boys in the State of California were unable to pass standard reading and writing tests.[12] This startling failure to educate a major minority segment of the State of California citizenry has not been met with curiosity or rage, but with deafening silence! There has been no outcry from the Congressional Black

---

11   "John C. Calhoun." Wikipedia. Wikimedia Foundation, Inc., July 31, 2018. en.wikipedia.org/wiki/John_C._Calhoun.

12   Matthew Bernstein. "75% Of Black Boys Fail Reading Test In CA, Liberals Use Minorities For Votes & Then Ditch Them." Teddy Stick, June 5, 2017. teddystick. com/75-of-black-boys-fail-reading-test-in-ca-liberals-use-minorities-for-votes-then-ditch-them.

Congress, who for decades has colluded with the National Labor Education Union to ensure limited access to quality schools for our nation's most vulnerable children. There has been silence from the mainstream media, who portray themselves as compassionate overseers and "all in" for social justice. There has been nothing from the Black Lives Matter coalition, who seem to be ignorantly disconnected regarding the value of the millions of Black lives not shot by Black and White policemen.

The most devastating silence for advocacy of the children of poor Black Americans has been the voice most trusted within urban Black community, the former President of the United States, Barack Hussein Obama. His eight years of prioritizing powerful Liberal organizations above the wellbeing of his own race can be seen with his very first Executive Order in office. Within weeks of being sworn in, President Obama, without fanfare, signed legislation to reward the Progressive/Socialist National Education Labor Union. President Obama's Executive Order, with a supporting bill denying funding, was introduced by Illinois Senator Dick Durbin; thus, the Democratic Party ended a successful pro-urban children's school choice lottery program. Due to its overwhelming success, for years this program had garnered the support of Democrats, Republicans, Independents, and thousands of poor parents vying for a coveted spot for their children. Only 1,800 Black students per year were chosen out of tens of thousands of applicants, but even this paltry number was still too high for our first Black president, Barack Obama. While graduation rates in D.C. Public Schools hovered around 55 percent, students who used this "school choice" voucher to attend private school had a ninety-one percent graduation rate.[13]

Noting that nine out of ten voucher recipients were Black, a *Washington Post* editorial declared in September 2013 that it was "...bewildering, if not downright perverse, for the Obama administration to use the banner of civil rights to bring a misguided suit that would block these disadvantaged students from getting the better educational opportunities they are due."[14] Liberal Columnist Juan Williams called the decision to end the program, "Obama's outrageous sin against our kids."

Once he had successfully ended the educational opportunity for over 1,800 poor Black children per year in D.C., President Obama attempted to do the same to poor Black children in the State of Louisiana. Fortunately, the courts prevented his administration from blocking school choice and schoolhouse

---

13   Lindsey Burke. "Obama's Budget Ends Funding for D.C. Opportunity Scholarship Program." *The Daily Signal*. February 13, 2012, Online edition, sec. Education. dailysignal.com/2012/02/13/presidents-budget-eliminates-funding-for-d-c-opportunity-scholarship-program.

14   Jason Bedrick. "Obama's War on School Choice." *National Review*. January 28, 2016, Online edition, sec. Politics & Policy. nationalreview.com/article/430446/obama-against-school-choice.

doors in Louisiana. The Fifth Circuit Court of Appeals threw out the suit in a blistering decision by Judge Edith Jones, who called the administration's argument "disingenuous." The majority held that the lower court's order complying with the administration's wishes went "beyond correcting—and indeed has nothing to do with—the violation originally litigated in [the case]" and noted that even the Department of Justice admitted that its position "amounted to a fishing expedition."

After four years of investigation, the Obama DOJ, in late 2015, quietly terminated its targeting of the oldest school voucher program in the nation. The investigation stemmed from complaints by the American Civil Liberties Union and Disability Rights Wisconsin, which claimed in 2011 that Milwaukee's voucher program supposedly discriminated against children with disabilities.[15]

Given a pass from scrutiny over the eight years of the Obama Administration were the public school overseers of our urban communities, the National Educational Union. The following articles are a small sample of the failure to educate Black and other minority students:

- 2013 Milwaukee Journal Sentinel, Black students near bottom in the nation on benchmark math, reading test.[16] Nation's report card posts stagnant education scores in Wisconsin.
- June 2017 a study was released stating that seventy-five percent of Black boys in the State of California were unable to pass standard reading and writing tests.[17]
- 2012 study reported State of New Jersey: "Nearly all of Newark's most disadvantaged elementary and middle school students attend failing district and charter schools."[18]
- 2017 report shows that Michigan ranks last in education, wellbeing for African American children. African American fourth graders in Michigan are reading at the lowest rate in the country.

15   *Ibid.*
16   Lydia Mulvany. "Black Students near Bottom in Nation on Benchmark Math, Reading Test." *The Journal Sentinel.* November 8, 2013, sec. Education. archive. jsonline.com/news/education/states-black-students-rank-lowest-in-reading-math-scores-b99136626z1-230903121.html.
17   Grace Carr. "Report: 75% Of Black California Boys Fail To Meet Reading And Writing Standards." Political news. Dailycaller.com, June 5, 2017. dailycaller. com/2017/06/05/report-75-of-black-california-boys-fail-to-meet-reading-and-writing-standards.
18   Jessica Calefati. "Report: Nearly All of Newark's Most Disadvantaged Students Attend Failing Schools." *New Jersey Real-Time News.* December 12, 2012. nj.com/news/index.ssf/2012/12/highest_need_newark_students_c.html.

> The math proficiency rate for eighth grade African American kids is tied with Alabama for the lowest in the country.[19]

- Baltimore's failing schools are a tragedy of criminal proportions.[20]
- Critics call Inside NYC schools "failure factories" in 2017.[21]

These reports are consistent throughout our nation, in *every* urban community. Because of this consistency of Black scholastic failure, there can be only one of two conclusions regarding the impacted Black race:

Conclusion #1—These test results, denoting an innate lack of intelligence in Black children is *very natural*. It is, after all, a "Black thing" in which Blacks think and act with their skin. It is, therefore, their lack of intelligence, partly due to the trauma of slavery by their great, great, great grandparents, that this should be accepted and expected.

Conclusion #2—These test results are *unnatural,* and the Black Community has been targeted for decades by its White and Black Socialist/ Marxist overseers. This conclusion accepts a premise that the strategy of "Black misery" has been imposed purposefully through Democratic policies to "GET OUT THE VOTE." Decades of failure within urban Black schools are consistent nationwide. The single common denominator is the educational oversight by appointed Black administrators and elected Black Socialist/ Marxist slave masters (i.e., politicians).

A question of priority should be asked of the Congressional Black Caucus, in which one of its members exhibited his "passion" for the plight of non-assimilating illegal immigrants. Cory Booker, the Democratic Senator from New Jersey, stated recently that he was "frankly seething with anger" over President Trump's comments about the condition of Haiti and the entrance of illegals into our country from there. Booker spoke of his "tears of rage" for these non-Americans.

As a ten-year veteran of the NFL locker room, and someone who has been aware for decades of the filthy woman-demeaning lyrics by hip hop "hero"

---

19   WXYZ staff. "Michigan Ranks Last in Education, Well-Being for African American Children." WXYZ Detroit. October 25, 2017, Online edition, sec. Analysis. wxyz. com/news/michigan-ranks-last-in-education-well-being-for-african-american-children.

20   Armstrong Williams. "Baltimore's Failing Schools Are a Tragedy of Criminal Proportions." *The Hill.* September 13, 2017, Online edition, sec. Opinions. thehill. com/opinion/education/350315-baltimores-failing-schools-are-a-tragedy-of-criminal-proportions.

21   Susan Edelman. "Inside the NYC Schools Critics Call 'Failure Factories.'" *New York Post.* September 2, 2017, Online edition, sec. Metro. https://nypost. com/2017/09/02/inside-the-nyc-schools-critics-call-failure-factories.

Jay-Z, I've asked myself what kind of man responds to a description of any country that is not America with tears of rage? Booker's response highlights the justification for the title of my first book, *Liberalism or How to Turn Good Men into Whiners, Weenies and Wimps.*

Many caring Americans would ask Senator Booker about his tears of rage when he read about the dimming future of American-born children of his own race in his state of New Jersey or the Democratic state of California? In 2012, it was reported in Booker's state of New Jersey that "nearly all of Newark's most disadvantaged elementary and middle school students attend failing district and charter schools."[22] In the same article reporting New Jersey's educational malfeasance is a picture of Senator Booker sitting with the Newark superintendent, an adviser and longtime friend, with no outrage, not seething with "tears of rage" but grinning from ear-to-ear.

A fair question that should be asked of Cory "Tears of Rage" Booker and the other silent members of the Congressional Black Caucus: what if the seventy-five percent of failing boys in the state of California were *not* poor and Black? What if instead they were Hispanic, illegal immigrants, or transgender? The guaranteed response from Booker and the rest of his royalty class Black elitists would be "shock and awe" and a demand for a Congressional investigation, a national dialogue and a call to action. In some convoluted way, with the backing of the mainstream media, Booker and the ever-compliant Black Caucus would call a press conference on the Capitol Building steps to lay the blame at the feet of a racist President Trump, White Christian Conservatives, and Uncle Tom Black Conservatives for somehow forgetting their Black roots.

All would be accused of denying non-White Americans and illegals their Constitutional right to progress in our country. On the topic of migration, the Left has long taken the Black community for granted and has forgotten that it too is a community of non-Whites and centuries-old legal Americans. If this train of thinking seems a little incoherent, remember this is the *modus operandi* of Black and White Socialist/Marxists, the total suspension of common sense and critical thinking. Is there any wonder why denying poor Black children a quality education that would teach common sense and critical thinking is so important to their political survival?

The bigotry of low expectations has been a spirit that has defined the Democratic Party since its pre-Civil War beginning. Every past Black generation has been at war against those who would attack and undermine the Black race of a healthy self-perception. Unfortunately, this has not changed over the last generation. With the aid of Socialists/Marxists within and royalty class Black Democratic elitists, the demeaning low expectations for Black Americans has found acceptance in our society.

---

22   Jessica Calefati. "Report: Nearly All of Newark's Most Disadvantaged Students Attend Failing Schools."

With the decades of messaging from the progressive Left, there is no surprise by most Americans, Blacks and Whites, that 75 percent of Black boys in California cannot read and write, or that 70 percent of Black men are abandoning their own children, or that 83 percent of Black teen males remain chronically unemployed nationwide...93 percent unemployed in the Liberal Land of Chicago.

It is also no surprise that 1,800 Black mothers daily will opt to sacrifice their baby and their own motherhood to White Socialist/Marxist abortionists; or that 40 percent of Black boys will drop out of high school and another 40 percent will drop out of college; or that the percentage of Black entrepreneurship ranks at the bottom of all other races, a paltry 3.8 percent, or that of the 100,000 youth incarcerated in juvenile correction centers annually, a majority of whom are Black, over 70 percent (70,000) will return to this system within a year after release. Due to this successful messaging and acceptance of the soft bigotry of low expectations, Americans throughout our country simply yawn and turn the channel.

Ota Benga, a Mbuti pygmy, was known for being featured in an anthropology exhibit at the Louisiana Purchase Exposition in St. Louis, Missouri in 1904, and in a human zoo exhibit in 1906 at the Bronx Zoo. Benga had been purchased from Black African slave traders by the explorer Samuel Phillips Verner, a businessman hunting African people for the exposition.[23]

Mr. Verner was associated with Madison Grant, a progressive lawyer and advisor to KKK member and future Democratic President, Woodrow Wilson. Grant was also a well-known promoter of eugenics, the settled science of the era that claimed that the White race was superior genetically to the darker races.

Based on the conclusion of the scientists of the day, the anthropometricists and psychometricists, the intelligence tests of the pygmies proved that they "behaved a good deal in the same way as the mentally deficient person, making many stupid errors and taking an enormous amount of time," nor did they do very well in sports competition—in Bradford and Blume's words, "the disgraceful record set by the ignoble savages."[24]

These progressive Democrats gave Benga a home in the primate cage at the Bronx Zoo. They dressed him like a savage and made him carry around a baby orangutan like it was his child. Their purpose was to demonstrate scientific proof that evolution was true and that the White race was clearly far ahead of Blacks on the evolutionary scale. Over 40,000 Americans were

---

23   "Caged in the human zoo: The shocking story of the young pygmy warrior put on show in a monkey house – and how he fueled Hitler's twisted beliefs." *Dailymail. October 31, 2009.* Retrieved May 23, 2014.

24   Phillips Verner Bradford, and Harvey Blume. *Ota Benga: The Pygmy in the Zoo.* Reprint. New York: Dell Publishing, 1993.

exposed to this "scientific truth," setting in place a false perception of the Black race that would last for generations.

Christians were outraged and spoke out against the evil of caging a human being in a zoo. The response from the Socialist/Marxist in charge was to ridicule them as being "non-scientific persons" who failed to understand that the pygmy was not rated very high by scientists on the human scale. The Christian community was determined to free Benga, and the zoo finally relented and allowed him out of his cage. He wandered the zoo freely but was mocked, tripped, and laughed at. Children tormented him without mercy, and he soon became resentful and angry. Benga made himself a bow and arrow and began shooting at visitors. Once he succeeded in wounding a few of his tormentors, he was eventually granted freedom.

Benga became a Christian, was baptized, and his English vocabulary rapidly improved. He learned how to read and occasionally attended classes at a Lynchburg seminary. He was popular among the boys and learned several sports such as baseball. Every effort was made to help him blend in. Even his teeth were capped to help him look more normal. Seemingly he had adjusted, but inwardly he had not. Eventually, he became despondent. He checked on the price of steamship tickets to Africa and concluded that he would never have enough money to purchase one. Later employed as a laborer in a tobacco factory in Lynchburg, VA, he grew increasingly depressed, hostile, irrational, and forlorn. When people spoke to him, they noticed that he had tears in his eyes. He told them he wanted to go home. Concluding that he would never be able to return to his native land, on March 20, 1916, Benga committed suicide with a revolver (Sanborn, 1916). In Ward's words: "Ota...removed the caps from his teeth. When his small companions asked him to lead them into the woods again, he turned them away. Once they were safely out of sight, he shot himself."[25]

This degrading "settled scientific" imagery promoted by the Democratic Party at the turn of the century was followed in 1915 by another successful progressive strategy. With the onset of the new era of motion picture films in 1915, it was President Woodrow Wilson who introduced for the first time *The Birth of a Nation*. This pro-KKK propaganda portrayed the Black man with racist imagery indicative of the beliefs of the Darwinist KKK member and racist Woodrow Wilson.[26]

The early 1900s Liberal/Progressive Democrat's vision of the Black race in the 1904 Brooklyn Zoo and through early pro-KKK motion pictures was: "...depicted in circuses, minstrel shows, song, and in twentieth century films

25   *Ibid.*

26   William Keylor. "In Their Own Words: The Long-Forgotten Racial Attitudes
      & Policies of Woodrow Wilson," March 4, 2013. bu.edu/news/2013/03/04/
      in-their-own-words-the-long-forgotten-racial-attitudes-policies-of-woodrow-
      wilson.

and radio programs and in popular culture...as lazy and silly bumpkins, high-strutting dandies who foolishly mimicked White elites, or simple-minded and contented 'darkies' who simply loved their White patrons..."[27] and "intellectually challenged, sexually and emotionally undisciplined, uneducated, unkempt, lazy, cowardly, criminals, baby factories, irresponsible, disloyal, angry and oppressed... (but boy do dey love to sing and dance...)"

Black Entertainment TV (BET). has molded the perception of an entire generation of Black Youth for two decades. Since 2000, BET has been one-hundred percent directed and controlled by media giant Viacom and its White Socialist Democrat owner, Sumner Redstone. The glorifying of the race-degrading gangster rap and hip hop subculture, and later the Marxist inspired Black Lives Matter movement, have all metastasized within the Black community through Viacom's use of BET as its Black-faced façade.

Today's Black urban culture has been subtly defined by messages targeting "at-risk" Black youth. The two decades-long promotion of violent, visionless, and misogynic gangster rap entertainment has resulted in the rise of a generational subculture of Black criminality. Through its lyrics, videos, and hero-worshipping, it has glorified for young Black boys and girls the failure of both manhood and womanhood. In the process, this debased culture further denigrates the Black family as it presents role models Black men who represent abject failures in every other past generation. This niche of BET (Viacom, Inc.) role models are comprised primarily of uneducated and inarticulate rappers who are irresponsible fathers, disloyal partners, and drug/sex addicts who eventually run out of places on their faces and necks to place their tattoos. They do not respect women enough to keep their pants from falling to their knees. As they demean and objectify Black women they refer to the mothers of their own children as "Baby Mamas." This violent, narcissistic, and anti-family culture has destroyed millions of Black lives and has left millions upon millions feeling hopeless and angry.

Viacom is the world's ninth-largest broadcasting, cable, and media company behind Comcast, The Walt Disney Company, Time Warner, 21st Century Fox, Bertelsmann, Dish Network, Sony, and Vivendi. Since its three billion dollar buyout from its original owner Robert Johnson in 2001, BET has been the most trusted source of entertainment and current news. Streamed into the homes of poor at-risk Black boys and girls, seventy percent of whom are fatherless, Viacom has been relentless in its demeaning messaging that will guarantee additional generations of irresponsible men and fatherless children.

Since the end of the Civil War in 1865, every generation of Black Americans has fought against the demeaning narrative now seen *daily* on BET. Their fight can be seen through video journals of the Civil Rights era. It can be seen in confrontational settings during hot southern summer marches and

27   Ronald L.F. Davis, Ph.D. "Surviving Jim Crow." James River Armory, n.d.

while sitting at "White-only" segregated lunch counters. Fighting this racist perception narrative to the civil rights leaders was as important as their fight against tangible racist Jim Crow laws and KKK terrorists. Their fight was for respect, dignity, and positive self-perception, and could be seen through their dress attire of White shirts, dark ties, dress slacks, and dress shoes during the heat of summer marches. Their courage and discipline were shown in their non-violent response to violent racist attacks. They articulated themselves succinctly as men of education. In the process of doing this they garnered the respect of Americans nationwide.

It was this same generation of visionary Black men, leaders during the 1960s civil rights era, who had earlier led America in its post-WWII growth. They led our country in the growth of its middle class (over 50 percent), the percentage of its men committed to family and marriage (over 70 percent), the percentage of entrepreneurs (over 40 percent), and in the percentage of men committed to higher education.

As we fast-forward to our present millennial era of unparalleled technology, found consistently in today's progressive education is the redaction of the success of these past generations of Black men and women. Missing are stories highlighting their success in *commanding* (not *demanding*) respect, and of their contributions that allowed for the healing of our country's racial divide. Instead, a narrative of Black impotency and oppression by another more powerful race has replaced the history of a race led by proud, educated, visionary men. As an instructional reminder, it is important to remember the words of Socialist founder, Karl Marx: "The first battleground is the rewriting of history."

Deleting from American history the sacrifice and contribution of millions of Black Americans has been where today's Socialist/Marxist Left has had their greatest success. How disappointing it would be for our past builders to see what we've allowed to happen to their great legacy.

CHAPTER 4

SOCIALISM VS. CAPITALISM: WHICH IS THE MORAL SYSTEM?

"The first battlefield is the rewriting of history."

—Karl Marx, Socialist and author of The Communist Manifesto[28]

"The goal of Socialism is Communism."

—Vladimir Lenin

Socialist founder Karl Marx viewed Christianity as a trap that tricks people into willingly falling into it and an element that promotes Capitalism. The Christian Bible encourages subservience through teachings such as "the first

---

28   "The Communist Manifesto." Wikimedia Foundation, Inc., n.d. en.wikipedia.org/wiki/The_Communist_Manifesto.

shall be last and the last shall be first" and "turn the other cheek." A core concept of the Bible is that there is an afterlife in which the immortal souls of people will be rewarded or punished according to how they acted during their life.

In part, teachings such as these discourage revolution because morally dubious acts, such as revolutions, involve killing and stealing of property, and partly because the importance of what one has during their life is significantly less if there are much greater rewards in an afterlife. The ultimate consequence of these teachings is that the lower classes are repressed by their own hand and refuse to rise up and free themselves."[29]

The following article is reprinted in its entirety with the permission of C. Bradley Thompson:

> *Throughout history there have been two basic forms of social organization: collectivism and individualism. In the twentieth-century collectivism has taken many forms: Socialism, fascism, Nazism, welfare-statism and Communism are its more notable variations. The only social system commensurate with individualism is laissez-faire Capitalism.*
>
> *The extraordinary level of material prosperity achieved by the Capitalist system over the course of the last two- hundred years is a matter of historical record. But very few people are willing to defend Capitalism as morally uplifting. It is fashionable among college professors, journalists, and politicians these days to sneer at the free-enterprise system. They tell us that Capitalism is base, callous, exploitative, dehumanizing, alienating, and ultimately enslaving.*
>
> *The intellectuals' mantra runs something like this: In theory Socialism is the morally superior social system despite its dismal record of failure in the real world. Capitalism, by contrast, is a morally bankrupt system despite the extraordinary prosperity it has created. In other words, Capitalism at best, can only be defended on pragmatic grounds. We tolerate it because it works.*
>
> *Under Socialism a ruling class of intellectuals, bureaucrats and social planners decide what people want or what is good*

29   Paul Bendor-Samuel. "Marx and Nietzsche: Christianity as the Disease of Man." Evolution & Revolution (blog), April 11, 2010. evolutionrevolutionatrhodes. blogspot.com/2010/04/marx-and-nietzsche-christianity-as.html.

for society and then use the coercive power of the State to regulate, tax, and redistribute the wealth of those who work for a living. In other words, Socialism is a form of legalized theft. The morality of Socialism can be summed-up in two words: envy and self-sacrifice. Envy is the desire to not only possess another's wealth but also the desire to see another's wealth lowered to the level of one's own. Socialism's teaching on self-sacrifice was nicely summarized by two of its greatest defenders, Hermann Goering and Benito Mussolini.

The highest principle of Nazism (National Socialism), said Goering, is: "Common good comes before private good."

Fascism, said Mussolini, "is a life in which the individual, through the sacrifice of his own private interests, realizes that completely spiritual existence in which his value as a man lies."

Socialism is the social system, which institutionalizes envy and self-sacrifice: It is the social system, which uses compulsion and the organized violence of the State to expropriate wealth from the producer class for its redistribution to the parasitical class.

Despite the intellectuals' psychotic hatred of Capitalism, it is the only moral and just social system. Capitalism is the only moral system because it requires human beings to deal with one another as traders–that is, as free moral agents trading and selling goods and services based on mutual consent. Capitalism is the only just system because the sole criterion that determines the value of thing exchanged is the free, voluntary, universal judgment of the consumer. Coercion and fraud are anathema to the free-market system. It is both moral and just because the degree to which man rises or falls in society is determined by the degree to which he uses his mind. Capitalism is the only social system that rewards merit, ability and achievement, regardless of one's birth or station in life.

Yes, there are winners and losers in Capitalism. The winners are those who are honest, industrious, thoughtful, prudent, frugal, responsible, disciplined, and efficient. The losers are those who are shiftless, lazy, imprudent, extravagant, negligent, impractical, and inefficient.

Capitalism is the only social system that rewards virtue and punishes vice. This applies to both the business executive and the carpenter, the lawyer and the factory worker. But how does the entrepreneurial mind work? Have you ever wondered about the mental processes of the men and women who invented penicillin, the internal combustion engine, the airplane, the radio, the electric light, canned food, air conditioning, washing machines, dishwashers, computers, etc.?

What are the characteristics of the entrepreneur? The entrepreneur is that man or woman with unlimited drive, initiative, insight, energy, daring creativity, optimism and ingenuity. The entrepreneur is the man who sees in every field a potential garden, in every seed an apple. Wealth starts with ideas in people's heads. The entrepreneur is therefore above all else a man of the mind. The entrepreneur is the man who is constantly thinking of new ways to improve the material or spiritual lives of the greatest number of people.

And what are the social and political conditions, which encourage or inhibit the entrepreneurial mind? The free-enterprise system is not possible without the sanctity of private property, the freedom of contract, free trade and the rule of law. But the one thing that the entrepreneur value over all others is freedom—the freedom to experiment, invent and produce. The one thing that the entrepreneur dreads is government intervention. Government taxation and regulation are how social planners punish and restrict the man or woman of ideas.

Welfare, regulations, taxes, tariffs, minimum-wage laws are all immoral because they use the coercive power of the state to organize human choice and action; they're immoral because they inhibit or deny the freedom to choose how we live our lives; they're immoral because they deny our right to live as autonomous moral agents; and they're immoral because they deny our essential humanity. If you think this is hyperbole, stop paying your taxes for a year or two and see what happens.

The requirements for success in a free society demand that ordinary citizens order their lives in accordance with certain virtues—namely, rationality, independence, industriousness, prudence, frugality, etc. In a free Capitalist society, individuals must choose for themselves how they will order their lives and the values they will pursue. Under Socialism, most of life's decisions are made for you.

Both Socialism and Capitalism have incentive programs. Under Socialism there are built-in incentives to shirk responsibility. There is no reason to work harder than anyone else because the rewards are shared and therefore minimal to the hard-working individual; indeed, the incentive is to work less than others because the immediate loss is shared and therefore minimal to the slacker. Under Capitalism, the incentive is to work harder because each producer will receive the total value of his production—the rewards are not shared. Simply put: Socialism rewards sloth and penalizes hard work while Capitalism rewards hard work and penalizes sloth.

According to Socialist doctrine, there is a limited amount of wealth in the world that must be divided equally between all citizens. One person's gain under such a system is another's loss.

According to the Capitalist teaching, wealth has an unlimited growth potential and the fruits of one's labor should be retained in whole by the producer. But unlike Socialism, one person's gain is everybody's gain in the Capitalist system. Wealth is distributed unequally but the ship of wealth rises for everyone.

Sadly, America is no longer a Capitalist nation. We live under what is more properly called a mixed economy—that is, an economic system that permits private property, but only at the discretion of government planners. A little bit of Capitalism and a little bit of Socialism.

When government redistributes wealth through taxation, when it attempts to control and regulate business production and trade, who are the winners and losers? Under this kind of economy, the winners and losers are reversed: the winners are those who scream the loudest for a handout and the losers are those quiet citizens who work hard and pay their taxes.

Because of our sixty-year experiment with a mixed economy and the welfare state, America has created two new classes of citizens. The first is a debased class of dependents whose means of survival is contingent upon the forced expropria-

tion of wealth from working citizens by a professional class of government social planners. The forgotten man and woman in all of this is the quiet, hardworking, law-abiding, taxpaying citizen who minds his or her own business but is forced to work for the government and their serfs.

The return of Capitalism will not happen until there is a moral revolution in this country. We must rediscover and then teach our young the virtues associated with being free and independent citizens. Then and only then, will there be social justice in America.

— C. Bradley Thompson is Assistant Professor of Political Science at Ashland University and Coordinator of Publications and Special Programs at the John M. Ashbrook Center for Public Affairs.

American Exceptionalism defines the boundless opportunities to serve and to resolve and offer solutions in an economic system that rewards such activities, without limits. The economic pillar of Capitalism/free enterprise is predicated on freedoms that unleash men's creativity and that reward his ingenuity and tenacity.

In the early 1900s, the Black community stood at a crossroads. Given two options, one would lead toward *American Exceptionalis*. The other, delivered through strategy and stealth, pulled it away from Capitalism's moorings, leading to decades of dependency and big government Socialism. To right the ship, it will be necessary to better understand the empowerment of Capitalism, the compassion of the American culture, and the morality intrinsically imbedded within both.

CHAPTER 5

THE NAACP STRATEGY: THE TROJAN HORSE

The Deepest Betrayal Begins with Ultimate Trust

"Hundreds of years ago Greece and Troy were at war. The Greeks came in their ships to attack Troy. For ten long years, they besieged Troy, but the Trojans would not surrender. There were strong and high walls around the city of Troy. No enemy could enter the city when the gates were closed. The Greeks made several attempts to break down the walls and the gates but failed each time.

"The Greeks built a huge wooden horse and placed it on a large platform with wheels underneath. A few of the bravest Greek warriors including Ulysses hid themselves in the hollow stomach of the horse. When the people of Troy opened the

gates and came out, they could only see the wooden horse left behind by the Greeks. They thought it was the idol of some Greek God.

"They gazed at the gigantic horse in admiration and excitement and soon dragged it into the city of Troy. The capture of the wooden horse was, to them, a symbol of their victory over the Greeks. They celebrated their success with feasting and merrymaking. "The danger is over, at last. We can sleep in peace now," they said to one another. Late at night, they went to sleep.

"In the dead of night, when the Trojans were fast asleep, the Greek warriors inside the stomach of the horse came out quietly. They opened the gates of the city for other Greeks to enter. The Greek ships which had pretended to sail away, now turned back quickly in response to the signal from their leaders inside Troy. Soon, thousands of Greek soldiers rushed into the city. They killed thousands of Trojans—men, women and children, burnt their houses and looted the city.

"Even before the Trojans were fully awake, their magnificent city was in ruins. Before they could realize what was happening, Troy was in the hands of the Greeks. Thus, the Greeks succeeded in punishing the Trojans for their refusal to hand over Helen to them. The architect of their great victory was the brainy and wily leader, Ulysses, who brought the long-drawn war to a close by this masterstroke of cunning and foul play."[30]

The story of the National Association for the Advancement of Colored People (NAACP) is the tale of two visions. One is represented by a legacy of courageous Black men and women who, for decades, were willing to sacrifice all for equal opportunity for their race. Many made the ultimate sacrifice for this cause. The communities in which they were raised believed in the promise of America. They were partakers of America's free enterprise system and were steadily progressing toward self-sufficiency and independence.

The other tale of the NAACP is one of stealth and deceit. As with the Greek Trojan Horse, the attainment of trust was but the first step to a devastating betrayal. The founders of this organization understood that only through

---

30   Arun. "History of Trojan Horse." Interesting Facts (blog), September 26, 2007. arunsreenivas.wordpress.com/2007/09/26/history-of-trojan-horse.

strategy and stealth could the ideology of Liberalism find a foothold within the early 1900 Black community.

For close to a century, the Black American intellectual, W.E.B. Du Bois, has been depicted as a driving force, a co-founder, and one of the original leaders of the NAACP. Though he was accepted and embraced within the integrated intellectual circles of his day, the portrayal of him as a visionary NAACP leader is false. It is true that he was influential in perpetuating within his race a new strategy of integration. However, he was also a staunch believer in Communism and an admirer of Adolph Hitler and Joseph Stalin.[31]

The true visionary NAACP leaders were its twenty-one original creators— wealthy White liberal, Socialist, and humanist members of the executive board. They ran this new and influential "Black" organization from behind the curtains, and with them resided all power of decision for strategies, priorities, and direction. As has been the history of Marxism/Socialism in the countries of China, Cuba, East Germany, Soviet Union, Vietnam, and so on, it is an ideology that takes advantage of desperate groups of humanity to further its cause. Thus, with the formation of the NAACP, White opportunists converged with Black desperation to create a force designed to confront not only the apartheid, Jim Crow culture of the era, but to also further the notion of "an empowered working class that controlled all aspects of ownership and production."[32] The goal of Socialist adoption in 1910, as it is with today's NAACP leadership, has remained the endgame. Nowhere is this more evident than in its coalescing support by the NAACP for a Socialist/Marxist presidential candidate for the United States.

Interestingly, an organization whose reputation was built on the belief of Black leadership and vision, would take seventy-five years to elect a Black man to the role of NAACP president. Its first three White presidents were known for their Socialist ties: Moorfield Story (1910–1915), Joel Spingarn (1915–1940), and Arthur Spingarn (1940–1966).[33]

In 1910, Du Bois was persuaded to join the NAACP after it was already established. He was given a place on the board, free office space, a salary, and the title Director of Publicity and Research. Translation: he was the editor and messenger for *Crisis* magazine. His assignment was to deliver the board's message to the Black community. His articles required the approval of at

---

31   Dr. Melvin Johnson. "NAACP's Founders Were White Socialists!" Religion. Thinking Out Loud (blog), July 11, 2012. blogs.christianpost.com/thinkingoutloud/naacps-founders-were-White-Socialists-10757.

32   *Ibid.*

33   Matt Smith. "The NAACP Was Founded by Communists/Socialists and Continues to Be Tool for the Radical Left Wing Socialists." Story Reports Comments (blog), July 17, 2010. storyreportscomments.blogspot.com/2010/07/naacp-was-founded-by.html.

least two members of the all-White NAACP executive board before they could be released.[34]

The concept of the NAACP began in 1909 with Mary White Ovington, a wealthy White Socialist, atheist, and editor. She solicited the help of Oswald Garrison Villard, editor of *The Nation*, a newspaper self-described as the "flagship of the left" and William English Walling, also a Socialist and writer. Together they conceived a strategy that would change the course of American race relations for the next one hundred years. As a means of gaining entry to the Black community, they devised a name for their all-White organization that would allow them access: The National Association for the Advancement of Colored People (NAACP).

At that time, the Black community was moving in a direction that was the antithesis of forced integration. Its leader and respected advocate, Booker T. Washington, was a conservative Capitalist and educator. He had developed a network of wealthy White philanthropists who were funding hundreds of Southern Black schools and colleges. His message was one of self-sufficiency, believing that integration between the races would be a natural consequence of increased value of skills, entrepreneurship, and moral values within the Black community. The progress of this self-reliant culture had become obvious with the success of the Black colleges throughout the country. It could also be seen with the success nationally of Black-owned businesses. This entrepreneurial spirit was highlighted at America's first business network convention, hosted by the Negro Business League in 1910.[35]

Booker T. Washington founded the Negro Business League in 1900 with the support of Andrew Carnegie, spotlighting many self-made millionaires and, in 1913, had as their guest speaker the president of the United States, Theodore Roosevelt.[36]

So, in 1910, the NAACP was created. There were no "colored people" involved, consulted, or any with controlling power. A small group of very wealthy White Socialist liberals/ progressives and atheist/humanists took it upon themselves to implement a strategy for Black race relations that had never been used in the history of mankind, called "integration."

The dichotomy between the two visions of the NAACP can be seen in the life and contribution of the NAACP's first Black president in 1975, William Montague Cobb. Born in 1904, W. Montague Cobb was a pioneering 20th-century American scholar, a medical doctor trained in anatomy and the first Black American Ph.D. in physical anthropology. As a scientist, he refuted the

---

34   "Who Is the Founder of the NAACP?," n.d. answers.com/Q/Who_is_the_founder_of_the_NAACP.

35   *Ibid.*

36   "National Negro Business League." Wikimedia Foundation, Inc., June 16, 2018. en.wikipedia.org/wiki/National_Negro_Business_League.

myths of physical and mental differences between the races. While chair of the anatomy department at Howard University's College of Medicine, Dr. Cobb was instrumental in the passage of the Civil Rights Act of 1964 and the establishment of Medicare in 1965. At Howard University, he built one of the world's foremost collections of human skeletons for the study of comparative anatomy. He also introduced creative new teaching methods. He is recognized as the first major historian of American Blacks in the medical field.

He received his bachelor's degree from Amherst College in 1925 and his MD from Howard University. In 1932, he was awarded a Ph.D. in anatomy and physical anthropology from Western Reserve University. He served as president of the National Medical Association (NMA) and of its Washington, D.C. chapter. He was editor of the *Journal of the National Medical Association* from 1949 to 1977. He chaired the Department of Anatomy at Howard University College of Medicine, authored 1,100 publications on diverse topics, and taught more than 6,000 anatomy students.[37]

Dr. Cobb was a great example of our last great generation's tenacity, grit, intelligence, and ability to reach for and obtain the American Dream. His success was earned at the height of the era of legal institutional racism in our country. Unfortunately, the progress that he worked for and envisioned has been undermined by the same organization that he trusted and to which he was committed. The opportunities that was available to him growing up as a Black youth in a Washington, D.C. neighborhood have long been eradicated by the policies of the ideology of Liberalism—with the full support and protection of his NAACP.

The irony of this great Black American's life's work begins by looking at the Washington, D.C. community in which he was raised. His community had accepted the premise that its progress would parallel other cultures and races that had embraced what can be best described as the American Way. The American Way is available to all who live in this country, regardless of race, creed, or color. It's a seeking spirit that asks questions, pushing boundaries in a way that is only possible in a free society where citizens are encouraged to think. It is a spirit that disregards one's present status and instead challenges all to dream big and envision beyond all obstacles, seen and unseen. It is a spirit that yearns for education and demands more than conventional thinking. Most important, it's a spirit that encourages its citizens to see one another the way that God does: from inside-out instead of outside-in. This vision will forever be embedded within our country's founding documents, highlighted by three words: "We the People."

Based on what is known of the Black community at the time of the founding of the NAACP, a question arises that needs an answer. Would the 1900

37   "William Montague Cobb." Wikimedia Foundation, Inc., June 28, 2018. en.wikipedia.org/wiki/William_Montague_Cobb.

Black American community have willingly accepted an allegiance with a 100 percent White-run and -controlled organization whose fundamental beliefs were totally contradictory to its own? Within the segregated Washington, D.C. community of Dr. Cobbs could be found the same messages of success principles as found in my segregated Tallahassee community fifty years later. The values and vision of our community were obvious, as were the need of stealth and deceit for entry by the ideology of Liberalism.

The 1990s Black Community and Judeo-Christian Values

Religion played a major role in the lives of Black Americans. The church was often the center of their social lives, offering in many cases the only place to gather that was free of White authority, especially in the South. In churches, Black Americans were able to gather and speak freely about what concerned them, including illegal and immoral practices of Whites against them. Another attraction was identifying gospels in the Bible with their own oppression and recognizing that the Bible related a personal, historical context of their lives in the South.[38] The church was usually the first community institution to be established. Starting around 1800 with the African Methodist Episcopal Church, African Methodist Episcopal Zion Church, and other churches, the Black church grew to be the focal point of the Black community.[39]

Churches served as neighborhood centers where free Black people could celebrate their African heritage without intrusion by White detractors. It was the center of education, where as early as 1800, they educated the freed and enslaved Blacks.[40]

As will be discussed later, a Supreme Court ruling in 1947 would forever change the obligation traditionally taken by the Black church to ensure the education of its own children. A combined effort of group of atheists, the anti-Christian ACLU, and a former KKK member would introduce to the US Constitution a new tenet. It was a concept never mentioned in our founding documents: the separation of church and state.

I was fortunate to have been introduced to my oldest known ancestor who arrived in America in the belly of a slave ship. The connection to the Christian faith and commitment to the education of our race can be seen through the remarkable life of this proud and educated American citizen.

My great, great-grandfather Silas Burgess was born in Africa in early 1848. He was brought to America in the hold of a slave ship with his mother

---

38   Debbie McKenna. "Early 1900's Black American South." Debbie McKenna (blog), October 2, 2010. dmckenn2.umwblogs.org/the-color-purple/page-5.

39   Albert J. Raboteau. *Canaan Land: A Religious History of African Americans*. Illustrated, Reprint. Religion in American Life. Oxford, UK: Oxford University Press, 2001.

40   *Ibid.*

and younger brother. They were sold like cattle at the infamous Potters Mart Auction House, in Charleston, SC. The plantation owner who purchased him was a Mr. Burgess. After many beatings, rapes, and bearing a child by this owner, Silas's mother informed him that she could no longer endure the torture. She told him, "You are the oldest, Silas. You must take care of the children. I must leave and never return." She then prepared a large meal, left all that she owned of value, prayed with her children, and left, never to be heard of or seen again. Whether my great, great, great-grandmother's plans were to escape or to commit suicide will forever be left to speculation.

Soon after she left, the plantation owner went looking for her. He commented, "When I find her I am going to give her a beating she will never forget." Great, great-grandfather Silas was eight years old at the time. He later escaped with the help of some male elders and made his way to Craft's Prairie, Texas, where he got his first job building the railroad.

He was described as a very spiritual and loving human being who was fiercely independent and highly respected by the entire community. I was fortunate to experience firsthand these same traits in his great-grandson, my dad. Great, great-grandpa Silas raised his large family on some hundred-and-one acres of farmland, which he paid off within two years. He was politically active as a member of the Republican party and served the spiritual needs of his community as a Primitive Baptist minister. He founded Zion Hill, the first church and school for Black Americans in the entire region. The church building served as a school where children were taught subjects from the first to seventh grades.

He prayed often to God asking that his seed not want for bread. His last prayer was beneath a giant family oak tree. It was a prayer for health and well-being of the generations to come. His prayer has since come to fruition, as his progeny have been granted opportunities for higher education and being part of the American middle class. One of his great, great, great-grandsons played football and graduated from Notre Dame and, like me, played a few years in the NFL. Another great, great, great-grandson played football and graduated from Yale University and like his mother is entering the medical profession. Yet another very determined and tenacious great, great, great-granddaughter, is a single mother who has earned her master's degree and is contracted to leave within weeks of this writing to teach in China. This is but a small sampling of the opportunities made available to just one side of my ancestral family by an educated, grateful, proud Christian, and former slave. My great, great-grandfather Silas represented the "fiercely independent" spirit and the trajectory of his race at the turn of the 1900s.

How did this mindset of pride in education, community, country, free enterprise, and God of the post-Civil War Black community compare with the 1910 ideology of the White organization that would lead it into the 20th century? One of the NAACP's original founders was John Dewey, a humanist and founder of today's public school system. The words humanist and atheist/agnostic are synonymous. It is a theological view that holds that there either isn't a god or that there is no way of knowing.[41] Dewey was consistent in his antagonism to God, as with the 1933 signing of the Humanist Manifesto, a document that contains a complete and thorough denial of God. It sets forth man as master of his fate and declares his utopia to be achievable.[42]

His political activities included being president of the Teachers' Labor Union and co-founder and advocate of the American Civil Liberties Union (ACLU). His political linkage would explain the decades of commitment of the NAACP to the Education Labor Union and his anti-God ACLU, to the detriment of millions of poor Black children. It was with the support of Dewey's ACLU that a group of atheists argued successfully before the Democratic former KKK member and anti-Catholic Supreme Court Chief Justice Hugo Black. This was the 1947 Everson v. Board of Education case. Legal battles concerning the separation of church and state began in laws dating to 1938 that required religious instruction in school or provided state funding for religious schools.[43]

The Catholic Church was a leading proponent of such laws and the primary opponent was the ACLU. The ACLU led the challenge in which Justice Hugo Black wrote, "The First Amendment has erected a wall between church and state.... That wall must be kept high and impregnable."[44] It was not clear that the Bill of Rights forbids state governments from supporting religious education, and strong legal arguments were made by religious proponents arguing that the Supreme Court should not act as a "national school board," and that the Constitution did not govern social issues. However, the ACLU and other advocates of the separation of church and state persuaded the Court to declare such activities unconstitutional. Historian Samuel Walker wrote that the ACLU's "greatest impact on American life" was its role in persuading the Supreme Court to "constitutionalize" so many public controversies.[45]

It should be noted that the Supreme Court justice Hugo Black's definition of a high and impenetrable wall between church and state is nowhere written or referred to in the US Constitution. It was part of a letter that Thomas Jefferson wrote to Christian parishioners.

---

41   "Secular Humanism." Wikipedia. Wikimedia Foundation, Inc., July 10, 2018. en.wikipedia.org/wiki/Secular_humanism.

42   "John Dewey the Humanist." News. Upstream Politics, February 5, 2013. upstre-ampolitics.wordpress.com/2013/02/05/john-dewey-the-humanist/.

43   "American Civil Liberties Union." Wikipedia. Wikimedia Foundation, Inc., August 10, 2018. en.wikipedia.org/wiki/American_Civil_Liberties_Union.

44   Daniel Dreisbach. "The Mythical 'Wall of Separation': How a Misused Metaphor Changed Church–State Law, Policy, and Discourse." Conservative issues. The Heritage Foundation, June 23, 2006. heritage.org/research/reports/2006/06/the-mythical-wall-of-separation-how-a-misused-metaphor-changed-church-state-law-policy-and-discourse.

45   "American Civil Liberties Union." Wikipedia.

*"Believing with you that religion is a matter which lies sole-
ly between man and his God, that he owes account to none
other for faith or his worship, that the legislative powers of
government reach actions only, and not opinions, I contem-
plate with solemn reverence that act of the whole American
people which declared that their legislature should 'make no
law respecting an establishment of religion, or prohibiting
the free exercise thereof,' thus building a wall of separation
between Church and State."[46]*

In this letter, Jefferson was responding to a letter he had received from
the Danbury Baptists of Danbury, CT. They were a minority denomination in
that area and were subjected to persecution for their beliefs. They feared that
if the government were to adopt a state religion, as it had done in England,
that their minority views would be trampled, and they themselves subject
to further persecution. Jefferson wrote his letter to them to reassure them
that they would remain free to worship as they wished, without needing to
fear government interference in their religious beliefs or practices. In fact,
he borrowed the term "wall of separation" from the famous Baptist minister
Roger Williams.[47]

"Separation of Church and State." These five little words, in their misuse,
have become the rallying cry of atheists, agnostics, the ACLU, and others who
wish to remove God from the public forum. This anti-God segment of our
nation believes that a free expression of faith in God is incompatible with any
government institution, practice, program, or official.[48]

The 1947 (ACLU-led) ruling has impacted the Black community in several
ways. It ended the 150-year influence of Black churches, like the Zion Hill of my
great, great-grandfather Silas. As with every other community, it also impacted
the community's ability to use its combined religious and public resources to
provide the education it deemed important for its own children. The long-term
impact of the 1947 ruling can be seen in the increasingly aggressive bullying
and intolerance of the ideology of Liberalism that is offended by any display of
the Christian religion in a public venue.

---

46   "U.S. Constitution." USConstitution.net, June 1, 2010. usconstitution.net/jeffwall.
      html.

47   John M. Barry. "God, Government and Roger Williams' Big Idea." *Smithsonian
      Magazine*, January 2012. smithsonianmag.com/history/god-government-and-
      roger-williams-big-idea-6291280.

48   *Ibid.*

NAACP—The ACLU Influence

- The ACLU court case—In June 2002, the 9th Circuit Court of Appeals ruled in favor of California atheist Michael Newdow, saying that the United States Pledge of Allegiance is unconstitutional because it contains the words "under God."[49]
- The ACLU and Americans United for Separation of Church and State have successfully sued to have displays of the Ten Commandments removed from government-owned property.[50]
- The ACLU attacked the governor of Alabama for having voluntary Bible studies in his office. They are leading the way in removing prayer and religious symbols from public schools. They are doing all of this under the banner of their favorite catch phrase—"separation of church and state."[51]

As the NAACP dutifully sides with the ACLU and other atheist groups that continue attempts to eliminate any reference to Judeo-Christian values we're left to question, is this what the predominantly Christian Black community had envisioned in 1910? Did they sacrifice their blood, sweat, and tears so that one day America would be a society that allowed the legal intimidation and bullying of their great, great, great progeny by the ACLU, Socialist/liberals, and atheists? Would past great generations have tolerated organizations that supported and cheered the PC bullying, the NAACP, and the Democratic Party? Could those Christian faith-based pioneers have foreseen the day when granting salutations of Merry Christmas to non-Christians would be paramount to hate speech? Would they have ever excused, as did the NAACP and the Royalty Black Class, any political party that would vote to delete the word "God" from their National Convention Platform? Would they tolerate the boos, jeers, and shaking of fists by the party's 2012 Democratic National Convention delegates as the amendment was passed to restore a mention of God?[52]

What would our past generations say as they observed the power that the ideology of Liberalism has over the actions of many of today's Black Christian ministers. Those who profess their faith in Jesus Christ and then cowardly stand in silence or boldly walk arm-in-arm with anti-God Socialists and political atheists. The subservience of many within the ministry highlights the unequivocal demands of the ideology of Liberalism, for it is satisfied with no

---

49   B.A. Robinson. "Religious Tolerance Menu, Site Map." Religious Tolerance, September 29, 2003. religioustolerance.org/nat_pled3.htm.

50   "American Civil Liberties Union." Wikipedia.

51   *Ibid.*

52   WND staff. "Democrats Boo Vote To Restore 'God.'" WorldNetDaily (WND). September 5, 2012. wnd.com/2012/09/democrats-boo-idea-of-mentioning-god.

less than total and absolute allegiance. Do we, as did our ancestors, defend our freedom to profess our faith or do we cower to the ideology of Liberalism and put our faith in the backseat? Will our Christian ministers lead as they have throughout the past proud history of the Black community's fight for freedom or will they follow a new ideological master? There is no gray line or place for ambivalence for the Black race. The choice is simple: "we either stand as a faith-based race or we fall as one that is not."

As Christians, we must remain fervent in our prayers that we, as a race and as a nation, remain steadfast and valiant, trusting only in the Savior and His promises. As we do so, we will be an influence for good. We will be blessed individually, but more importantly, we will be a blessing to others; those of the Christian faith as well as those who are not.

Based on history, we can assume some things regarding our Black ancestors of the 1800s–1960s. First, they were not lukewarm whiners, weenies, and wimps regarding their faith. Second, their vision was never in concert with the vision of the NAACP, whose present policies remain consistent with the ideology of those who stood behind the curtain in 1910. The NAACP was, after all, an organization of twenty-one wealthy White liberals, progressives, Socialists, humanists, and atheists whose core values were antithetical to the values of the community they purported to represent for the next one hundred years. As an organization formed on the strategy of stealth, the NAACP is ultimately symbolic of the Greek Trojan Horse for community of Christian, Capitalist, patriotic, and independent Black Americans.

The 1900s Black Community Family and the Role of the Father

In 2012, the U.S Census Bureau released a report that studied the history of marriage in the United States. They discovered some startling statistics. When calculating marriage by race, from 1890 until the 1960s, the study found that African-Americans age thirty-five and older were more likely to be married than White Americans. Not only did they swap places during the 1960s but in 1980 the number of never married African-Americans began a staggering climb from about 10 percent to more than 25 percent by 2010. During this time, the percentage for White women remained under 10 percent and just over 10 percent for White men.[53]

These statistics show that since the 1960s, there have been an increasing number of Black men not committing to their family. A 1965 report by NY Democratic Senator Patrick Moynihan, "The Negro Family: The Case for National Action," supports these statistics. In the report, Moynihan attempted to sound the alarm of the detrimental impact that the ideology of Liberalism's

---

53   "African American Employment." Metrics. Black Demographics, July 2018. black-demographics.com/economics/employment.

policies of federal welfare was having on the Black family. One of many conclusions was that, "The steady expansion of welfare programs could be taken as a measure of the steady disintegration of the Negro family structure over the past generation in the United States."[54]

As early as 1965, Moynihan argued "without access to jobs and the means to contribute meaningful support to a family, Black men would become systematically alienated from their roles as husbands and fathers. This would cause rates of divorce, child-abandonment and out-of-wedlock births to skyrocket in the Black community—leading to vast increases in the numbers of female-headed households and the higher rates of poverty, low educational outcomes, and inflated rates of child abuse that are associated with them."

The report concluded that the structure of family life in the Black community "constituted a 'tangle of pathology...capable of perpetuating itself without assistance from the White world,' and that 'at the heart of the deterioration of the fabric of Negro society is the deterioration of the Negro family. It is the fundamental source of the weakness of the Negro community now...the matriarchal structure of Black culture weakened the ability of Black men to function as authority figures. This particular notion of Black familial life has become a widespread, if not dominant, paradigm for comprehending the social and economic disintegration of late twentieth-century Black urban life."[55]

Democratic Senator Monahan's report was prophetic. How did the NAACP respond? The senator was maligned and ignored. As predictable with the ideology of Liberalism's methods of silencing and intimidating opposing thought, he was accused of infusing his report with racist assumptions.[56]

The report was sharply attacked by Black civil rights leaders as examples of White patronizing, cultural bias, or racism. It was condemned or dismissed by the NAACP and other civil rights groups. Black leaders such as Jesse Jackson and Al Sharpton accused Moynihan of relying on stereotypes of the Black family and Black men. They said the report implied that Blacks had inferior academic performance and portrayed crime and pathology as endemic to the Black community. They failed to recognize that both cultural bias and racism in standardized tests had contributed to apparent lower achievement by Blacks in school. The report was criticized for threatening to undermine the place of civil rights on the national agenda, leaving "a vacuum that could be filled with a politics that blamed Blacks for their own troubles."[57]

---

54   "The Negro Family: The Case For National Action." Wikipedia. Wikimedia Foundation, Inc., June 23, 2018. en.wikipedia.org/wiki/The_Negro_Family:_The_Case_For_National_Action.

55   Ibid.

56   Robin Marie Averbeck. "The Good Old Liberals." Jacobin Magazine, March 2015. jacobinmag.com/2015/03/moynihan-report-fiftieth-anniversary-liberalism.

57   Ibid.

James Farmer, civil rights leader and honorary vice chairman of the Democratic Socialists of America, noted, "By laying the primary blame for present-day inequalities on the pathological condition of the Negro family and community, Moynihan has provided a massive academic cop-out for the White conscience and clearly implied that Negroes in this nation will never secure a substantial measure of freedom until we learn to behave ourselves and stop buying Cadillacs instead of bread."[58] In 1987, Hortense Spillers, a Black feminist academic, criticized the Moynihan report on semantic grounds for its use of "matriarchy" and "patriarchy" when describing the African-American family. She argues that the "terminology used to define White families cannot be used to define African-American families because of the way slavery has affected the African-American family."[59]

Psychologist William Ryan, in his 1971 book, *Blaming the Victim*, also criticized the Moynihan report. He said it was an "attempt to divert responsibility for poverty from social structural factors to the behaviors and cultural patterns of the poor."[60]

Every segment of American sociality teaches importance of individual accountability and the mastering of actions/ attitudes as stepping stone for success. Honesty, hard work, preparedness, and a positive attitude are imperative. Most assuredly, these were the principles that the White liberal Ryan taught his own children, for he envisioned their future as successful and productive citizens. The ideology of Liberalism has a different standard for urban Black Americans, lowering expectations of them and considering such an act as compassionate. Acceptance of lower expectations of a race is not compassionate, but rather debilitating, condescending, and extremely racist.

When our children reach the age of maturity, capable of understanding lessons of personal accountability, responsibility and critical thinking, we teach them. For our special needs children, these lessons are tailored to match their capability to learn. This is an act of compassion and a wise acknowledgment of the personal limitations of the special needs child. This best summarizes the perspective of the ideology of Liberalism toward the urban Black community. Viewed as children, incapable of making necessary changes in personal conduct and choices, they suggest that personal accountability be negated from the success equation. The ideology of Liberalism then convinces its followers that their failing status has nothing to do with personal choices, i.e., dropping out of school, having babies out of wedlock, the lack of personal people skills or education, dismal work habits, or inappropriate appearance and dress. After imposing for decades its multiple anti-Black policies, the ideology of Liberalism then blames individual failure on racist White conservatives and their policies.

---

58   *Ibid.*
59   *Ibid.*
60   "The Negro Family: The Case For National Action." Wikipedia.

The consequence of condescendingly low expectations placed on the poor is seen in every community dominated by the ideology of Liberalism. It is also seen in every Socialist and Communist country around the world. In this environment, it is seen as a predictable constant...the poor remains forever and hopelessly bound and dependent in poverty.

From its beginnings in the early 1960s until 1996, federal welfare was an open-ended entitlement that encouraged long-term dependency. There was widespread agreement that it was a terrible failure. It neither reduced poverty nor helped the poor become self-sufficient. It encouraged out-of-wedlock births and de-emphasized the work ethic. The pathologies it engendered were passed from generation to generation.[61] Regardless of its obvious failure, the ideology of Liberalism continued have its way in the Democratic-controlled House and Senate, as members continued to block any welfare reform that would stem the growing government dependency of the Black underclass. It was the Democratic Party's view that ending dependency of recipients on the federal government welfare program equated to a lack of compassion for those who were dependent on it. With the increasing statistical evidence of the detrimental impact of welfare on the Black family unit, every Socialist/Liberal organization, including the NAACP, demanded the status quo...no change!

After decades of a Democratic-controlled House and Senate (1955–1980) and (1987–1995),[62] welfare reform was finally passed in 1996 by Democratic President Bill Clinton, supported by a Republican-controlled House and Senate. The Personal Responsibility and Work Opportunity Reconciliation Act fulfilled Clinton's 1992 campaign promise to "end welfare as we have come to know it."[63]

Because of this reform, thirty-one years after the predicted devastation of federal welfare programs, welfare and poverty rates declined during the late 1990s. This led many commentators to declare that the legislation was a success. An editorial in the ultra-liberal magazine *The New Republic* opined: "A broad consensus now holds that welfare reform was certainly not a disaster—and that it may, in fact, have worked much as its designers had hoped.[64]

After five decades of dominance, the ideology of Liberalism media and the Royalty Class Black Man introduced terminology that would have

61   Michael Tanner, and Tad DeHaven. "TANF and Federal Welfare." Analysis. Down-sizing the Federal Government, September 1, 2010. downsizinggovernment.org/hhs/welfare-spending.

62   "What Years Did Democrats Control Both House and Senate?" Forum. Answers.com, n.d. answers.com/Q/What_years_did_democrats_control_both_house_and_senate.

63   "Personal Responsibility and Work Opportunity Act." Wikipedia. Wikimedia Foundation, Inc., July 7, 2018. en.wikipedia.org/wiki/Personal_Responsibil-ity_and_Work_Opportunity_Act.

64   Jonathan Chait. "Fact Finders." *The New Republic*, February 28, 2005. newrepub-lic.com/article/61829/fact-finders.

been considered highly offensive by early 1900 Black Americans. It was the assignment of segments of Americans to a hopeless status called "the permanent underclass." Defined as "people who are at the bottom of a society having become victims of the poverty trap. This class is largely composed of the young unemployed, long-term-unemployed, chronically sick, disabled, old, or single mothers...who are therefore, unable to rise out of it."[65]

America's Promise

One of the unique features of the Promise of America is the access it gives each of its citizens to upward mobility. It provides the freest environment on the face of the earth for anyone to choose to climb if he or she wishes, with a caveat that risk and failure are intrinsic parts of the equation. An increasing number of Americans demand the presence of an arbitrator who will guarantee them equal results while negating all pain. This is the false premise of Communism and Socialism, but was never the vision of Capitalism, which can be summarized "Where There Is No Pain, There Is No Gain." The American promise is one that grants multiple opportunities to try and, if necessary, start anew. A serendipity of the American Way is access to an unseen source of strength needed to transition through growth, called hope. The promise of the American Way is predicated on an understanding that we're only required to do our best to maximize our own full capability. This gives us faith in a fair resolution as we inch our way to the other side of defeat, disappointment, and betrayal. It is a journey that every American must take, making personal choices along the way as to whether they will remain on the thruway or take one of its many off-ramps. If the choice is to remain steady, principled, and not to "grow weary in well doing" happiness is assured through the adoption of attributes such as faith, forgiveness, diligence, patience, and charity.

This is the message of conservatism. This was also the belief of the Black communities of the early to mid-1900s, summarized in three cumulatively powerful words, "We Shall Overcome."

How does this compare with the ideology of Liberalism? As we reread the definition of America's "permanent underclass," we can see how this ideology envisions those who are convinced to depend on it most. It sees a large segment of Americans as permanently too incompetent, too lost, too poor, too Black, too uneducated, too single, too angry, too hopeless, and too hapless ever to find themselves out of poverty. It is this same segment of Americans that have been left reeling from the decades of anti-Black policies imposed on them, keeping them poor. Policies that predictably undermined the expectations of men to fulfill their divine roles, as it simultaneously undermined women's expectation

---

65   "Underclass." BusinessDictionary.Com. WebFinance, Inc. Accessed August 1, 2018. businessdictionary.com/definition/underclass.html.

for a loyal, competent, and committed partnership. As the Royalty Class Black Politicians blame others for this downward trajectory of the community that they oversaw, they confidently demand continued loyalty by promising more of the same. Only within the ideology of Liberalism/Socialism are expectations placed on individuals based on their external attributes and status. Its influence grows only as it convinces its believers to view others from outside-in versus inside-out, dividing and highlighting their differences versus celebrating their commonality.

It is the ideology of Liberalism that refuses to acknowledge the basic underpinning of the American culture, which envisions a lineage of each individual to an all-powerful and omnipotent God. This spiritual heritage unveils an unlimited human potential, making it impossible to assign a permanent economic status to any free American.

Yes, economic limitations and misery can be mandated, as it has been in the godless regimes of Cuba, China, Russia, North Korea, and Iran. Mandating constraints on rights and freedom has never been the American Way. Ours is the one country that has for two centuries protected the agency to choose one's own path. It is the country that also acknowledges that with freedom of choice comes immutable consequences based on those choices. Because personal choices within a Capitalist society define our financial status, neither wealth nor poverty is guaranteed or permanent in America. Those who choose to live with hope, a tenacious work ethic, honesty, and an empathetic spirit towards others will be blessed with their personal version of the American dream.

Those who choose the route of laziness, self-centered narcissism, dishonesty/betrayal, and lack of vision—the poverty of mind, body, and soul awaits them. Regardless of our choice, there is a coinciding link to immutable consequences. The Law of Seed and Harvest remains in force and, like the Law of Gravity and the Law of Inertia, it is eternally predictable.

The fickle status of wealth is reported almost daily in our reality-TV culture. Outside the arena of sports and entertainment, the stories of Black Americans obtaining long-lasting, real success through the utilization of traditional success principles are very rare. Those who have done so through the free market/ Capitalism remain unheralded. It is not beneficial to the ideology of Liberalism to celebrate Black Americans who have, through their own ingenuity, tenacity, and willpower, proven that the American Way works. The message that poverty is a choice and not a permanent condition is a dichotomy to its very existence. It is a dagger that strikes at its very core when an individual recognizes that government dependency is akin to mental, emotional, and spiritual slavery. Like a malignant cancer this form of dependency eats away the essence and value of the soul. It is worse than physical slavery because it enslaves the human will, necessary to fight for and win freedom.

Therefore, it is imperative for the survival of the ideology of Liberalism that the successful voices of conservative Black Americans are ignored or silenced. If they become too vocal and too visible they are, with collaboration of the Royalty Class Black Man and the White liberal elitist's BET, demeaned, discredited, and destroyed, if possible. Understood by the ideology of

Liberalism is the threat that these independent- thinking Americans pose to their dependable base of urban Black Americans. The message that escape is possible from the sweet enticement of government dependency and its Siamese twin, poverty, could inspire others to also seek self-sufficiency.

Such is the case of conservative Black American, Star Parker. Star was a single welfare mother in Los Angeles, California. After accepting Jesus Christ in her life, she returned to college, earned a BS degree in marketing, and launched an urban Christian magazine. The 1992 Los Angeles riots destroyed her business and yet served as a springboard for her focus on faith-based and free market alternatives to empower the poor. As a social policy consultant, Star gives regular testimony before the United States Congress, and is a national expert on major television and radio shows across the country. Currently, Star is a regular commentator on CNN, MSNBC, and FOX News. She has debated Jesse Jackson on BET, fought for school choice on *Larry King Live*, and defended welfare reform on *The Oprah Winfrey Show*.[66]

Star has written three books, *Pimps, Whores and Welfare Brats* (1996), *Uncle Sam's Plantation* (2003), and *White Ghetto* (2006). In 1995, she founded the Center for Urban Renewal and Education (CURE),[67] which works with Black religious and community groups on social policy issues like school choice.[68] She is also a syndicated columnist for Scripps-Howard News Service, offering weekly op-eds to more than 400 newspapers worldwide.[69]

Star represents the possibilities, the rags-to-riches middle-class American dream, for millions of near-hopeless Black Americans. She is independent, smart, articulate, courageous, accomplished, and proof that poverty in America is a choice. It does not have to be permanent after all. She is a great example, a role model, and a voice in the wilderness for millions of young Black girls in a community sorely lacking hopeful messaging.

What has been the response of the pro-welfare ideology of Liberalism to this successful Black American woman who has successfully broken the chains of welfare? There is no better example of the condescending, misogynist, and racist based spirit of the ideology of Liberalism than the comments of White liberal blogger, Gaius Publius. Typical of a liberal White racist, he accepts the premise that he is an expert on the acceptable degrees of Blackness. From his exalted perspective, he sees his role as a judge capable of defining for Americans those who are truly worthy of being called Black. Consistent with

66   "Star Parker Biography." All American Speakers Bureau, n.d. allamericanspeak-ers.com/celebritytalentbios/Star-Parker#sthash.a7DfvJmP.dpuf.

67   "Cure: Center for Urban Renewal and Education." Awareness. Urban Cure, n.d. urbancure. org.

68   "Star Parker." Wikipedia. Wikimedia Foundation, Inc., July 26, 2018. en.wikipedia.org/wiki/Star_Parker.

69   "Star Parker Biography." All American Speakers Bureau.

White liberal racist is the liberty and comfort that he takes in disrespecting Black womanhood.

As America's smallest minority segment, with the audacity to step out of place, the independent Black woman is granted the highest degree of disdain from White liberal racist. As Publius verbally assaults and demeans another successful Black role model, he is also confident of the praise forthcoming from his fellow backslapping liberal PC collaborators. He will travel home to his integrated community of liberals, expecting the wink and nod from the ever-predictable Royalty Class Black Man.

This is the gang cowardice that is typical of liberal White racism. And though it is not politically correct to call a Black American who has stepped out of their place, "a nigger," this group of White liberal men gleefully use such terms as Uncle Tom, Oreo, Porch Monkey, and so on to accommodate their racist disdain. They will, after all, have the blessings and cover of their good Black people, the Royalty Class Black Man.

Imagine the racist, misogynistic, and disrespectful comments made of another Black woman of our day, First Lady Michele Obama. There are both Black and White Americans who will never see this correlation, because they have unfortunately accepted the basic premise of the ideology of Liberalism. This premise states that the sacred nature of the liberal ideology requires loyalty that is much deeper than that required for the honor and respect of Black womanhood. Where has this liberal premise found its most secure home? With the whiners, weenies, and wimps called the Royalty Class Black Man.

Gaius Publius, representative of White liberal racism, defines for Americans "a good Black" versus "a self-loathing bad Black," or as he calls us... Uncle Toms. The following are his comments about national leader, successful vocal Christian, and Black role model, Star Parker:

- An African-American unemployed single mother who got abortions the way normal people use tissues and who was arrested multiple times on multiple charges.
- A right wing huckster pedaling Republican nonsense-for-pay.
- Her specialty is phony moralizing and African American self-loathing, as in her pathetic autobiography
- She pimps full-time for the GOP.
- Widely considered one of the most prominent Uncle Toms of the GOP.
- The Republican Party cleaned her up nicely before they sent her out to talk trash about poor people and tell everyone that they should read the Bible and hope for a better life in Heaven.[70]

---

70   DownWithTyranny. "Palin Picks Another Loser: Star Parker." Down with Tyranny! (blog), June 18, 2010. downwithtyranny.blogspot.com/2010/06/palin-picks-another-loser-star-parker.html#sthash.MannNUKP7.dpuf.

I believe in the resiliency of the Black race. Though its manhood has been under attack for over sixty years, there are still millions of real Black men alive and well throughout our nation. These are men who are proud of their race, their heritage, our women, and who are willing to defend them all. It will be these men who will demand—not beg, plead, or negotiate—for the end of the disgraceful and degrading liberal attacks on Black American women. Whether our women have reached successful pinnacles of national visibility or not, it is time for this debauchery to end.

It is time we call out every Black and White elitist who chooses to disrespect Black women because they believe their racist misogyny is funny and in vogue. The age of covering for obnoxious, White liberal racism is over. As the ideology of Liberalism attacks and demeans Black womanhood it shines an insightful light on its view of Black men, who is also viewed with disrespect. From the perspective of the 1900s, Black community and my proud 1960s segregated community of Tallahassee, Florida, we ask: What kind of man "remains in his place" as our women are being verbally abused and assaulted? The answer from every other proud generation of men: whiners, weenies, and wimps...

NOTE: For the White liberal racists who have taken solace in the predictable cover granted to you by the Royalty Class Black Man while you, with smug confidence and no thought of consequence, denigrate our Black womanhood, those days are over. The resurrection of the Black community will have within it men who will ensure the light of exposure and free market consequences.

The vision of the early 1900 Black community for the role of manhood was simple and straightforward. Considered a divine one, it was based on loyalty and faithfulness as a husband, dedication and leadership as a father, and as the ultimate defender of his family, community, and country. The idea of self-sacrifice has been intrinsic as it came with the territory. This was never the vision of the Black man by the White liberals, Socialists, and humanists—the founders of the NAACP. Their ideals from the beginning were a contradiction—an organization steeped in Socialism and atheism is a dichotomy of one founded in Capitalism by a community of devout Christians. From this divergence of ideals and values came the strategic need for the Trojan Horse called the NAACP.

The Presence of the NAACP

Where was the NAACP during the last fifty years as federal welfare programs undermined the Black family, as predicted in early 1965, and saw the increase in hopelessness and the abandonment by neutered Black males? As the facts began to surface about the deepening and ever-devastating urban dependency, where was the NAACP pro-growth community strategy and their MAN-UP campaign? Where was the message that is consistent within every other successful minority culture of self-sufficiency, education, work ethic, and the use of "commonsense" people skills? For decades the NAACP has remained in lock step, 100 percent predictable and loyal to the ideology of Liberalism and the White leadership of the Democratic Party. "Not once" has it broken rank and shown any backbone to side with the millions of Black Americans who have believed in them. Instead, multiple generations of trusting poor Americans have suffered through decades of NAACP-supported liberal anti-Black policies imposed on them.

As recently as the mid-1960s, the Black community ranked at the top of the scale for many of America's positive success indicators, i.e., education, marriage percentage, growth of its middle class, religious commitment, percentage of entrepreneurs, and so forth. Fifty years later, it ranks at the top of every national negative indicator: illiteracy, crime, murder, abortion, child abandonment, child abuse, unemployment, lack of entrepreneurs, and so on. What has been the cost according to the misery index and lives lost as the ideology of Liberalism has dominated every urban city government? Each of these present war zones has been led and dominated by liberal/Socialist Black politicians, liberal/Socialist Black public school administrators, liberal/Socialist pro-union, anti-Black employment policies, and Socialist market strategies. And yet, typical of an ideology that refuses to embrace the concept of personal accountability, it lays the blame for the lack of Black progress at the feet of the White race and conservatism.

Unfortunately, since the formation of the NAACP in 1910, conservative values, once the bedrock of the early 1900s Black community, have had an ever-diminishing influence. Standing behind the curtain of the Crisis were twenty-one White Socialists, liberals, and atheist founding executive board members. Their first actions were directed at attacking Capitalism by maligning the foremost Capitalist and educator of that day, Booker T. Washington. They successfully set in place his reputation within the Black community as an Uncle Tom. They then set about over the following decades to undermine the loyalty that the Black community once had for the Republican Party.

Booker T. Washington, an American hero, laid the foundation for more progress by the Black race than any other man in 20th-century history. It is his Tuskegee University that will be known throughout the annals of time for its contributions to WWII, the legendary Tuskegee Airman. It is also the University that has given to the American marketplace millions of talented Black graduates since 1881. It was through his collaboration with Andrew Carnegie that, in 1900, the nation's first business network was established. This Black Business Network served as the foundation for the exploding Black middle class throughout the 1940s, 1950s, and early 1960s. Through his collaboration with other wealthy philanthropists, millions of dollars were sent to support Black high schools and colleges throughout the South and to fund secret lawsuits against racist policies. This financial support was extended for decades after his death in 1915. In 1901, he was the first Black American invited to the White House, where he dined with the Republican President Theodore Roosevelt. In his last years, he was warned to slow down his work pace due to health concerns. He dismissed these warnings and died at his beloved Tuskegee just days after an arduous fundraising tour throughout the Northeast. His death was due to the complications from exhaustion and high blood pressure. This is the man whom the ideology of Liberalism, the NAACP, and the Royalty Class Black Man have successful tainted as an Uncle Tom. His sin? As an accomplished Capitalist, educator, bridge builder, and Christian, he delivered a message of independence, self- reliance, and sufficiency, defining him as a conservative. To the ideology of Liberalism this is equivalent to putting a large silver cross in the face of Count Dracula.

Likewise, through persistent and effective messaging, the ideology of Liberalism has been successful in tainting the Republican Party as racist. This was the party whose only reason for existence in 1860 was to present to the country its first anti-slavery platform. Its first presidential candidate, Abraham Lincoln, fulfilled that promise. It has throughout the 1900s consistently advanced pro-Black policies of anti-slavery, pro-Reconstruction, anti-KKK, anti-segregation, pro-civil rights, pro-God, pro-Capitalist, pro-school choice, pro-traditional family, pro-job opportunity (anti-Davis-Bacon), and pro-Judeo-Christian values. This is the party that the progressive education and the Socialist Royalty Class Black Man, has cast as racist. It has been Black Conservative Americans with these views that have been cast as Uncle Toms. Of interest is that every pro-Black policy listed here, other than pro-Civil Rights, the liberal/Socialist Democratic Party have stood adamantly opposed to.

The NAACP, with its effective messaging, has obscured the real roles played by the Democratic and Republican parties regarding to the progress of Black Americans. It was the Democratic President Woodrow Wilson who ordered the segregation the United States Navy and it was General Dwight D. Eisenhower, later a Republican president, who allowed African-American soldiers to join the White military units to fight in combat for the first time—the first step toward a desegregated United States military.[71] It was Republican President Eisenhower, in 1957, who sent the 101st Airborne to Little Rock, Arkansas, to enforce the integration mandate. Many in the Democratic establishment convulsed with rage.[72] The support of the 1867 Post Civil War Reconstruction Act and passage of the 1965 Voting Rights Act illustrate the convoluted, yet effective messaging of the ideology of Liberalism.

The post-Civil War Reconstruction period was a defining moment that cemented the loyalty of the early Black community to the Republican Party. During the Republican-legislated Reconstruction era, which began in 1867, newly-enfranchised Blacks gained a voice in government for the first time in

---

71   "Desegregation." Wikipedia. Wikimedia Foundation, Inc., June 8, 2018. en.wikipedia.org/wiki/Desegregation#In_the_U.S._military.

72   Kasey S. Pipes. "Eisenhower Was Key Desegregation Figure." Politico, September 18, 2007. politico.com/story/2007/09/eisenhower-was-key-desegregation-figure-005885#ixzz41CLzr1ZA.

American history, winning election to Southern state legislatures and even to the U.S. Congress.

Within a decade, however, reactionary forces, including the Democratic Party's terrorist organization, the Ku Klux Klan, reversed the changes wrought by Reconstruction and restored White supremacy in the South.[73] Considerable violence and fraud accompanied elections during Reconstruction, as the White Democrats used paramilitary groups (the KKK) from the 1870s to suppress Black Republican voting and to turn Republicans out of office. In North Carolina's Wilmington Insurrection of 1898, White Democrats conducted a *coup d'état* of city government, the only one in United States history. They overturned a duly elected biracial government and widely attacked the Black community, destroying lives and property. Ultimately, White Democrats achieved widespread disenfranchisement by law: from 1890 to 1908, Southern state legislatures passed new constitutions, constitutional amendments, and laws that made voter registration and voting more difficult. They succeeded in disenfranchising most of the Black citizens. The Republican Party was nearly eliminated in the region for decades.[74]

---

73   History.com staff. "Reconstruction: Compromise of 1877." History.com, 2009. history.com/topics/american-civil-war/reconstruction.

74   "Disenfranchisement after the Reconstruction Era." Wikipedia. Wikimedia Foundation, Inc., September 9, 2018. en.wikipedia.org/wiki/Disenfranchisement_after_the_Reconstruction_Era.

On August 6, 1965, the Civil Rights Voting Rights Act was signed into law. In the Senate, 94 percent of Republicans voted in favor, while just 73 percent of Democrats voted for it. In the U.S. House of Representatives, 82 percent of Republicans voted in favor compared to 78 percent for the Democrats. Senator Everett Dirksen (R-IL), co-author of the 1965 Voting Rights Act, helped outmaneuver Democrat opposition: "There has to be a real remedy. There must be something durable and worthwhile. This cannot go on forever, this denial of the right to vote by ruses and devices and tests and whatever the mind can contrive to either make it very difficult or to make it impossible to vote."

The 1965 Voting Rights Act achieved for African-Americans a major goal of the GOP's Reconstruction Era-civil rights agenda, which the Democrats had blocked a century earlier.[75]

The 1900s Black Community and Capitalism

Dr. Cobb's father, William Elmer Cobb, moved to Washington from Selma, Alabama, in 1899 to work for the Government Printing Office. He later established his own printing business supporting his segregated community. His entry into the Black middle class was consistent with the prevalence of the entrepreneurial mindset of that day.[76]

In that same 1900 neighborhood where Dr. Cobb's father was able to pursue his American dream, it is now impossible for a Black man, with the same skills and ambition, to do the same. It is also impossible for young Black teenagers in these urban communities to get work experience under the tutelage of members of their own race. William Julius Wilson, a sociologist, has published numerous works about the problems of poverty caused by the loss of good-paying industrial jobs, as well as the migration of residential populations, jobs, and related facilities to the suburbs.[77]

This absence of good-paying jobs and entrepreneurial opportunities within the urban Black communities can be laid at the feet of anti-Black/pro-Union policies supported by the NAACP and the Congressional Black Caucus. Since 1931, the White leadership of the labor unions, the White leadership of the Democratic Party, and the first White Board members of the NAACP have successfully colluded to protect an anti-Black law called the Davis-Bacon Act. The Davis-Bacon Act requires that federal construction contractors pay their workers "prevailing wages" (union wages). The law was passed during the height of the Great Depression with the intent to protect White workers, who belonged to White-only unions, from competing against non-unionized Black

---

75   Michael Zak. "Republicans Passed the 1965 Voting Rights Act." General / Chat. Free Republic, August 6, 2010. freerepublic.com/focus/f-chat/2565711/posts.

76   "William Montague Cobb." Wikimedia Foundation, Inc., June 28, 2018.

77   "The Negro Family: The Case For National Action." Wikipedia.

workers. The act continues to have discriminatory effects today by favoring disproportionately White, skilled, and unionized construction workers over disproportionately Black, unskilled, and non-unionized construction workers. Because the Davis-Bacon Act was passed with discriminatory intent and continues to have discriminatory effects, its enforcement violates the Constitution's guarantee of equal protection of the law.[78]

The passage of the Davis-Bacon Act only exacerbated the financial woes of the early 1930s Black community. Its cause and effect continue today as it deprives the community of Black entrepreneurs, job opportunities for Black laborers, and the tax base derived from both. While Black and White unemployment rates were similar prior to passage of the Davis-Bacon Act, they began to diverge afterwards. This problem persists today. In the first quarter of 1992, the Black unemployment rate was 14.2 percent, even though the overall national rate was only 7.9 percent.[79]

Davis-Bacon restricts the economic opportunities of low-income individuals in several ways. Minority contracting firms are often small and non-unionized and cannot afford to pay the "prevailing wage." The act requires contractors to pay unskilled laborers the prevailing wage for any job they perform, essentially forcing contractors to hire skilled tradesmen, selecting workers from a pool dominated by Whites.[80]

Thus, the Davis-Bacon Act constitutes a formidable barrier to entry into the construction industry for unskilled or low-skilled workers. This is especially harmful to minorities. Work in the construction industry usually pays extraordinarily well compared to other entry-level positions. Such jobs could provide plentiful opportunities for low-income individuals to enter the economic mainstream. The law's impact on the ability of minorities to find work in the construction industry has been particularly devastating. The Department of Labor's initial set of regulations did not recognize categories of unskilled workers except for union apprentices. As a result, contractors had to pay an unskilled worker who was not part of a union apprenticeship program as much as a skilled laborer, which almost completely excluded Blacks from working on Davis-Bacon projects. This effectively foreclosed the only means by which unskilled Blacks could learn the necessary skills to become skilled workers.[81]

As unskilled workers must be paid the same wage as a skilled worker, the contractor is forced to pay laborers considerably more than the market value

78   David E. Bernstein. "Cato Institute Briefing Paper No. 17: The Davis-Bacon Act: Let's Bring Jim Crow to an End." Research. Cato Institute, January 18, 1993. cato. org/publications/briefing-paper/davisbacon-act-lets-bring-jim-crow-end.

79   John Frantz. "Davis-Bacon: Jim Crow's Last Stand." Politics. Foundation for Economic Education, February 1, 1994. fee.org/articles/davis-bacon-jim-crows-last-stand.

80   *Ibid.*

81   *Ibid.*

for their work. For example, in Philadelphia, electricians working on projects covered by the Davis-Bacon Act must be paid 37.97 dollars per hour in wages and fringe benefits. The average wage of electricians working for private contractors on non-Davis-Bacon projects is 15.76 dollars per hour, with some laborers working for as little as 10.50 dollars per hour. Thus, even minority open-shop contractors have no incentive to hire unskilled Black workers.

Ralph C. Thomas, former executive director of the National Association of Minority Contractors, stated that a minority contractor who acquires a Davis-Bacon contract has "no choice but to hire skilled tradesmen, the majority of which are of the majority." As a result, Thomas said, "Davis-Bacon closes the door in such activity in an industry most capable of employing the largest numbers of minorities.[82]

Urban community residents watch as state and federally funded projects are built all around them. Consistent is the presence of predominantly White-only union laborers whose members take and spend their paychecks in their own neighborhoods, supporting their own neighborhoods and schools. Also consistent is the lack of opportunity and job experience for Black teenagers. This ensures that the young Black male will consistently lack responsible role models, mentors, and Black entrepreneurs, most of whom would hire their own if they had the opportunity. There is also no place in this community for inquisitive Black youth to learn and experience Capitalism, as is found in other minority communities, such as Asian, Indian, Chinese, Japanese, Cuban, Mexican, and so on.

Black Americans' unemployment rates are high in every urban community throughout our country. In Chicago, unemployment of Blacks has reached a high of 25 percent, while the rate among the White Americans is 7 percent, and among Latinos, 12 percent.[83] Chicago is the bastion of Liberalism and the home of the prominent Royal Class Black Problem Profiteer, Jesse Jackson. The unemployment rate among teenaged Black males there is an astounding 92 percent.[84] This equates to ninety-two out of every hundred Black teenage males in one of our nation's largest cities being denied the opportunity to work and learn successful life skills. If there is any wonder why Chicago leads the nation in the murder of Black citizens, the dire hopelessness of 92 percent jobless, fatherless, uneducated, visionless Black teenage males is a good place to begin

---

82   *Ibid.*

83   Adeshina Emmanuel. "Chicago's Black Unemployment Rate Higher than Other Large Metro Areas." *The Chicago Reporter*. November 16, 2014, sec. Employment and Labor. chicagoreporter.com/chicagos-black-unemployment-rate-higher-other-large-metro-areas.

84   National Urban League Wire. "Chicago's Black Male Teens' 92 Percent Unemployment Rate Leads Nation." I Am Empowered. January 28, 2014, sec. Newsroom. http://www.iamempowered.com/article/2014/01/28/chicagos-Black-male-teens-92-percent-unemployment-rate-leads-nation.

seeking an answer. This is the result of pure, unadulterated, unapologetic, and unaccountable Liberalism.

Aside from the racist Davis-Bacon Act, another very popular anti-Black/pro-union policy of the ideology of Liberalism is increasing the minimum wage. Politicians from both parties understand the devastating impact this policy has on millions of Black lives. Unskilled labor, which defines the Black male teenager, is impacted the most. With each increase of the minimum wage, Black teenagers are "automatically" priced out of reach of the small business owners who would normally hire them. So, between being legislated out of work by the liberal-backed Davis-Bacon Act, priced out of work by the liberal-backed minimum wage, and entering a competitive market with minimum education skills controlled by a liberal union public school, the Black teenager faces the perfect storm, liberal-induced. It keeps him unskilled, unemployed, and in time, unemployable.

The Black teenager has little to look forward to but a life of crime or dependency on federal government assistance. The liberal segments of both the Democratic and Republican parties understand the math and the common sense that drives this issue. The typical Royalty Class politician, Black and White, views the sacrifice of these millions of lives through multiple generations simply as the price of doing business. It sounds compassionate enough and guarantees a pathway to re-election.

Supporters of raising the minimum wage argue it will raise the earnings of low-income workers. Labor unions are among the most prominent of these supporters, a fact that makes little intuitive sense, because very few union members work for the minimum wage. Unions, however, are not just being altruistic when they push to raise the minimum wage. A higher minimum wage increases the expense of hiring unskilled workers. This makes hiring skilled union members more attractive and could raise the earnings of union members who compete with minimum wage workers by 20 to 40 percent. Meanwhile, non-union, low-skilled worker earnings (Black American youth) fall due to reduced working hours and fewer job opportunities.[85] This helps explain the 92 percent unemployment rate among Black American boys in the union-friendly, Davis-Bacon Act, high minimum wage bastion of Liberalism of Chicago, Illinois. Nationwide unemployment for Black male teens is 83 percent.[86]

85   Anthony Kim, and Tim Kane. "A Higher Minimum Wage Equals Less Economic Free-
      dom." Conservative issues. The Heritage Foundation, March 8, 2007. heritage.org/
      jobs-and-labor/report/higher-minimum-wage-equals-less-economic-freedom.
86   Ann Brown. "No Openings: 92% Of Black Male Chicago Youth Are Out Of
      Work." Entertainment. Madame Noire (blog), January 22, 2014. madamenoire.
      com/342987/92-young-black-males-chicago-unemployed.

The facts, according to the CBO (Congressional Budgeting Office), are that the lost jobs are broadly consistent with Employment Policies Institute earlier estimates. It found that at least 360,000 jobs—and as many as a million— would be lost from a 10.10 dollars minimum wage increase.[87]

High minimum wage rates lead to unemployment for teens. One of the prime reasons for this drastic employment drought is the mandated wage hikes that policymakers have forced on small businesses. Economic research has shown time and again that increasing the minimum wage destroys jobs for low-skilled workers while doing little to address poverty.[88]

High minimum wage rates price teens out of jobs. When the minimum wage gets boosted, employers frequently cut down on hiring teens who typically fill lower- priority positions. Nearly half of all minimum wage earners are teenagers or young people still living with their parents. Most of the work still gets done, but customers may get stuck standing in longer lines, and teens suffer because they've been priced out of the opportunity to work.[89]

Employers are unable to afford to hire more unskilled and inexperienced workers when the minimum wage increases. Ironically, one of the stated goals of the Fair Labor Standards Act (FLSA) is to "protect the educational opportunities of minors." However, as labor becomes more expensive for small businesses, managers are forced to hirer fewer workers, leaving unskilled teens and minorities out of luck.[90]

But, of course, the data/facts and impact on millions and millions of poor Black Americans, does not faze the empathy-free Royalty Class Black leadership of the NAACP. Their jobs and lifestyles are secured if their loyalties remain with the ideology of Liberalism.

Dr. Cobb's father's decision to leave the federal government job to pursue his own business is practically unheard of in today's Black community. There was a common mindset toward independence and private ownership during the early 1900s. In 1900, Booker T. Washington founded the National Negro Business League (NNBL), which was committed to the economic advancement of African Americans. NNBL promoted Black-owned businesses as the key to economic advancement. The League included Negro small business owners, doctors, farmers, craftsmen, and other professionals. It also maintained

---

87   Peter Coy. "The CBO Foresees Lost Jobs From a Higher Minimum Wage." *Bloomberg Businessweek*, February 18, 2014. bloomberg.com/bw/articles/2014-02-18/the-cbo-foresees-lost-jobs-from-a-higher-minimum-wage.

88   EPI staff. "Minimum Wage: Teen Unemployment, The Teen Unemployment Crisis: Questions And Answers, Why Is Teen Unemployment Rising?" Research. Employment Policies Institute, n.d. epionline.org/minimum-wage/minimum-wage-teen-unemployment.

89   *Ibid.*

90   *Ibid.*

directories for all major US cities and incorporated African-American contacts in numerous businesses.[91]

President Theodore Roosevelt was the featured speaker at NNBL's first National Business Network convention. In 1901, Booker T. Washington was the first Black American invited to the White House, where he dined with the president.

A 1907 photograph of businessmen commemorates the thirteenth annual meeting of Oakland's Afro-American Council, demonstrating the ongoing presence of a Black middle class. Some Black entrepreneurs—including several women—managed to find financial success through hard work and good fortune. Former slave Biddy Mason used the money she earned as a nurse to invest in Los Angeles real estate, becoming a wealthy philanthropist and founding the First AME Church. Mary Ellen Pleasant, another former slave, ran several businesses and restaurants in San Francisco and used her resources to fight for African-American civil rights.[92]

African-Americans today are overrepresented in the government sector. More than 20 percent of the Black working population over the age of sixteen are employees of federal, state, or local government, which is just over 5 percentage points higher than the national average. On the other end, a much smaller percentage of African-Americans are self-employed (3.6 percent) compared to the national average of 6.2 percent.[93]

In the present marketplace, government employment has become synonymous with unionized, safe, secure income and a great retirement with lifelong medical benefits. Why risk entering the free market and aspire for greater things when government unions give guarantees without apparent risk? All that is asked of the federal or state employee is to show up for their nine-to-five workday, take their guaranteed paid vacation and sick days, support the ideology of Liberalism through union dues, and vote for pro-labor union's Royalty Class Black politicians.

The downside to a lifestyle dependent on government jobs is the possibility of a reduction in forces due to bloated size and/or inefficiency. This has had a major impact on the government-dependent Black middle class in Chicago. In Chicago, the Black middle class relies heavily on employment

---

91   Joseph Bernardo. "National Negro Business League (1900 -)." Archive. Black-Past.org, n.d. blackpast.org/aah/national-negro-business-league.

92   California Cultures staff. "The Struggle for Economic Equality, 1900-1950s." Historical. Calisphere, 2005. calisphere.universityofcalifornia.edu/calcultures/ethnic_groups/subtopic1b.html.

93   "African American Employment." Metrics. Black Demographics, July 2018. black-demographics.com/economics/employment.

with the city and the school district. It has suffered disproportionately amid massive layoffs.[94]

Leading the Black community away from the independent seeking voice of Capitalism represented by Booker T. Washington was the subtle and patient message of the ideology of Liberalism. Once delivered through the NAACP's *Crisis*, and now through Viacom's BET, the message of Socialism and atheism is finally showing a sense of brashness. Empowered by decades of dominance, the ideology of Liberalism no longer feels the need to hide in the underbelly of the NAACP Trojan Horse, as they publicly fawn over every anti-American Communist despot around the world who is willing to buy their presence.

The Royalty Class Black Entertainers Jay-Z and Beyoncé derive their multimillions in wealth through the American free enterprise. Through the free market they delivered to the trusting Black urban community their hip-hop music promoting gangster lifestyle, sex, drugs, antisocial behavior, misogyny, anger, and Black racism. Once they'd acquired their financial freedom and wealth, they were the first to stand in line to celebrate the ruthless Cuban Communist dictators, the Castro brothers. As they flew their private jet to the Communist island to be treated like royalty, they were surely unaware of the boats below them full of desperate Cubans attempting to reach the free shores of America. An empathy-free and narcissistic soul is a typical attribute of the Royal Class Black.

And finally, stepping from behind the Socialist curtain 106 years in the making is the former head of NAACP, Ben Chavis. Chavis formally and proudly announced his endorsement for the agnostic, Socialist presidential Democratic candidate Bernie Sanders. Nowhere in the history of the world of Socialism is God allowed to reign. On the other hand, because it's steeped in atheism, it has been the source of persecutions of millions of Christian and members of other religious faiths. When Sanders was asked by talk-show host Jimmy Kimmel whether he believes in God, he replied: "I am what I am. And what I believe in, and what my spirituality is about, is that we're all in this together."[95] Unfortunately, due to the influence of the ideology of Liberalism, it appears these "I am what I am" and "we're all in this together" answers are enough today for many God-fearing Christians who are willing to vote for a person who does not believe in the Judeo-Christian core values that are at the center of every Christian's life. These answers would not have sufficed for the early 1900s proud Christian Black community, nor would it have held water in my proud, segregated 1960s community of Tallahassee, Florida.

---

94   Adeshina Emmanuel. "Chicago's Black Unemployment Rate Higher than Other Large Metro Areas."

95   Stoyan Zaimov. "Bernie Sanders Says He's Not an Atheist, Believes in God in His Own Way." *The Christian Post.* January 28, 2016, sec. Politics. christianpost.com/news/bernie-sanders-atheist-believes-god-156166/#5KjDAQxFMuxrpu5f.99.

Each of the Democratic candidates now stumble over themselves to fly to Harlem to kiss the ring of the master Royalty Class Black Problem Profiteer, Al Sharpton. It is through their faith in him that these candidates envision the shepherding of the urban Black vote. Ironically, this predicable procession unfolds every election cycle. This is the same Problem Profiteer who has made millions by promoting, articulating, and advocating for every anti-Black policy proposed by the "man behind the curtain." And yet he continues to have the full support of those who are purposely left ignorant by him. Thus, it is those within the socialized urban community, the fatherless, jobless, illiterate, dependent, and perpetually hopeless, frustrated, and angry who are left to ponder this truth: "The Deepest Betrayal begins with Ultimate Trust." Political free agency will put an end to the Royalty Class Black Man's elitist "Class over Race" representation.

The 1900s Black Community and Education

His father's success as a Capitalist, the owner of his own successful printing business, allowed Dr. Cobb to attend the all-Black Dunbar High School in Washington, D.C. Dunbar High boasted a remarkably high number of graduates who went on to higher education and whose general student body was rated as very successful. The school was considered the nation's best high school for African-Americans during the first half of the 20th century and was instrumental in making Washington, D.C. an educational and cultural capital.

As we consider the success of Black education institutions like Duncan during this era of increasing demand of integration, we must recognize the presence of a subtle message not missed by either race. Quality Black schools, communities, and businesses across the nation were never targeted for integration. The demand from the NAACP was that only White schools and businesses would forcibly share their property and resources, not Blacks. With this demand is the subtle admission of the innate inferiority of Black property/resources. As is the central theory of free-market supply and demand, the higher the demand, the higher the evaluation of the product being supplied. As the ideological demand for the transfer of Black students to White schools and tax-paying Black middle class to White communities, the result was a devaluation of Black schools, teachers, coaches, administrators, and property left behind. Thousands of talented and experienced Black Americans lost their livelihoods during this initial period of integration. The Black middle class took a hit with an increase of once-successful Black businesses within the community closing. Apparently viewed as a necessary sacrifice for the cause, the NAACP was silent in its protest during this big economic hit on the Black community. Following desegregation and demolition of the original facility, Dunbar High School's prestige dropped notably. Through the years the school, with an enrollment of 98 percent Black Americans, has continued to perform below standards and was among a list of failing schools identified for turnaround or closure.[96]

If he had known, would Dr. Cobb have supported an organization whose strategy was based on a premise that every Black-owned and -controlled entity was innately inferior to White-owned entities? Did he expect that success in this integration endeavor would mean in the mass exodus of the Black middle class, as they did in the 1970s TV series *The Jeffersons*, "moving on up and out" of their own community? Would he have agreed to give credibility to an organization whose values were the antithesis of his father's pro-Capitalist generation, controlled by White liberals, Socialists, and atheists that would leave his once-proud alma mater a dismal educational failure?

The educational opportunity that was once offered to Dr. Cobb's 1920 student body is no longer available in any school system in the country that is now predominantly Black. Was that the vision of this extraordinary and dedicated educator? The NAACP commitment to the policies of the ideology of Liberalism, and its extension the teacher labor unions, has assured that Dunbar High School, once one of our nation's best high schools, will remain what it is today, a simple footnote.

The ideology of Liberalism has a strong foothold within today's public educational system. The ideals of the pro-union and pro-ACLU founders, John Dewey and Mary Ovington, can be seen in the present policies of the NAACP. Its total commitment to ideology has betrayed the community that trusted them. As it was with the lost jobs for thousands of Black educators due to its integration push, it has for decades sacrificed the education for millions of Black American children at the altar of labor unions.

There is no better illustration of this loyalty to "Class over Race" than with the "very first executive action" by the first Black president of the United States after taking his oath of office. Though 99.9 percent of the Black urban community supported his candidacy and continues to support his presidency, President Obama's very first action in office was one of gratitude to the White-controlled education labor union. He defunded a very successful school choice program that supported over 2,000 Washington, D.C. inner-city Black children every year. With a graduation rate over 91 percent and close to this percentage electing to go on to college, Republicans, Democrats, Independents, and parents praised the program.[97]

Because school choice presents a competitive environment demanding lower cost, lower tolerance of incompetency, and measurable accountability,

---

96   "Dunbar High School (Washington, D.C.)." Wikipedia. Wikimedia
      Foundation, Inc., July 31, 2018. en.wikipedia.org/wiki/Dunbar_High_
      School_%28Washington,_D.C.%29.

97   "D.C. Opportunity Scholarship Program." Wikipedia. Wikimedia Foundation, Inc.,
      August 26, 2017. en.wikipedia.org/wiki/D.C._Opportunity_Scholarship_Program.

the labor union stands adamantly against it. None of these criteria are in the best interest of their members. In his first act as president, Obama stood with the 100 percent backing of the NAACP and Royalty Class Black Politicians to end the school choice vouchers for D.C.'s poor Black children. They prioritized instead the protectionist policies of dues-paying labor union adults. The results of these anti-choice policies, very popular with the Democratic party, are drastically fewer Black children in successful "state-of-the-art" schools. Instead, as in the private school that President Obama's daughters attend, there is a concentration of the children of the Black and White wealthy elitists—"Class over Race."

Once the Washington, D.C. school choice programs ended, and the poor urban children were sent back to their failing and dangerous public schools, President Obama's Department of Justice then proceed to sue Louisiana's very successful school voucher system. Consistent with the ideology of Liberalism is its empathy-free policies, of which the anti-school choice targeting of the poor and the powerless is a prime example.

The NAACP Strategy

W.E.B. Du Bois deserves all the credit for disseminating, through the NAACP magazine *Crisis*, the new concept of integration and creating the belief in the minds of the urban Black men that he did have a right to receive what no male group had ever received in all human history: integration rights into another male group's established society. Prior to 1909, the idea of one race demanding a share in the proceeds, property, and work of another race had never been a consideration.[98] All minorities, including Black Americans, instead addressed the barriers of exclusion, prejudice, and bigotry by creating value within. They supported their own enterprises, built and expanded their own communities, and educated their own children. Prior to this new messaging, Blacks had never marched in protest of the current "separate" living arrangements.[99] By 1917, most Northern urban Black newspapers followed the lead of the *Crisis* and demanded that integration was a legitimate right for their people.

Three White members of the society elites met in February 1909 with representatives of the Black community to gauge how receptive they would be to their new integration agenda. Overton had known Du Bois from Harvard and was aware of his Northern Black professional group, the now-defunct Niagara Movement They had organized earlier to protest Booker T. Washington's strategy and demand that White Americans commit to race-nullification, among other things. Ovington, Walling, and Villard were able to

---

98 "Who Was the Founder of the NAACP?" Answers.com, n.d. answers.com/Q/
     Who_was_the_founder_of_the_NAACP.

99 *Ibid.*

persuade this group of Black professionals that integration would expedite social justice. Once they knew the idea of integration would be supported the NAACP was created in 1910. Its initial executive committee board was comprised of twenty-one wealthy White Socialists, liberals, and at least one humanist. Most founding members were accomplished journalists, authors, and editors but Du Bois would be given the role as editor and be the face of the organizations magazine, *Crisis*. The founder and *The Nation* owner Villard funded the NAACP's budget and provided free office space in *The Evening Post* building for Du Bois.[100]

The only thing required of him from the board was that he mail copies of his *Crisis* articles to each of the executive board committee members for their approval before publishing. The board seemed very myopic regarding the message that was delivered to the Black community.

Through the NAACP's *Crisis*, a campaign was launched to diminish Booker T. Washington's influence and his fundraising efforts for Tuskegee. Among the disagreements between Du Bois' class of Northern Royalty Class Black Professionals and Booker T. Washington was their opposition to the mission of Tuskegee University and its "Industrial Education." They considered work related to farming, agriculture, and other work/businesses that required manual labor as demeaning and too closely related to slavery. Their preference was programs and curriculum emphasizing liberal arts, like those taught at Ivy League universities like Harvard. As Du Bois' group of Northern Black professionals, the Talented Tenth, attacked the character and agenda of Washington, they also inhibited his ability to raise funds for very successful All-Black Tuskegee University.

Although White liberals established the NAACP, it became a Black parallel system to the liberal White system of power distribution. The NAACP was never a radical organization. It represented an expression of a class and regional division within the Black population. Northern or Northern-educated Blacks and the Black professional class were the primary supporters of the NAACP and, in this sense, it was an elitist organization. The NAACP is not a supporter of mass movements, such as those that would have been favored by Vernon Johns and Martin Luther King, Jr. Tuskegee University and the NAACP reflected the political continuum and distribution of power between conservatives and liberals. More importantly, neither Whites nor Black liberals were interested in radical change. That is still true of the situation today.[101]

Not surprisingly, when the new and revolutionary NAACP was launched, though it was created and run by White people, it wasn't in any way popular

---

100   "NAACP: A Century in the Fight for Freedom: Founding and Early Years." Archive. Library of Congress, n.d. loc.gov/exhibits/naacp/founding-and-early-years.html.

101   "Chapter 20. The Second Extension Of Equality: The Progressive Era." The Vernon Johns Society, n.d. vernonjohns.org/vernjohns/sthprgrs.html.

among the numerically and culturally dominant White population. In fact, White Americans steadfastly rejected the agenda. This attitude was likely rooted in simple and logically sound reasoning that Blacks, being a distinct people, should be separate and thereby achieve self-reliance, which would produce a feeling of empowerment as a people. This was Booker T. Washington's desire and pursuit. White philanthropists also believed Blacks should be separate and a self-reliant people, and therefore did not offer financial help to the NAACP in its formative years.

Du Bois became the favorite of another prominent atheist and liberal, Margaret Sanger. As a proponent of the KKK, pro-eugenicist, racist, and founder of Planned Parenthood, she took the NAACP strategy to new heights. A brilliant strategist, she invited Du Bois and a host of other prominent middle-class Royalty Class Black Professionals to join her board(s) as she began her abortion foray on the Black community of Harlem in 1929. The "NAACP Strategy" model, for which he served as the prototype, has been for over one hundred years an effective means of delivering the message of Socialism to the Black community by an avowed Socialist. It is a message controlled by others who have remained hidden behind the curtain. For over a century, those providing the message have been the antithesis of the Black, Christian, Capitalist, visionary, and family-centered community of the early 1900s.

That model of stealth, the Trojan Horse, is still in use today by some of our nations' largest media corporations. An example is Viacom, a multi-billion-dollar media corporation. Ninety percent of the voting shares are owned by the ultra-liberal/progressive ideologue, Sumner Redstone.[102] In 2001, Viacom purchased BET (Black Entertainment TV) for three billion dollars. The purchase of BET negated all influence of messaging to the Black community by Black Americans. No Black American serves on the controlling Viacom executive board of directors, which oversees the BET programming. Though purchased in late 2000, it's been controlled and directed since 2001 by a White corporation, Viacom. But BET is still perceived by its Black audience as Black-controlled. Viacom later employed a strategy that led to the bankruptcy of Roberts Broadcasting, the last Black-owned and -operated, full-power TV station in our country.[103]

Roberts Broadcasting programming featured ordinary portrayals of African-Americans. As mentioned previously, in 2006 there were eighteen African-American-owned and -operated full-power commercial TV stations,

---

102   Peter Elkind, and Marty Jones. "The Disturbing Decline Of Sumner Redstone (Part 1 Of 3)." Fortune.Com, May 5, 2016. http://fortune.com/sumner-redstone-part-1/.

103   Joseph Torres, and S. Derek Turner. "Number of Black-Owned TV Stations Plummets to Zero." *Pittsburgh Courier*, n.d., sec. Business. newpittsburghcourieronline.com/2013/12/30/number-of-black-owned-tv-stations-plummets-to-zero.

representing just 1.3 percent of all such stations. In 2013, there were none. Predictably, there is silence from the Royalty Class Black Problem Profiteers regarding concerns of lack of Black American leadership and influence in the exclusive White executive boardrooms of corporate media.[104]

James Winston, the executive director of the Washington-based National Association of Black Owned Broadcasters expressed concern about the sale of BET. He stated, "There will not be African-American ownership at the very top, and I think that makes a difference." In 2010, James spoke before the House of Representative Oversight and Government Reform Committee regarding the policies being implemented that were forcing Black entrepreneurs out of the industry. It should be noted that the liberal Democratic Party controlled the House and Senate under the leadership of the first Black president, also a Democrat. Even after hearing the concerns of the National Association of Black Owned Broadcasters, nothing was done. As is the priority of the Royalty Class Black Politician, who has never risked entry into the free market, there is no empathy for the Black entrepreneur. They remain unaware and unmoved that it was the Black Capitalist who was responsible for the rise of a robust 1940s, 1950s, and 1960s middle class.

> *"Unfortunately, in recent years we have seen a substantial decline in the number of minority companies owning broadcast stations. This decline has been precipitated by government policies that encouraged the consolidation of the industry into the hands of a few large conglomerates, the credit crisis which has resulted in the bankruptcies of several African American owned companies, and a flawed Arbitron audience measurement service that fails to adequately estimate Black audiences."*
>
> *—James L. Winston[105]*

Viacom paid former BET owner Robert L. Johnson more than 2.3 billion dollars and assumed nearly 600 million dollars of BET's debt; at the time, BET was generating 225 million dollars in revenue. It made him America's first Black American billionaire.

---

104 *Ibid.*

105 "Testimony of James L. Winston, Executive Director and General Counsel of the National Association of Black Owned Broadcasters, Inc., Hearing On 'The 2010 Census Communications Contract: The Media Plan In Hard To Count Areas' Before the Oversight and Government Reform Committee Information Policy, Census, and National Archives Subcommittee of the United States House of Representatives," February 24, 2010. oversight.house.gov/wp-content/uploads/2012/01/20100224winston.pdf.

The purchase granted Viacom entry into an established and trusting venue, the Black urban market. This environment, already accepting of the filthy language, anti-authority, and anti-women messaging of gangster rap was ripe for the ideology of Liberalism. It was also a cause of collaboration by the Royalty Class Black, once a whiff of super wealth was in the air. Johnson was quick to note that the deal had received the blessing of the Royalty Class Black Problem Profiteers. He mentioned that in considering this deal he talked to several leaders in the Black community, including Rev. Jesse Jackson. Together they concluded that selling to Viacom would provide a "boon to the Black community."

How personally becoming a billionaire and leaving all future control of Black messaging to a powerful White liberal controlled corporation is "a boon to the Black community" has yet to be explained. The fact is that Johnson was not creating new jobs for Black Americans nor was he spending his money in Black American communities, supporting Black American business. As a wealthy member of the Royalty Class Black and a loyal Democrat, he remained supportive of the anti-Black entrepreneur Davis-Bacon Act, the anti-employment for unskilled Black teen labor, high minimum wage initiatives, and the anti-school choice education for poor Black children. The statement that his wealth is a "boon to the Black community" is a stretch if looked at in a conventional way.

Translated into the language of Royalty it becomes clear his real meaning. What Black billionaire Robert L. Johnson really meant was that his wealth was "a boon" for the Royalty Class Black and the ideology of Liberalism. What can be counted on within the small circle of wealthy Royalty members is their support for one another. There will be very sizable charitable "tax write-off "checks clearing the bank account of our Royalty Class Billionaire written to the "nonprofit" organizations of the Royalty Class Black Problem Profiteers who will "pay themselves" and use the remainder as a "tax write off" in their get out the vote effort. Their goal...to once again get the hopeless and desperate underclass Black motivated for another voting cycle to re-elect a retread of the Civil Rights "oldie but goodie" Royalty Class Black Politicians.

"Let's make those old, White, racist, rich Republicans pay for what they've done to you" is the masterful message that has always worked; it has for decades. The Royalty Class Black Politician then shows gratitude to the hopeless but trusting constituents by submissively voting for every anti-Black liberal policy demanded of them by powerful liberal-controlled corporations, like the all-White corporate board of Viacom (BET). This is the true "boon" that Johnson envisions, White and Black liberal elitists racing to the top for more trappings...power, wealth, lifestyle, and bragging rights in their wealthy integrated neighborhoods of other Royalty—"Class over Race."

Since none of them will be spending their money with Black-owned businesses located in the Black community, it once again shows the deceit and betrayal of this empathy-free class of Americans.

"We are proud to be combining with Viacom to better serve the African-American community," Johnson said. "This provides a beacon for others. This is an opportunity for the Black community to receive more information, more entertainment and more relevant news."[106] What Johnson fails to mention is that the entertainment, information, and relevant news is now fed unfiltered into the young urban Black community without input from concerned, caring, and visionary Black Americans. Johnson remained employed until 2006 but was not offered a seat on the corporate executive board. Like his model, W.E.B. Du Bois, he became the trusted face of a White-owned corporation with its own agenda for the Black community (never good, by the way, for the Black community). Like W.E.B. Du Bois, Johnson was simply another highly-compensated employee without control. For the ideology of Liberalism, regardless of the elaborate Black facade, control will always remain in the hands of "the man behind the curtain." This defined the subtlety of the "NAACP Strategy."

This truth became apparent to the very loyal W.E.B. Du Bois in 1932 when he found himself no longer in sync with the White-controlled NAACP board of directors. After sixteen years of loyalty as editor of *The Crisis* delivering the board's message of integration and Socialism to the Black community, Du Bois began to see the merit in Black segregation. During the years of the Great Depression when the Black community was the most vulnerable, he saw segregation as an effective strategy to bind Blacks together economically.[107] He recognized that integration was financially hurting the Black community as Blacks continued to support White businesses, forsaking their own. His new understanding of segregation as a beneficial strategy would encourage Black patrons to support their own community's Black-owned businesses. For this radical departure from the NAACP White executive board's mission, Du Bois was fired.[108] He was later re-hired but fired again for the last time, prior to the beginning of WWII.

W.E.B. Du Bois' legacy will rest on the divisiveness that he brought to his race as he convinced a significant number of them of the premise of the atheist-based science of eugenics. This pseudo-science suggests that some of the Black race, based on mixed skin tone, European hair, intelligence, or classical education, were genetically superior to others (the Talented Tenth). If only he

---

106   Luisa Beltran. "Viacom Pays $2.3B for BET: Media Giant Buys BET, Making John-
       son Second-Largest Individual Shareholder." Finance. CNN Money, November 3,
       2000. money.cnn.com/2000/11/03/deals/viacom.

107   Lynne Duke. "That Was Then This Is Now." *The Washington Post.* Decem-
       ber 18, 1994, sec. Lifestyle. washingtonpost.com/archive/lifestyle/maga-
       zine/1994/12/18/that-was-then-this-is-now/02545c32-9172-4064-a5c1-
       eda3dd0dd210.

108   *Ibid.*

could get the "ignorant" Black people from reproducing, the Talented Tenth would "raise up those deemed worthy." His legacy will be his facilitation of the Socialist and atheist message of the White NAACP founders that would lead his race away from the path of self-sufficiency and independence. It helped that he was a believer, a Socialist, and atheist. The free enterprise message of Capitalism that had been a bridge to the American Dream for every other American other cultures/race, was not to be taught to his community. Instead, Black Americans have been guided to see themselves as a consumer race instead of one that manufactures and produces value of their own. It has been messaged subtly over decades that others' property and presence is of more value than their own. This has facilitated the acceptance of the debilitating dependency of Socialism in every US urban community.

His legacy will be his introduction into the Black community of the Black Widow spider and deadly abortionist, Margaret Sanger. Abortion is now the leading killer of Black Americans and has morphed into the most hideous forms of infanticide...partial birth abortion, selective sex abortions, and now "live birth" abortions, advocated in 2003 by then Senator Barack Obama.[109]

Perhaps after being fired twice from the NAACP and his diminishing presence in a post war of patriotic and Capitalist Black Americans, Du Bois felt alone with a sense of betrayal by his former circle of White liberal and intellectual Socialists. He was, after all, based on his own predictions as a young man to be the savior of his race. It's possible that it was this reflection that caused him to muse near the end of his life, "In my country for nearly a century I have been nothing but a *nigger.*"[110]

Unfortunately for W.E.B. Du Bois, it took his entire ninety-year lifetime to recognize the empathy-free ways of his chosen ideology. At the end of his life, no longer valued by his former comrades as an all-star player, this does confirm another age-old eternal truth: "You reap what you sow."

109   Warner Todd Huston. "Obama Lied About Vote Against Live-Birth Abortion Ban, Media Mum." Conservative issues. NewsBusters (blog), August 13, 2008. news-busters.org/blogs/nb/warner-todd-huston/2008/08/13/obama-lied-about-vote-against-live-birth-abortion-ban-media.

110   "Du Bois, 91, Lauds China." *The New York Times.* March 5, 1959, Online edition, sec. Archives. archive.nytimes.com/www.nytimes.com/books/00/11/05/spe-cials/dubois-china.html.

W.E.B. Du Bois

A staunch believer in Communism and admirer of Adolf Hitler and Joseph Stalin.[111]

> *"One can hardly exaggerate the moral disaster of [religion]. We have to thank the Soviet Union for the courage to stop it."*
>
> —W.E.B. Du Bois

> *"Capitalism cannot reform itself; it is doomed to self-destruction. No universal selfishness can bring social good to all."*
>
> —W.E.B. Du Bois

> *"Communism—the effort to give all men what they need and to ask of each the best they can contribute—this is the only way of human life. It is a difficult and hard end to reach—it has and will make mistakes, but today it marches triumphantly on in education and science, in home and food, with increased freedom of thought and deliverance from dogma. In the end Communism will triumph. I want to help bring that day."[112]*
>
> —W.E.B. Du Bois

The following are the original founders of the NAACP. Their occupations are diverse, ranging from Journalist, editors, attorneys, college professors, wealth social and political reformers, Magazines owners and Labor Unionist advocates. Each was essentially Socialist in philosophy and seized the opportunity to advance the Socialist-progressive movement by incorporating the Black struggle and anti-racism efforts during the early 1900s.[113] With another

---

111 W.E.B. Du Bois. "On Stalin." Archive. Marxists.org, March 16, 1953. marxists.org/reference/archive/stalin/biographies/1953/03/16.htm.

112 "W.E.B. Du Bois." Wikiquote, April 21, 2018. en.wikiquote.org/wiki/W._E._B._Du_Bois.

113 W.E.B. Du Bois. "On Stalin."

common theme of atheism, two of the NAACP White founders also founded the nemesis to Christian organizations, the ACLU. As a Socialist opportunist, John Dewey was associated with fifteen Marxist front organizations,[114] known as the father of the progressive, union-controlled public school system, and the pro-labor union advocate.

Small wonder that a bewildered Marcus Garvey stormed out of NAACP headquarters in 1917, muttering that it was a White organization.[115]

1910 White Founders and Executive Board Members of the NAACP

Ray Stannard Baker

Socialist: White executive board member of the NAACP. Journalist, author, and biographer of Woodrow Wilson. After supporting President Theodore Roosevelt, Baker flirted briefly with Socialism for several years before embracing the candidacy of Woodrow Wilson in 1912. Serving as Wilson's press secretary at Versailles, he eventually published fifteen volumes on Wilson and internationalism.[116]

John Dewey

ACLU founder and father of modern public school system. Atheist, Socialist, and humanist: White executive board member of the NAACP.

---

114 Stanley Kurtz. "How Little Socialists Are Made." EagleForum.Org, July 2018. eagleforum.org/publications/efr/july18/how-little-socialists-are-made.html.

115 S. Francis. "Jews, Blacks, and Race." The Occidental Press, 2006. kevinmacdonald. net/Jews&Blacks.pdf.

116 Robert Bannister. "Ray Stannard Baker: A Guide to Resources." Archive. Swarth-more.edu, August 24, 2000. swarthmore.edu/SocSci/rbannis1/Baker/index.html.

"You can't make Socialists out of individualists. Children who know how to think for themselves spoil the harmony of the collective society, which is coming, where everyone is interdependent."[117]

—John Dewey

"Faith in the prayer-hearing God is an unproved and outmoded faith. There is no God and there is no soul. Hence, there are no needs for the props of traditional religion. With dogma and creed excluded, the immutable truth is also dead and buried. There is no room for fixed, natural law or moral absolutes."[118]

—John Dewey

"Change must come gradually," he wrote. "To force it unduly would compromise its final success by favoring a violent reaction." In other words, implementing Socialistic ideas had to be done slowly; otherwise those who truly cared about educating children would become angry and resist.[119]

John Dewey, known as "the father of progressive education," was an avowed Socialist and the co-author of *The Humanist Manifesto*. The U.S. House Committee on Un-American Activities discovered that he belonged to fifteen Marxist front organizations. He taught the professors who trained America's teachers.[120]

Joel E. Spingarn

Chairman of the board of directors

Socialist: White executive board member of the NAACP. Named after himself, in 1914 he established the coveted Spingarn Medal awarded yearly by the NAACP. According to recent revelations by the *Memphis Commercial Appeal* newspaper he was also a spy for the United States Army. Spingarn was hired in May 1918 and given the rank of major in the Military Intelligence Division (MID). Spingarn ran "a small unit of undercover agents" who were looking for "proof of subversion." The MID opened 100,000 pieces of mail a week and

117   Stanley Kurtz. "How Little Socialists Are Made."
118   John Dewey, "Soul-Searching," *Teacher Magazine*, September 1933, p. 33
119   David Fiorazo. "The NEA Agenda? How John Dewey, Socialism Influenced Public Education." David Fiorazo: Author, Speakerm Radio Host (blog), February 21, 2013. davidfiorazo.com/2013/02/the-nea-agenda-how-john-deweySocialism-influenced-public-education.
120   Stanley Kurtz. "How Little Socialists Are Made."

monitored Black publications. According to the *Appeal*: "The documents show Spingarn, who remained NAACP chairman during his tenure at MID, used his post to obtain critical information for MID, such as a list of the organization's 32,000 members."[121]

William English Walling

Chairman of the NAACP Executive Committee (1910–1911)

Socialist: White executive board member and co-founder of the NAACP. Author of the book *Labor-Union Socialism and Socialist Labor-Unionism* (1912). In 1908, Walling published *Russia's Message*, a book inspired by the social unrest he and his wife had observed in Russia. He joined the Socialist Party (1910–1917), his books included *Socialism as It Is: A Survey of the World-Wide Revolutionary Movement* (1912/1918). He published two other books on Socialism by 1914, *The Larger Aspects of Socialism* and *Progressivism and After*.[122]

Charles Edward Russell

Socialist: White executive board member of the NAACP. Author and Pulitzer Prize winner. *Why I Am a Socialist* (1910): "This is the offer of Socialism: the righting of the centuries of wrong the producers have suffered, the dawn of a genuine democracy, peace instead of war, sufficiency instead of suffering, life raised above the level of appetite, a chance at last for the good in people to attain their normal development."

Mary White Ovington

Socialist: White co-founder of the NAACP. A suffragist and journalist, Ovington joined the Socialist Party of America in 1905 where she met Socialists A. Philip Randolph, Floyd Dell, Max Eastman, and Jack London. London argued that racial problems were as much a matter of "Class as of Race."[123]

Henry Moskowitz

Socialist: White executive board member of the NAACP. In 1917 Moskowitz served as the Commissioner of Public Markets in New York City. He was the founding Executive Director of the League of New York Theatres,

---

121 NOI Research. "Should Your 'Best Friends' Spy On You? The NAACP And Joel E. Spingarn." Nation of Islam Research Group (blog), July 4, 2016. noirg.org/articles/should-your-best-friends-spy-on-you-%E2%80%A8the-naacp-and-joel-e-spingarn.

122 "William English Walling." Wikipedia. Wikimedia Foundation, Inc., September 18, 2017. en.wikipedia.org/wiki/William_English_Walling.

123 "Mary White Ovington." Wikipedia. Wikimedia Foundation, Inc., July 29, 2018. en.wikipedia.org/wiki/Mary_White_Ovington.

---

which eventually became The Broadway League, the organization known for producing the Tony Awards.[124]

Florence Kelley

Marxist: White executive board member of the NAACP. Kelley, the daughter of United States congressman, William D. Kelley, was born on September 12, 1859. She studied at Cornell University and the University of Zurich. While in Europe she became a follower of Karl Marx and Friedrich Engels. Over the next few years she worked on an English translation of Engels's *The Conditions of the Working Class in England* that was eventually published in the United States in 1887. Kelley moved to New York City where she started the Intercollegiate Socialist Society.[125]

Lincoln Steffens

Socialist: White executive board member of the NAACP. Steffens was a New York reporter who published a book titled *The Shame of the Cities*. He is remembered for investigating corruption in municipal government in American cities and for his early support for the Soviet Union. He once famously said upon arriving back from Russia after the revolution, "I have been over into the future, and it works."[126]

124 "An NAACP Crisis Timeline: 1909-1954." *The New Crisis*, July 1999. questia.com/magazine/1P3-44716911/an-naacp-crisis-timeline-1909-1954.

125 "Florence Kelley (1859 – 1932): Social Reformer, Child Welfare Advocate, Socialist and Pacifist." *Social Welfare History Project*, April 3, 2008. socialwelfarehistory.com/people/kelley-florence.

126 John Simkin. "Lincoln Steffens." Spartacus Educational, April 2013. spartacus-educational.com/Jsteffens.htm.

Clarence Darrow

Socialist/Atheist: White executive board member of the NAACP. Darrow was a lawyer and unionist. In September 1905, Darrow joined with Jack London, Upton Sinclair, and Florence Kelley to form the Intercollegiate Socialist Society. Its stated purpose was to "throw light on the world-wide movement of industrial democracy known as Socialism."[127] "Socialism at least recognized that if man was to make a better world it must be through the mutual effort of human units; that it must be by some sort of co-operation that would include all the units of the state."[128]

As part of a public symposium on belief held in Columbus, Ohio, Darrow delivered a famous and powerful speech, which was later titled "Why I Am an Agnostic," on agnosticism, skepticism, belief, and religion. In the speech, Darrow thoroughly discussed the meaning of being an agnostic and questioned the doctrines of Christianity and the Bible. He concluded that "the fear of God is not the beginning of wisdom. The fear of God is the death of wisdom. Skepticism and doubt lead to study and investigation, and investigation is the beginning of wisdom. In the November 18, 1915 edition of the Washington Post, Darrow stated: "Chloroform unfit children. Show them the same mercy that is shown beasts that are no longer fit to live."[129]

127 "League for Industrial Democracy." Wikipedia. Wikimedia Foundation, Inc., July 14, 2017. en.wikipedia.org/wiki/League_for_Industrial_Democracy.

128 John Simkin. "Clarence Darrow." Spartacus Educational, April 2013. spartacus-educational.com/USAdarrow.htm.

129 "Clarence Darrow." Wikipedia. Wikimedia Foundation, Inc., August 7, 2018. en.wikipedia.org/wiki/Clarence_Darrow.

Jane Addams

Socialist: White executive board member of the NAACP. In 1889 Addams co-founded Hull House and in 1920 she was a co-founder for the ACLU. In 1931 she became the first American woman to be awarded the Nobel Peace Prize and is recognized as the founder of the social work profession in the United States.[130] Co-founder of the labor union Women's Trade Union League.[131]

William Dean Howells

Socialist: White executive board member of the NAACP. Editor of *The Atlantic Monthly*. Howells was a Christian Socialist whose ideals were greatly influenced by Russian writer Leo Tolstoy. He joined a Christian Socialist group in Boston between 1889 to 1891.[132]

Lillian Wald

Socialist: White executive board member of the NAACP. Wald was an employer and protégé to abortionist Margaret Sanger.[133] Born in Cincinnati, Ohio, on March 10, 1867, Wald became a nurse. Inspired by the work of Jane Addams and Ellen Starr at Hull House in Chicago, she joined Mary Brewster

130   "Jane Addams." Wikipedia. Wikimedia Foundation, Inc., July 29, 2018. en.wikipedia.org/wiki/Jane_Addams.

131   Kevin Rogers. "1903: Jane Addams Becomes Vice President of National Women's Trade Union League." World History Project (WHP), n.d. worldhistoryproject. org/1903/jane-addams-becomes-vice-president-of-national-womens-trade-union-league.

132   "William Dean Howells." Wikipedia. Wikimedia Foundation, Inc., February 9, 2018. en.wikipedia.org/wiki/William_Dean_Howells.

133   Jack Hansan. "Lillian D. Wald (1867 – 1940) — Nurse, Social Worker, Women's Rights Activist and Founder of Henry Street Settlement." Social Welfare History Project, n.d. socialwelfarehistory.com/people/wald-lillian. socialwelfarehistory. com/people/wald-lillian.

to establish the Henry Street Settlement in New York City in 1893. After WWI, Wald campaigned for Socialist candidates and was closely associated with left-wing abortionist, trade unionist, and anarchist, Emma Goldman.[134]

The Original NAACP White Founders/ Executive Board Members[115]

Mary White Ovington	Socialist	Journalist, *New York Evening Post*
Oswald Garrison Villard	Progressive	Owner of magazine, *The Nation*
William English Walling	Socialist	Wealthy Publisher, *Russia Message*
Dr. Henry Moscowitz	Progressive	Physician
Morefield Storey	liberal/Democrat	Lawyer and Publicist
Joel Spingarn	Progressive	Professor at Columbia
Arthur Spingarn		Lawyer and NAACP President
Inez Milholland	Socialist	World War I correspondent
Jane Addams	Socialist	Philosopher, sociologist, author
Florence Kelley	Marxist	Social and political reformer
Sophonisba Breckinridge	Progressive	University of Chicago Professor
John Haynes Holmes	Socialist	Pacifist Unitarian minister
Charles Edward Russell	Socialist	Author and Pulizer Prize winner
John Dewey	Humanist/Atheist	The Father of Public Education
William Dean Howells	Socialist	Editor of the *Atlantic Monthly*
Lillian Wald	Socialist	Nurse, Author, Humanitarian
Clarence Darrow	Socialist/Atheist	Lawyer, ACLU Leader
Lincoln Steffens	Progressive	Reporter, New York Evening Post
Ray Stannard Baker	Progressive	American journalist and author
Fanny Garrison Villard	Socialist	Wealthy wife of Publisher
Walter Sachs	Socialist	

---

134   John Simkin. "Emma Goldman." Spartacus Educational, August 2014. spartacus-educational.com/USAgoldman.htm.

CHAPTER 6

PLANNED PARENTHOOD: THE SOPHISTRY OF MARGARET SANGER

The masthead motto of M. Sanger's newsletter, The Woman Rebel, reads:

"No Gods, No Masters"

"Consistent with her deep belief of racial supremacy and purity of the Aryan race" Margaret Sanger is responsible, more than anyone else, for keeping alive international racism. Sanger played the attractive hostess for racist thinkers all over the world. Organizing the First World Population Conference in Geneva in 1926, she invited Clarence C. Little, Edward A. East, Henry Pratt Fairchild, and Raymond Pearl—all infamous racists."[135] In 1931, Sanger founded the Population Association of America with Fairchild as its head. Fairchild, formerly the secretary-treasurer of the American Eugenics Society and the leading academic racist of the decade, wrote *The Melting Pot Mistake*, which denigrated the Jews, referring to them as the inferior new immigrants who would threaten the native Nordic stock.[136]

Today, on an average, 1,876 Black babies are aborted daily in the United States. Though minority women constitute only about 13 percent of the U.S. female population (aged fifteen to forty-four), they underwent approximately

---

135   Margaret Sanger, *Birth Control Review*, November 1926, birthcontrolreview.net/Birth%20Control%20Review/1926-11%20November.pdf.
136   Allan Chase, *The Legacy of Malthus*, Illini Books, March 1980, p. 656.

36 percent of the abortions. According to the Alan Guttmacher Institute, Black women are more than five times as likely as White women to have an abortion.[137]

As the results of one hundred years of steady, progressive, and effective messaging, Planned Parenthood has gained support from segments of Americans that just decades ago would have been deemed impossible. The ideology of Liberalism has convinced close to 50 percent of Americans of all religious faiths, colors, and backgrounds of the merits of embracing the beliefs of Planned Parenthood's founder Margaret Sanger. Once deemed unacceptable, her views of Black Americans and other minorities as akin to "human weeds," "reckless breeders," "spawning...human beings who never should have been born"[138] have been safely tucked away categorized under the PC term of "choice."

Over the course of several decades, our nation's once-intrinsic ideals that value each soul as one of promise has eroded away. We've watched an organization, through shrewd patience and sophistry, gain credibility and admiration doing singularly what all former racist groups—the KKK, the Confederate Army, thousands of heinous slave owners, and Jim Crow-era lynch mobs—could not do combined. On a scale matched only by the Nazi government's genocide machine, American abortionists have killed over sixteen million Black babies since 1972. Based on a 2010 census, there are approximately forty million Black Americans, representing 12.3 percent of the U.S. population. This is down from 14.8 percent of the population in 2000.[139] This represents 40 percent of the present Black population that has been aborted for profit or convenience at the altar of the ideology of Liberalism. Sadly, even with the knowledge of its racist beginning, its disproportional racist impact on one American race and growing scientific evidence of the long-term emotional and physical toll it takes on Black mothers, this tenet of the ideology of Liberalism remains entrenched so effectively it has embedded itself into the core of our soul and consciousness. And unlike all the generations before us... we simply don't care.

As a sociopathic chameleon, Sanger was able to simultaneously and effectively ingratiate herself into two separate and opposing groups, the White racist KKK organization and the Black racist Royalty Class Professionals. This sense of sophistry attests to her talent in fulfilling the superiority needs of her diverse audiences. The science of eugenics allowed Royalty Class Black Elitists to accept their superior status to others of their race, those they deemed darker and less-educated. This perception was based on their perceived superior

---

137   "Approximate Number of African American Deaths Since 1973," 2012, black-genocide.org/black.html.

138   Margaret Sanger, *Pivot of Civilization, The*, Brentano's Publisher, New York, 1922.

139   "African American Population Report," 2017, blackdemographics.com.

genetic value of their mixed ancestry. White racists accepted their superiority based on their hatred of anyone different from themselves.

Scientific Racism—This form of racism is based on genes, rather than skin color or language. The issue is not color of skin or dialect of tongue, but quality of genes. Therefore, if Blacks, Jews, and Hispanics demonstrate a good quality gene pool—as long as they act White and think White—they are esteemed equal with Aryans. If they are, as Margaret Sanger said, 'the best of their race,' then they can be [counted] as valuable citizens." By the same token, individual Whites who show dysgenic traits must have their fertility curbed right along with the other inferiors and undesirables. Scientific racism is equal opportunity. Anyone with a defective gene pool is suspect. And anyone who shows promise may be admitted to the ranks of the elite.[140]

Racial Supremacy—Sanger organized the First World Population Conference in Geneva in 1926, inviting Clarence C. Little, Edward A. East, Henry Pratt Fairchild, and Raymond Pearl—all infamous racists." In September 1930, she invited Nazi anthropologist Eugene Fischer, whose ideas were cited by the Nazis to legitimize the extermination of Jews, to meet with her at her home.[141]

History of Planned Parenthood

Planned Parenthood itself reports that of the 132,314 abortions it did in 1991, 23.2 percent were on African-Americans, 12.5 percent were on Hispanics, and seven percent were on other minorities. Thus, the total abortions on minorities are 42.7 percent. But minorities comprise only 27.6 percent of the U.S. population. Therefore, relative to population percentage, Planned Parenthood strategically aborts minorities at a three times higher rate than Whites.

> *"When an organization has a history of racism, when its literature is openly racist, when its goals are self-consciously racial, and when its programs invariably revolve around race, it doesn't take an expert to realize that the organization is indeed racist."*
>
> *—Black financial analyst William L. Davis[142]*

---

140   "The Negro Project: Margaret Sanger's Eugenic Plan for Black Americans," Concerned Women for America, 2001, legislative, cwfa.org/the-negro-project-margaret-sangers-eugenic-plan-for-black-americans.

141   Lynn K. Murphy, Life Research Institute, June 1994, "Planned Parenthood's Racism," ewtn.com/library/PROLIFE/PPRACISM.txt.

142   *Ibid.*

1916—Margaret Sanger, a member of the Socialist Party of America,[143] opened the first birth control clinic in Harlem. The clinic serviced the poor immigrants who heavily populated the area, i.e., those deemed by Sanger as "unfit" to reproduce.[144]

May 1926—The KKK. "I accepted an invitation to talk to the women's branch of the Ku Klux Klan…I saw through the door dim figures parading with banners and illuminated crosses…I was escorted to the platform, was introduced, and began to speak…. In the end, through simple illustrations, I believed I had accomplished my purpose. A dozen invitations to speak to similar groups were proffered."[145]

1939—The Negro Project: "We should hire three or four colored ministers, preferably with social-service backgrounds, and with engaging personalities. The most successful educational approach to the Negro is through a religious appeal. We don't want the word to go out that we want to exterminate the Negro population and the minister is the man who can straighten out that idea if it ever occurs to any of their more rebellious members."—Margaret Sanger[146]

2002—The Born-Alive Infants Protection Act (BAIPA). The state of Illinois and federal legislature eventually passed BAIPA, which was meant to make death "by neglect" of babies born alive but unwanted by their mother illegal.[147] Three attempts were made in the Illinois legislation 2001, 2002, and 2003 to provide legal protection for "babies born

143   John Simkin, "Socialism in the United States," Spartacus Educational Publishers Ltd., September 1997, updated August 2014, spartacus-educational.com/USASocialism.htm.

144   Patatlci, "Planned Parenthood and Racism," excerpts from Margaret Sanger's "The Negro Project," Life Coalition International, February 2012, lifecoalition.com/?p=101.

145   *Ibid.*

146   Margaret Sanger, speaking about "The Negro Project," 1939.

147   Warner Todd Huston, "Obama Lied About Vote Against Live-Birth Abortion Ban, Media Mum," RedState, August 2008, redstate.com/diary/warner_todd_huston/2008/08/14/obama-lied-about-vote-against-live-birth-abor.

alive." All three attempts were opposed by then Illinois Senator Obama.[148]

2012—"After-Birth Abortion." (Live Birth Abortion/ Infanticide). Alberto Giubilin, a philosopher from the University of Milan, and Francesca Minerva, an ethicist from the University of Melbourne, have made the case that since both the unborn baby and the newborn do not have the moral status of actual persons and are consequently morally irrelevant, what they call "after-birth abortion" should be permissible in all the cases where abortion is unborn or newly born, including cases where the newborn is perfectly healthy.[149]

2015—Selling of Baby Body Parts. In the fourth undercover investigative video of Planned Parenthood, officials discussed the harvesting and selling of aborted baby parts (internal organs and tissue). A medical assistant and the doctor is shown in a Planned Parenthood office picking organs from a dead baby out of a glass pie dish and saying, "here's the heart...this is part of the head...here's some intestines."[150]

Who would have guessed in 1916 that a decision by the Black community in Harlem, New York, to open its doors to the first abortion center would progress within one hundred years to the election of a Black president who would defend the practice of "live birth abortion," a United States Justice Department that would not investigate the selling of body parts of babies statistically killed to maximize their market value, and Democrat and pro-abortionist Republicans who refuse to do anything about this abortion cartel?

---

148 Jess Henig, "Obama and 'Infanticide': The facts about Obama's votes against 'Born Alive' bills in Illinois," FactCheck.org, August 2008, factcheck. org/2008/08/obama-and-infanticide.

149 Peter Baklinski, "Ethicists justify infanticide in major medical journal," LifeSite, February 2012, lifesitenews.com/news/shock-ethicists-justify-infanticide-in-major-medical-journal.

150 Michael W. Chapman, "Planned Parenthood & Baby Body Parts Video: 'Was That Crack the Little Bits of the Skull?' – 'Here's the Heart,'" CNS News, July 2015, cnsnews.com/news/article/michael-w-chapman/planned-parenthood-baby-body-parts-video-was-crack-little-bits-skull.

The Nature of Eternal Laws

There are eternal laws of nature that serve as touchstones by which all human progress is measured, i.e., math, science, chemistry, and so on. Each law is predictable, irrefutable, and cannot be altered by man's wishes or wisdom. Regarding our relationship to these laws, as individuals or collectively as a nation, it is simple. We can choose the blessing that comes from understanding and respecting them, or we can choose to work through the consequences of our ignorance. As per the Law of Gravity, the effects of eternal laws are both reliable and predictable. Always present, the Law of Gravity cannot be changed or altered by the laws of man. It can be suspended temporality, by other eternal laws that are counteractive to it, like The Law of Lift or Momentum; in time through, regardless of time, race, creed, or color, the Law of Gravity will again claim its own, for what goes up must come down.

So it is, too, with the Eternal Law of Seed and Harvest. The blossoming of an apple tree is tied inexplicably to the planting of an apple seed, the fruition of a tomato plant originates with the sowing of a tomato seed...it is immutable. In keeping with this law, the planting of the seed of bigotry, deception, and evil begets the fruit of bigotry, deception, and evil. The seed and fruit thus described is called Planned Parenthood, the sower of the seed, its founder, Margaret Sanger.

As we consider the documented goals of this organization and its founders, it will be helpful to understand the soil in which the seed of Planned Parenthood was planted. During the late 1800s Americans' hearts, minds, and souls were receptive to a new scientific theory whose influence would be felt throughout the world. The world was in the process of embracing the wisdom of two men who introduced new theories to explain both the origin of man and how through artificial means man could improve the species. The consequence of Darwinism and eugenics would, over the following century, result in the suffering and loss of millions of lives. The country's acceptance of their racist-based science would stunt America's heart and prolong for decades the acceptance of its minority groups as equals. The seed of Darwinism, sowed by a White intellectual atheist, was founded on a premise that man began as a primitive ape, progressed in time to a primitive, subhuman Black race, and ultimately to its greatest creation, the White race. A naturalist, Charles Darwin's thinking and writing about evolution and natural selection would cause him to reject evidence of God in nature and ultimately renounce the Bible, God, and the Christian faith.[151]

---

151 John M. Brentnall and Russell M. Grigg, "Darwin's slippery slide into unbelief," Creation.com, February 2009, creation.com/charles-darwins-slippery-slide-into-unbelief.

The seed of eugenics, again sowed by a White intellectual atheist, was predicated on an idea that later in the 1800s there would be a need to control inferior populations through population control. Defined in this manner, "The essence of evolution is natural selection; the essence of eugenics is the replacement of 'natural' selection by conscious, premeditated, or artificial selection in the hope of speeding up the evolution of 'desirable' characteristics and the elimination of undesirable ones."[152]

This philosophy of "survival of the fit" would lead eugenicist believers adamantly opposed to charities that saved or improved the lives of the downtrodden. Francis Galton, a cousin of Charles Darwin, who coined the word, believed that "the proper evolution of humanity was thwarted by philanthropic outreach to the poor: misguided charity encouraged the "unfit" to bear more children."[153] This spiritually devoid science, over the next one hundred years, would lead to the demeaning of life and the subsequent mistreatment and extermination of minorities around the world. As governments worldwide declared classified groups as "inferior class" and subhuman, these groups would be treated with untold cruelty, actions justified by the science of Darwinism and eugenics. It is in this environment in which millions within "civilized" societies would tolerate in full sight, man's inhumanity to man, tolerance that would eventually empower the century's greatest tyrants and mass murderers Hitler, Stalin, and Mussolini.

The acceptance of these theories led to a hardening of America's heart and spirit. What followed was a callous consciousness that would evolve to self-centered elitism. It is this spirit of elitism that today defines the ideology of liberalism, Socialism, Communism, and the progressive movement.

Margaret Sanger's embrace of the race-based science of Darwinism and eugenics combined with a mix of atheism and Marxism proved to be a potent concoction resulting in what could be best described today as a sociopath, an individual "devoid of conscience." She spent her entire adult life gaining the trust of the Black race, as she would simultaneously spend her life's resources attempting to eliminate them. Her view of the Australian Aborigine people is instructive of her racist and evil personality. Like many eugenicists of her era, Sanger saw Australian aborigines as under-evolved and of little value except where they could be studied to gain better knowledge of evolution. She certainly believed that they, and other Black people, should not be allowed to enter the White gene pool. She had a strong drive to promote contraception and negative eugenics (to prevent the birth of "weaker" human elements.) "It is said that a fish as large as a man has a brain no larger than the kernel of an almond. In all fish and

---

152   Nathan Emmerich, "Bioethics, public intellectuals, and political biology today," *History of the Human Sciences*, Dublin City University, Belfast, April 2018.

153   *Ibid.*

reptiles where there is no great brain development, there is also no conscious sexual control. The lower down in the scale of human development we go the less sexual control we find. It is said that the aboriginal Australian, the lowest known species of the human family, just a step higher than the chimpanzee in brain development, has so little sexual control that police authority alone prevents him from obtaining sexual satisfaction on the streets."[154]

Sanger the Siren

In Greek mythology, sirens were dangerous creatures, portrayed as seductresses who lured nearby sailors with their enchanting music and voices to shipwreck on the rocky coast of their island. There is no better example of the bewitching and destructive nature of ideology of Liberalism than Planned Parenthood. It has been for the Black community, its most seductive siren.

No organization in our history has torn at the fiber of the family as has Planned Parenthood. Its founder, Margaret Sanger was both genius and beguiling in her strategy, both heartless and ruthless in her betrayal. An atheist, Socialist. and racist, she was able, over the course of her life, to seduce the support of some of the most educated and successful Black Americans of her day. She was able to accomplish what the KKK found impossible to do over decades of intimidation, for as evil as were the KKK's many atrocities, they could not defeat the determined, courageous, and united Black community. Sanger, on the other hand, relied on stealth networking to disarm the community she had targeted. Some of those she used were enthralled as she fed their egos with platitudes and prominence as others were attracted by her feigned concern for their race. Her international, multibillion-dollar organization today continues to reward prominent members of Black community. Those who give their allegiance to her program are granted political power, wealth, acceptance, and face time on BET, MSNBC, and other liberal media outlets.

Peddling her wares wrapped in pretty packages labeled "women's health" and "family planning," her program has been a plague on the Black community for over one hundred years. It has hardened the very soul of a race that continues to kill hundreds of thousands of its own babies each year.

Sanger—In Her Own Words

To understand Sanger's program and strategy it will be instructive to hear directly from her own words:

---

154   Margaret Sanger, *What Every Girl Should Know*. Max N. Maisel, New York, 1916, p. 47.

Ku Klux Klan

"I accepted an invitation to talk to the women's branch of the Ku Klux Klan...I saw through the door dim figures parading with banners and illuminated crosses...I was escorted to the platform, was introduced, and began to speak.... In the end, through simple illustrations I believed I had accomplished my purpose. A dozen invitations to speak to similar groups were proffered."[155]

Human Waste

"[Slavs, Latin, and Hebrew immigrants are] human weeds... deadweight of human waste...[Blacks, soldiers, and Jews are a] menace to the race...Eugenic sterilization is an urgent need...We must prevent multiplication of this bad stock."[156]

Large Families

"The most merciful thing that a large family does to one of its infant members is to kill it."[157]

Human Weeds

On Blacks, immigrants and indigents: *"human weeds," "reckless breeders," "spawning...human beings who never should have been born."[158]*

Charities

"Organized charity itself is the symptom of a malignant social disease. Those vast, complex, interrelated organizations aiming to control and to diminish the spread of misery and destitution and all the menacing evils that spring out of this sinisterly fertile soil, are the surest sign that our civilization has bred, is breeding and perpetuating constantly increasing numbers of defectives, delinquents and dependents."[159]

---

155 Margaret Sanger, *Margaret Sanger: An Autobiography*. Maxwell Reprint Co., University of Michigan, 1938, p.366.

156 M. Sanger, *Birth Control Review*, Volumes 18–21. American Birth Control League, University of Michigan, 1933.

157 Margaret Sanger, *Women and the New Race*. Eugenics Publishing Company, 1920, 1923.

158 M. Sanger, Birth Control Review.

159 Margaret Sanger, *Pivot of Civilization, The*. Brentano's Publishers, New York, 1922.

On the Extermination of Blacks

"We do not want word to go out that we want to exterminate the Negro population," she said, "if it ever occurs to any of their more rebellious members."[160]

"The mass of significant Negroes still breed carelessly and disastrously, with the result that the increase among Negroes... is in that portion of the population least intelligent and fit."[161]

Catholics

The "salvation of American civilization"—the sterilization of those "unfit" to procreate. She condemned the "irresponsible and reckless" rates of procreation among those "whose religious scruples prevent their exercising control over their numbers." "There is no doubt in the minds of all thinking people that the procreation of this group should be stopped."[162]

Board of Directors

Sanger was relentless and productive in networking her way into the Black community with the help of respected Black intellectual professions. She and other eugenicist of her day believed that lighter-skinned races were superior to darker-skinned races. There were other Royalty Class Black Professionals like W.E.B. Du Bois who held the same eugenicist philosophy as Sanger. It was this eugenic and evolutionary foundation that would initiate Du Bois' proposed Talented Tenth beliefs in which intellectuals, European-looking Blacks, like himself, would be looked upon as the saviors of their race.

It was this philosophy that justified his advocacy for abortion within his community and integration (race normalization) outside of it. These beliefs were predicated on the idea of evolutionary group of "betters" (Royalty Class Blacks) within the Black race, which would eventually "raise up" and (integrate or race neutralize themselves) themselves away from the remainder of their race.... Away from those who have been deemed not worthy of acceptance by the Royalty Class. According to W.E.B. Du Bois "...developing the 'Best of this Race' that they may guide the Mass away from the contamination and death of the Worst, in their own and other races."

---

160   Whisperingsage, "Margaret Sanger Quotes." ThinkExist.com, 1999–2016, thinkexist.com/quotation/organized-charity-itself-is-the-symptom-of-a/397373.html.

161   Diane S. Dew, "In Her Own Words." Dianedew.com, 2010, dianedew.com/sanger.htm.

162   Margaret Sanger, *Pivot of Civilization, The*. Brentano's Publishers, New York, 1922.

More Sophism

W.E.B. Du Bois: Sanger's Harlem Birth Control Center: Board Member

Du Bois, in his article "Black Folk and Birth Control," said, "inevitable clash of ideals between those Negroes who were striving to improve their economic position and those whose religious faith made the limitation of children a sin." He criticized the mass of ignorant Negroes who bred "carelessly and disastrously so that the increase among [them]...is from that part of the population least intelligent and fit, and least able to rear their children properly." He called for a more liberal attitude among Black churches. He said they were open to "intelligent propaganda of any sort, and the American Birth Control League and other agencies ought to get their speakers before church congregations and their arguments in the Negro newspapers."[163]

Charles S. Johnson (Eugenist): Fisk University's First Black President: Board Member

Johnson served on the National Advisory Council to the BCFA, becoming integral to the Negro Project. He wrote eugenic discrimination was necessary for Blacks. He said the high maternal and infant mortality rates, along with diseases, like tuberculosis, typhoid, malaria, and venereal infection, made it difficult for large families to adequately sustain themselves.

Further, "...the status of Negroes as marginal workers, their confinement to the lowest paid branches of industry, the necessity for the labors of mothers, as well as children, to balance meager budgets, are factors [that] emphasize the need for lessening the burden not only for themselves, but of society, which must provide the supplementary support in the form of relief."[164]

Dr. Dorothy Ferebee (Eugenist): Black Physician and Sanger's Board Member

"For a eugenic....it was integral to the implementation of eugenics to eliminate the 'unfit'. Eugenics is "a science that deals with the improvement (as by control of human mating) of hereditary qualities of a race or breed." Negative eugenics focused on preventing the birth of those it considered inferior or unfit. The pseudo-science (racial hygiene theory) of negative eugenics influenced social policy and eugenics-based legislation via the Immigration Act of 1923, segregation laws, and sterilization laws, and led to the racial hygiene theory adopted by the Nazis."[165]

163 "Birth Control as a Solution." Blackgenocide.org, 2012, blackgenocide.org/archived_articles/negro03.html

164 *Ibid.*

165 "The Negro Project." Toomanyaborted.com, The Radiance Foundation, toomanyaborted.com/thenegroproject/

> *"The future program [of Planned Parenthood] should center around more education in the field through the work of a professional Negro worker, because those of us who believe that the benefits of Planned Parenthood as a vital key to the elimination of human waste must reach the entire population, also believe that a double effort must be made to extend this program as a public health measure to Negroes who need is proportionately greater."*[166]
>
> —Dr. Dorothy Ferebee, Chairman of the Family Planning Committee of the National Council of Negro Women

> *"Negro professionals fully integrated into the staff...who could interpret the program and objectives to [other Blacks] in the normal course of day-to-day contacts; could break down fallacious attitudes and beliefs and elements of distrust; could inspire the confidence of the group; and would not be suspect of the intent to eliminate the race."*
>
> —"Planned Parenthood as a Public Health Measure for the Negro Race," January 29, 1942, Dr. Dorothy Ferebee

There are many unsung heroes throughout this era as the Black community progressed from its former state of slavery. Nothing is more indicative of the courage of this generation than what can be seen through the efforts of the Black fraternities and sororities during that time. Indicative of this was the AKA Sorority, one of the many prominent national Black women's service organizations. Initiated by its International President, Ida Jackson, the AKAs from 1933 to 1940, became America's first mobile medical clinic servicing poor Blacks throughout the South.

The program, called The Mississippi Health Project, with the above-quoted Dr. Ferebee of Howard University Medical School appointed as director, would facilitate over forty-six Black female doctors participating over the summer months.[167]

Over a seven year period this program stands as one of the most impressive examples of voluntary work ever conducted by Black physicians in the Jim Crow South. Throughout the era of segregation, Black physicians in the South contributed their time, money, and expertise to improve the health of their communities. Their stated goals for the Mississippi Health Project reflected a commonalty with others, like Booker T. Washington, to uplift and offer a hand-up to self-sufficiency:

---

166   *Ibid.*

167   "Changing the Face of Medicine: Dr. Dorothy Celeste Boulding Ferebee." National Institutes of Health, 2007.

(1.) To improve the health of Negroes in a section of the country where medical services were limited;

(2.) To create and encourage Negro efforts for self-improvement; and

(3.) To stimulate a sense of pride and appreciation for the AKA service programs.[168]

It ended due to the fuel shortage at the beginning of WWII. These female doctors drove their own vehicles from the Northeast over Southern backwoods and rural roads delivering medical support, supplies and hygiene education to over 15,000 uneducated, indentured rural families throughout Mississippi.[169] It was initiatives by selfless Black leaders like Ida Jackson that would provide a window through word, deed, and example, for Southern rural Black Americans to see the American Dream in force. In the summer of 1934, Ida Jackson initiated the Summer School for Rural Teachers to train future teachers. She worked with a total of twenty-two student teachers and two hundred forty-three school children. In addition, she held night classes for forty-eight adults. By obtaining 2,600 books for the school's library, Jackson made it "the largest library owned by White or colored in all of Holmes County."[170]

Sanger's ability to network and befriend those within the leadership of the Black community can be seen in the contradiction of Dr. Dorothy Boulding Freebee. Dorothy Freebee would oversee a program that required a courageous commitment and charity to the most vulnerable of her race. That she would simultaneously sit on the advisory board of Planned Parenthood, whose founder was committed to "weeding out" the unfit of her race, is curious and inconsistent. As a eugenics proponent, Sanger's view on charity was very clear. "[Charity] conceals a stupid cruelty, because it is not courageous enough to face unpleasant facts.[171]

The composition of Sanger's Planned Parenthood board could very well highlight the sociopathic effectiveness of Sanger to befriend and persuade her victims of her "good intentions." It should be noted in Ferebee's talk, "Changing the Face of Medicine," it seemed to reflect Sanger's influence as she discusses "the elimination of human waste" when speaking of others of her race. Though many professional Blacks shared the preeminent philosophy of a genetically-superior Talented Tenth, many of the well-meaning Black middle class to upper-class were simply seduced into the web of the deceitful Black widow spider, whose motives were ultimately 180 decrees different from theirs.

---

168 AKA sorority, "The 1936 Mississippi Health Project in Bolivar County," Detroit and London: Gale Research Inc., 1992.

169 McNealey, Earnestine G., Pearls of Service: The Legacy of America's First Black Sorority, Alpha Kappa Alpha, Alpha Kappa Alpha Sorority, Chicago, 2006.

170 *Ibid.*

171 Margaret Sanger, *Pivot of Civilization, The*. Brentano's Publishers, New York, 1922.

Sanger was able to move her agenda though the community by understanding the different visionary camps within and being able to morph the message of her cause to be attractive to her victims. By giving the appearance of making their cause her cause, she increased her influence and the effectiveness in spreading her message. She would use Black professionals who deeply cared for their own community as her messengers, as indicated in the Mississippi Health Project. These visionary professionals would use their own financial resources to travel down hot and dusty rural Southern roads to serve and uplift the poorest and most downtrodden among their race.

Sanger would simultaneously tailor another message for the middle class elitists represented by W.E.B. Du Bois. These professionals perceived themselves superior to other members of their race based on education, professional occupation, being "light-skinned" and by their acceptance into White society's inner circles. By introducing Sanger as a friend, they proved to be the perfect Trojan Horse for Sanger's goal to ingratiate herself within the Black community.

Sanger's Strategy

Prior to 1939, Sanger's abortion outreach was limited to the Black community, her Harlem clinic, and speaking at Black churches. Her vision for the reproductive practices of Black Americans expanded after the January 1939 merger of the Clinical Research Bureau and the American Birth Control League to form the Birth Control Federation of America.

Dr. Clarence J. Gamble, of Procter and Gamble fame, was chosen as the Birth Control Federation of America, Southern Regional Director.[172] Best articulated by the racist abortionist, Dr. Gamble, is the strategy of Planned Parenthood, its perception, and its deception. In a November 1939 memorandum entitled Suggestions for the Negro Project, he recognized that Black leaders might regard birth control as an extermination plot, so suggested (to Sanger) Black leaders be placed in positions where "it would appear" they were in charge.

Another project Director lamented to Sanger: "I wonder if Southern Darkies can ever be entrusted with...a clinic. Our experience causes us to doubt their ability to work except under White supervision."[173]

Margaret Sanger might well have been one of the twentieth century's greatest strategists. She was among the America's first influential contributors to the concept of "personal relationship networking." Today social liberals consider

---

172 CWALAC Staff, "Margaret Sanger's Eugenic Plan for Black Americans." Sanctity of Life, Concerned Women for America Legislative Action Committee, 2001, cwfa.org/the-negro-project-margaret-sangers-eugenic-plan-for-Black-americans/#sthash.fBtDxRY1.dpuf.

173 *Ibid.*

her as one of the primary leaders and inspirations of the liberal social and sexual revolution of the 1960s.[174] U.S. Secretary of State Hillary Clinton said that she admires "Margaret Sanger enormously, her courage, her tenacity, her vision" and that she was "really in awe of" Sanger's early work in Brooklyn, New York.[175]

Though Sanger's strategy of sophistry has not changed over the last one hundred years, its size and scope, with its adoption by others of like minds and agenda, has. The success of the early White-managed Planned Parenthood and NAACP was predicated on their strategic use of Black Americans as façades, "giving the appearance" that they were in charge. This new century's version can now be seen in large and powerful corporations like Viacom (BET), Comcast/NBC (MSNBC), and the White-controlled labor unions (AFL/CIO) that strategically deliver their message to the masses through their employed Black spokesmen. Black ownership, Black control, and legitimate Black leadership have never been congruent with the ways of the ideology of Liberalism.

Sanger continues to cast a dark shadow over the Black community decades after her death as her legacy continues to "weed out the unfit" among Black Americans. As with her pre-1939 efforts had focused on the community of Harlem clinic and Black churches,[176] her present organization has retained that legacy. New research released by Protecting Black Life (an outreach of Life Issues Institute) reveals that seventy-nine percent of Planned Parenthood's surgical abortion facilities are located within walking distance of African-American and/ or Hispanic/Latino communities. The group has a new map (http://www.protectingblack life.org/pp_targets/) that serves as a powerful visual—illustrating in full color on a website portal integrated with Google Maps functionality just how Planned Parenthood targets minorities. This interactive site gives viewers an up close and personal look at just how close these facilities are to their neighborhoods.[177]

Sanger's organization has since 1973 been responsible for the deaths of over sixteen-million Black babies, 40 percent of the total number of Blacks living in America today. Some would consider the targeted elimination of that number of lives within one race genocide—not the Royalty Class Black Man.

174   "Margaret Sanger: A New Appraisal...." UKApologetics.net, 2005–2018, ukapolo-getics.net/10/sanger.htm.

175   Hilary White, "Secretary Clinton "In Awe" of Racist Eugenicist Margaret Sanger." Lifesitenews.com, April 2009, lifesitenews.com/news/archive/ldn/2009/apr/09040306.

176   CWALAC Staff, "Margaret Sanger's Eugenic Plan for Black Americans."

177   Steven Ertfelt, "79% of Planned Parenthood Abortion Clinics Target Blacks, Hispanics." Lifenews.com, October 2012, lifenews.com/2012/10/16/79-of-planned-parenthood-abortion-clinics-target-Blacks-hispanics.

Added to the NAACP/Sanger strategy is one of the ideologies of Liberalism's most effective plays. It requires an agreeable Black spokesman who is willing to do what is politically incorrect for White Americans to do. This involves silencing all competing and independent Black voices via personal attacks, vilifying and destroying reputations if necessary. Considered racist if these actions were taken by liberal White racist, the Royalty Class Black Man is given carte blanche to turn his vitriol onto successful members of his own race. Because his goal is not to find solutions for his own race through intellectual debates, the Royalty Class Black Man plays his appointed role as the ideology of Liberalism's attack dog. He displays his anger at new thought even though old thought has proven a dismal failure for the Black community (a boon for the Royalty Class). He then dutifully and predictably returns to his traditional and limited vocabulary of past intimidation terms like Uncle Tom, Oreo, Porch monkey, and so on. (Again, see Kevin Jacksons' book *Race Pimping* for a one-page list.)

The prototype is the accomplished intellectual and...the "best of his race," W.E.B. Du Bois. Today's ideology of Liberalism no longer requires a person of accomplishment or intelligence. It only needs a "willing opportunist," someone who can, on cue, rally the emotions of the hopeless and angry urban Black community when called upon. The same community is kept angry, through its anti-White messaging, by the "Black in Name Only," BET (Black Entertainment News Channel). The contracted Royalty Class Black Problem Profiteers, Jesse Jackson, and Al Sharpton fill the role of the erstwhile Socialist turned anti-American Communist Du Bois.

Sanger would continue throughout the decades to hone her message and deepen her influence into the Black professional network, as she prepared to implement her 1936 Negro Project. Ironically, if she were alive today she would silently detest most of the liberals who defend and honor her...Blacks, Jews, Christians, immigrants, and soldiers. She has left us with fifty years of documented writings, actions, and words that conclusively define her. She was an avowed atheist, eugenicist, Socialist, pro-Nazi supporter, pro-KKK supporter, anti-Catholic, and racist; yet, today's ideology of Liberalism view her as a saint and twist the truth like a pretzel to defend her.

Robin A. Brace, January 2010, UK Apologetics

"Margaret Sanger's ethics and moral evaluation were very deeply flawed and her seeming liking for vulgarity, bad taste and for provoking anger when it might have been avoided, often brought her into needless conflicts. Meanwhile her atheism, and her easy acceptance of racism and eugenics and her approval of the principle of euthanasia (if not the actual practice of gassing the physically and mentally unfit) mean that—overall—we must consider Sanger as an evil little lady who will not escape the judgment of God for her part in being one of the architects of the hideous moral revolution of the 1960s/1970s, a sexual revolution which, it is now clear, has caused enormous damage, including the utterly disgraceful fact of millions of aborted babies. This, we believe, will finally stand as one of the most hideous stains on 20th/21st century western society. Most 'enlightened' westerners don't even think of this as important, but there is a God in Heaven who is keeping an account."[178]

---

178   "Margaret Sanger: A New Appraisal...."

CHAPTER 7

THE CHINESE BAMBOO TREE

EVIL is the purposeful stealing of one's hopes, dreams, and future. PURE EVIL is the targeting of a race of millions and using human misery as a political strategy to steal their hopes, dreams, and future.

—Burgess Owens

On the Asian continent grows a tree that exemplifies the spiritual and physical Law of Seed and Harvest. This law can be identified in terms such as patience, persistence, vision, and faith, all integral to success.

The story of the Chinese bamboo begins with the planting of its tiny seed. After an entire year of watering, fertilizing, and cultivation, it shows no evidence of life. This cycle repeats itself for season two, three, and four. It is only after the fifth season of the application of patient and persistent does the Law of Seed and Harvest begin to bear fruit. Considered by the casual observer as an overnight miracle, the Chinese bamboo tree transitions overnight, as it blossoms ninety feet *within six weeks.*

It will be from this perspective that historians will view the trajectory of the Black community's journey in America. Recorded will be the miraculous blossoming of its seeds within fifty years of the end of slavery. Though fertilized with the nutrients of freedom, Capitalism, and Christian faith, the Black community had to endure an even longer season of hopelessness wrought by the parasitic weeds of Socialism/Marxism. The weed seed was planted with stealth and betrayal, and over time has darkened the hopes and dreams of millions of Black Americans.

The 1932 movie *The Wizard of OZ*, exemplifies *The Black American Journey. It* is now time we pull back the curtain of deceit and expose those who have, since 1910, been undermining the Black community and are now doing the same to our American society.

Killing Fields of Socialism

Venezuela, in South America, represents a country that once prospered due to its natural wealth in oil. It was a country that once freely elected its representatives. Over the last decades, Venezuela has been transformed. It is now a totalitarian Socialistic state where elections are no longer free, private property and businesses have been confiscated by the State, and anti-government speech results in death, torture and/or imprisonment. Its citizens must now choose between eating government-subsidized rabbits, their pets, or buffalo and horses from the zoo.[179] In this once free country powered by its free market, the only private market that is prospering is the growing numbers of young girls who are selling their bodies for sex in exchange for food.

"Now what we need is food, you know, you wake up with nothing to eat," a child prostitute said. "I've been two weeks just eating plantains and with nothing—boiled plantains, fried plantains, boiled plantains, with nothing. So what am I going to do? Get to work."[180]

With this dramatic change in a continent due south of us, and with knowledge of it a few keyboard clicks away on their smartphone, seventy-three percent of America's millennials cannot identify the correct meaning of Socialism.[181]

A recent survey showed that forty-four percent of America's young people favor Socialism over Capitalism, with seven percent opting for outright Communism and seven percent for fascism. This adds up to many young Americans who claim they would accept total government control over their economic lives! Capitalism, on the other hand, is viewed favorably by only forty-two percent of millennials. With over one hundred million citizens murdered by Communists and the Nazis during the 20th century, it appears that ancient history has gone down a memory hole.[182]

As our upcoming generation of leaders inch closer to repudiating their own Judeo-Christian free market system, we must ask the questions: *How?*

---

179   Yesman Utrera, "Pets on the Menu as Venezuelans Starve." Thedailybeast.com, The Daily Beast, November 2014, thedailybeast.com/zoo-animals-on-the-menu-as-venezuelans-starve.

180   Ben Kew. "Venezuela: Teenage Girls Turn to Prostitution to Fight Starvation." Political news. Breitbart, November 3, 2017. breitbart.com/national-security/2017/11/03/venezuela-teenage-girls-turn-prostitution-fight-starvation.

181   Shawn Langlois. "Poll: Millennials Desperately Need to Bone up on the History of Communism." MarketWatch, October 21, 2016. marketwatch.com/story/poll-millennials-desperately-need-to-bone-up-on-the-history-of-Communism-2016-10-17.

182   Robert Knight. "Socialism's Predictable Outcomes." *The Washington Times*. November 19, 2017, Online edition, sec. Opinion/Commentary. washingtontimes.com/news/2017/nov/19/socialisms-history-shows-it-delivers-misery-murder.

Why? Who? Or *What?* With access to more knowledge than at any other time in human history...

How have we allowed ourselves to devolve to a place where so little is known about our nation's history and its providential mission?

Why are so many young Americans turning away from America's culture of freedom?

What is at the root cause of the inter-generational change in our perception of the American Way?

As will be seen through the pages of *Why I Stand,* the Black American community has been the target of Socialism/Marxism since 1910. This ideological enemy is both deadly and destructive but is *not* distinctive of color or race. Instead, it infects the American culture with class *Elitism.*

Within fifty years of the Emancipation Proclamation, the Black community had established itself as this country's most competitive and impacting minority. This was a result of approximately four million newly-freed American citizens feeling a strong connection to the American Way. They successfully worked to become entrepreneurs, educators, professionals, and laborers. They built their communities based on a strong nuclear family unit and their Christian faith. They dreamed past their obstacles and tenaciously worked to progress. In the process they gifted their children with a bright vision of America's promise.

Since the surprise suicide attack on 9/11, the word "radicalization" has become part of our country's vocabulary. It is founded on a strategy of targeted propaganda resulting in the invoking of an illogical hatred. This strategy of targeting the Black community with anti-White, anti-family, anti-police, and anti-American propaganda has been a strategy of the Socialist/Marxists for decades. Millions of NFL fans throughout the 2016 and 2017 seasons witnessed very blessed and wealthy Black NFL players, some making over twelve million dollars annually, protesting the American flag. These young men have been taught to believe the American culture to be oppressive and racist. This belief, all too real to these young men, is a result of messengering or racialization over two decades by those who have been trusted to deliver its news and entertainment.

Radicalization is a process by which an individual or group comes to adopt increasingly extreme political, social, or religious ideals and aspirations that reject or undermine the status quo or reject and/or undermine contemporary ideas and expressions of freedom of choice.[183]

The "radicalization" of the Black community took time, patience, persistence, and has been an act of strategic betrayal from within. Its success has come through stealth and collusion between Black and White Socialist/

---

183   "Radicalization." Wikipedia, Last updated: 15 June 2018. en.wikipedia.org/wiki/
Radicalization.

Marxist politicians and activists. With its all too predictable support of legislative policies that has statistically been proven to undermine the core of the Black community, the Congressional Black Caucus has proven to be its most effective adversary. These elected members of Congress have for decades prioritized their own wealth, fame, and popularity over the welfare of their own race and country. The impact of their leadership has been on display for the last two seasons on the NFL sidelines. As they have colluded with wealthy White media and entertainment giants like Viacom, they've promoted within the urban community anti-White, anti-Capitalism, anti-Flag, anti-American propaganda. The result has been super wealthy young Black athletes and entertainers who feel totally justified to be ungrateful, oppressed, anti-American Socialists. As a result, this same collaborative effort has resulted in thousands of young Black students who passionately parrot the mantra of social justice Marxism. What is missing from this generation of Social Justice Warriors is the attitude of gratitude and love for our American Way. Instead, through consistent messaging of anger, judgment, and intolerance, they have been taught a deep sense of entitlement.

The blossoming of the ideological seed of Socialism/Marxism within the urban Black community has resulted in the exponential growth of crime, death, illiteracy, unemployment, child abandonment, abuse, and abortions. It can be measured throughout the decades, by the destruction of every institution that once stood as the cornerstone of the successful Black American community. This ideology has been the genesis of the demise of Black manhood, the disrespect for Black womanhood, the destruction of the Black nuclear family, Judeo Christian values, and any mention of God in the public square.

Historically, every country that has embraced the ideology of Marxist Socialism has inevitable incurred the same wrath of misery that is seen presently within the Black community. The only differential in each experiment is the name of the enlightened elitist leadership who demands of those who he oversees that they get it right and follow his lead. America's enlightened progressive Left have ensured that an entire generation of economic ignorance by not teaching America's own world leading system of free enterprise. The Democratic education unionists have strategically hidden the history of misery imposed upon millions and millions of men, women, and children by their ideology. Predictably, every totalitarian despot begins his reign with confident assurance to his own people of the coming utopia. What follows predictably is the wanton disregard and destruction of human life as they replace God with themselves. The insidious ideology of Socialist Marxism has left killing fields spewed throughout the world in the 20th century. They consist of the following:

The Killing Fields of Socialism/Communism[184]

- *Socialism:* 40–70 million killed in China under Chairman Mao, 1958–61
- *Socialism:* 20 million killed in USSR under Joseph Stalin, 1936–52
- *Socialism:* 40 million killed in USSR under other leaders
- *Communism:* 4 million killed in Cambodia under Pol Pot, 1975–79
- *Socialism:* 5.6 million killed in North Korea under Kim Il Sung
- *Socialism:* 1.15 million killed in Yugoslavia under Josip Tito, 1945–65
- *Communism:* 1 million killed in Ethiopia under Menghistu, 1975–1978
- *Communism:* 1 million killed in Indonesia under Suharto, 1966
- *Communism:* 1 million killed in Afghanistan under Brezhnev, 1979–1981
- *Socialism:* 800,000 killed in Rwanda under Jean Kambanda, 1994

---

184   Rock Kelo. "Socialism & Mass Murder in the 20th Century." Ceteris Paribus, June 2014. rickkelo.liberty.me/Socialism-mass-murder.

CHAPTER 8

AMERICA'S PROMISE

Pride in community, for those who grew up in the days of Jim Crow segregation, was not founded on the embellishment of opportunities lost due to racism, but instead was built on highlighting the great accomplishments in spite of it. The "can do" outlook that prevailed in past Black generations cleared the pathway to prosperity and celebrated a creative, courageous and self-respecting community determined never to be held back.

—*Burgess Owens*

At the end of the Civil War, at a cost of over 600,000 American lives, over four million slaves gained their freedom. This effort represented the loss of more American lives than all other American conflicts combined. The following decades of federal policies would represent the ebb and flow of efforts that would either correct past injustices or add to them.

As the Civil War came to an end, the doorway to the American promise of freedom and equality began to open. President's Lincoln Emancipation Proclamation and the congressional legislation of the Radical Republicans Coalition paved the way. The 1868 Fourteenth Amendment and the Wade–Davis Bill respectively upgraded the rights of African Americans and curtailed the rights of former Confederates. Andrew Johnson, the Democratic successor to President Lincoln, showed a heightened leniency toward the defeated ex-Confederates. Whereas Lincoln showed a leaning toward supporting the enfranchisement of all freedmen, Johnson opposed this.[185]

---

185   James M. Campbell, and Rebecca J. Fraser. *Reconstruction: People and Perspectives*. ABC-CLIO, 2008.

Johnson's interpretations of Lincoln's policies prevailed until the Congressional elections of 1866, which enabled the Radical Republicans to take control of policy. They removed former Confederates from power and enfranchised the Black freedmen. A Republican coalition came to power in nearly all the southern states and set out to transform society by setting up a free labor economy, using the U.S. Army and the Freedmen's Bureau. The Bureau protected the legal rights of freedmen, negotiated labor contracts, and established schools and churches. Thousands of northerners came south as missionaries, teachers, businessmen, and politicians. Hostile southern Democrats called them "carpetbaggers."

In early 1866, Congress passed the Freedmen's Bureau and civil rights bills and sent them to Johnson for his signature. The first bill extended the life of the bureau, originally established as a temporary organization charged with assisting refugees and freed slaves, while the second defined all persons born in the United States as national citizens with equality before the law. President Johnson vetoed the bills, but Congress overrode his veto. This historic Civil Rights Act was the first major bill in the history of the United States to become law through an override of a presidential veto. The Radical Republicans in the House of Representatives, frustrated by Johnson's opposition to Congressional Reconstruction, filed impeachment charges. The action failed by one vote in the Senate.[186]

In 1868, the newly elected Republican President Ulysses S. Grant, enforced the Enforcement Acts, Reconstruction legislation passed by his party to protect southern African Americans. The Enforcement Acts effectively combated and essentially eliminated the Democratic Party's terrorist group, the Ku Klux Klan. Unfortunately, there was a resurgence of the KKK in 1913, after the election of Democrat and KKK member, President Woodrow Wilson. This dark chapter of both subversive and overt attacks on the early thriving, patriotic, Christian and entrepreneurial Black community will be discussed in a later chapter.

Reconstruction Era

The period after the Civil War from 1865 to 1877 was called the Reconstruction period. Abraham Lincoln began planning for the reconstruction of the South during the Civil War as Union soldiers occupied huge areas of the South. Unfortunately, due to his assassination on April 15, 1865, Lincoln's vision for a compassionate federal outreach to the defeated south, combined with support for Black American assimilation, was not to be realized for another one hundred years.

---

186   "Reconstruction Era." Wikipedia, July 2018. en.wikipedia.org/wiki/Reconstruction_Era.

Under the administration of Democratic President Andrew Johnson, in 1865 and 1866 new southern state legislatures passed restrictive "Black codes" to control the labor and behavior of former slaves and other African Americans.[187] In Johnson's view, the southern states had never given up their right to govern themselves, and the federal government had no right to determine voting requirements or other questions at the state level.

Because of Johnson's leniency, many southern states successfully enacted a series of "Black codes" designed to restrict freed Blacks from competing with White laborers. These repressive codes enraged many in the North. As a result, many of the Radical Republicans refused to seat congressmen and senators elected from the southern states.

Under Johnson's Presidential Reconstruction, all land that had been confiscated and distributed to the freed slaves by the Union army or the Freedmen's Bureau (established by Congress in 1865) reverted to its prewar owners.

Apart from being required to uphold the abolition of slavery in compliance with the 13th Amendment to the Constitution, swear loyalty to the Union, and pay off war debt, southern state governments were given free rein to rebuild themselves. After northern voters rejected Johnson's policies in the congressional elections in late 1866, Republicans in Congress took firm hold of Reconstruction in the South. The following March, over Johnson's veto, Congress passed the Reconstruction Act of 1867, which temporarily divided the South into five military districts and outlined how governments based on universal (male) suffrage were to be organized. The law also required southern states to ratify the 14th Amendment, which broadened the definition of citizenship, granting "equal protection" of the Constitution to former slaves, before they could rejoin the Union. In February 1869, Congress approved the 15th Amendment (adopted in 1870), which guaranteed that a citizen's right to vote would not be denied "on account of race, color, or previous condition of servitude."

By 1870, all the former Confederate states had been readmitted to the Union, and the state constitutions during the years of Radical Reconstruction were the most progressive in the region's history. African American participation in southern public life after 1867 would be by far the most radical development of Reconstruction, which was essentially a large-scale experiment in interracial democracy unlike that of any other society following the abolition of slavery.

Blacks won election to southern state governments and the U.S. Congress during this period. Among the other achievements of Reconstruction were the South's first state-funded public school systems, more equitable taxation legislation, laws against racial discrimination in public transport and

---

187   "Reconstruction: Compromise of 1877." History.com, n.d. history.com/topics/american-civil-war/reconstruction.

accommodations, and ambitious economic development programs, including aid to railroads and other enterprises.[188]

Reconstruction Comes to an End

After 1867, an increasing number of southern Whites turned to violence in response to the revolutionary changes of Radical Reconstruction. The Ku Klux Klan and other White supremacist organizations targeted local Republican leaders, White and Black, and other African Americans who challenged White authority. Federal legislation passed during the administration of President Ulysses S. Grant in 1871 took aim at the Klan and others who attempted to interfere with Black suffrage and other political rights. White supremacy gradually reasserted its hold on the South after the early 1870s as support for Reconstruction waned. Racism was still a potent force in both the North and South, and Republicans became less egalitarian as the decade continued. In 1874, after an economic depression plunged much of the South into poverty, the Democratic Party won control of the House of Representatives for the first time since the Civil War.[189]

When Democrats waged a campaign of violence to take control of Mississippi in 1875, Grant refused to send federal troops, marking the end of federal support for Reconstruction-era state governments in the South. By 1876, only Florida, Louisiana, and South Carolina were still in Republican hands. In the contested presidential election that year, Republican candidate Rutherford B. Hayes reached a compromise with Democrats in Congress. In exchange for certification of his election, he acknowledged Democratic control of the entire South. The Compromise of 1876 marked the end of Reconstruction as a distinct period, but the struggle to deal with the revolution ushered in by slavery's eradication would continue in the South and elsewhere long after that date. A century later, the legacy of Reconstruction would be revived during the civil rights movement of the 1960s as African Americans fought for the political, economic, and social equality that had long been denied them.[190]

Reconstruction was a significant chapter in the history of civil rights in the United States, and in economic history. After Reconstruction ended, the South remained a poverty-stricken "backwater" dependent on agriculture.[191] White Southerners soon succeeded in re-establishing legal and political dominance over Blacks through violence, intimidation, and discrimination. Historian Eric Foner argues, "What remains certain is that Reconstruction failed, and that for

---

188   *Ibid.*
189   *Ibid.*
190   *Ibid.*
191   *Ibid.*

Blacks its failure was a disaster whose magnitude cannot be obscured by the genuine accomplishments that did endure."[192]

Success—The Old American Way

It was during the Reconstruction Period where the tenacity of the community of former slaves can be seen. Introduced to their faith through the unimaginable evil of slavery, these new Christians saw their forced journey to the promised land of America as providential. This perspective was best summarized by one of its foremost leaders of that day, former slave, Booker T. Washington:

> *"Then, when we rid ourselves of prejudice, or racial feeling, and look facts in the face, we must acknowledge that, not-withstanding the cruelty and moral wrong of slavery, the ten million Negroes inhabiting this country, who themselves or whose ancestors went through the school of American slavery, are in a stronger and more hopeful condition materially, intellectually, morally, and religiously than is true of an equal number of Black people in any other portion of the globe. This is so to such an extent that Negroes in this country, who themselves or whose forefathers went through the school of slavery, are constantly returning to Africa as missionaries to enlighten those who remained in the fatherland. This I say, not to justify slavery—on the other hand, I condemn it as an institution, as we all know that in America it was established for selfish and financial reasons, and not from a missionary motive—but to call attention to a fact, and to show how Providence so often uses men and institutions to accomplish a purpose."* [193]

This optimism and appreciation for American citizenship is embodied in the story of my first American ancestor, my great, great grandfather Silas Burgess. Silas arrived in America as a child in the belly of a slave ship. Years later, after escaping to freedom, he became a successful entrepreneur, teacher, leader, and a pillar of his community.

---

192 *Foner, E. Reconstruction: America's Unfinished Revolution, 1863-1877. Perennial Classics. HarperCollins, 2002. books.google.com/books?id=FhvA0S_op38C.*

193 West, M.R. *The Education of Booker T. Washington: American Democracy and the Idea of Race Relations.* Columbia University Press, 2006. books.google.com/books?id=BFViCwAAQBAJ.

American soil of the early 1900s had not yet been fully cultivated for total acceptance of Black Americans, as well as other non-White and non-Protestant communities; the seeds of freedom had been planted and were waiting for their season to blossom. This would be a consistent process with every new culture arriving to America. As with the Chinese bamboo tree, there would be the period of dormancy, a time of patience, faith, and endurance. This was a process experienced by all who would later, with gratitude, call themselves Americans. It would, however, take additional years for evidence of germination to become apparent.

Within fifty years after the Civil War, the American Dream was becoming a reality for Black Americans. Though institutional racism would remain an impediment for decades to come, access to the free market, education, and strong nuclear family units would bless millions upon millions throughout the years.

Teaching slaves to read and write was illegal and punishable by harsh beatings and death. Once free, though, they taught themselves and moved forward. By the end of the 1800s, this community had blossomed with its own pharmacists, scientists, inventors, physicians, academics, explorers, entrepreneurs, teachers, farmers, and laborers. Their entrepreneurial propensity produced millionaires nationwide, including America's first female millionaire, Madame CJ Walker, in 1915. Committed to a vision of hope, prosperity, and opportunities for their progenitors, they built their own institutions of education. By 1905, Tuskegee University, a Black Alabama college founded in 1885 by Booker T. Washington, was creating more self-made millionaires than Harvard, Princeton, and Yale combined.[194]

Here are the stories of some of those visionary pioneers:

Thomas L. Jennings (1791–February 12, 1856) was an African American tradesman and abolitionist in New York City, New York. He owned and operated a tailoring and dry-cleaning business, and on March 3,1821, he was granted a patent for a dry scrub process; the first African American to be granted a patent.[195]

George Crum—*Inventor of Potato Chips* (1824–July 22, 1914) was an American chef, hunter, guide, and cook. By 1860, Crum had opened his own restaurant called Crum's on Story Hill in New York. His cuisine was in high demand among Saratoga Springs' tourists and elites. His rules of procedure were his own and he "played no favorites." Guests were obliged to wait their turn, be they millionaire or wage-earner—Mr. Vanderbilt was obliged to wait

---

194   Marcus Noel. "'A Man Ahead Of His Time': What Booker T. Washington Under-stood About Entrepreneurship." Forbes.com, February 2017. forbes.com/sites/under30network/2017/02/23/a-man-ahead-of-his-time-what-booker-t-wash-ington-understood-about-entrepreneurship.

195   M. Bellis. "Thomas Jennings, the First African-American Patent Holder." ThoughtCo.com, June 2017. thoughtco.com/thomas-jennings-inventor-1991311.

an hour and a half for a meal. With none but rich pleasure-seekers as his guests, Crum kept his tables laden with the best of everything.

Bessie Coleman—*First African American Female Pilot* (January 26, 1892–April 30, 1926), a sharecropper's daughter, became interested in aviation in her early 20s. As an African American woman, she was denied admission to flight schools. She eventually learned to fly in France. In 1921, she became the first African American female pilot and the first to have an international aviation license.[196]

Doctor Charles Drew—*Blood Bank Inventor* (Born in 1904) was the African American inventor, physician, researcher, and surgeon who revolutionized the understanding of blood plasma, leading to the invention of blood banks. His system for the storing of blood plasma revolutionized the medical profession. He was chosen to set up a system for storing blood and for its transfusion, a project nicknamed "Blood for Britain."

This prototypical blood bank collected blood from 15,000 people for soldiers and civilians in World War II Britain and paved the way for the American Red Cross blood bank, of which he was the first director. In 1941, the American Red Cross decided to set up blood donor stations to collect plasma for the U.S. Armed Forces. When the Armed Forces ordered that only Caucasian blood be given to soldiers, Drew protested and resigned.[197]

Matthew Alexander Henson (August 8, 1866–March 9, 1955) was the first African American explorer with Robert Peary, completing seven voyages over a period of nearly twenty-three years (the North Pole among them). He was a navigator and craftsman who traded with the Inuit and learned their language. He was known as Peary's "first man" for these arduous travels.[198]

George Washington Carver (1860s–January 5, 1943) was an American botanist and inventor. His reputation is largely based on his promotion of alternative crops to cotton, such as peanuts and sweet potatoes. He wanted poor farmers to grow alternative crops both as a source of their own food and as a source of other products to improve their quality of life. He was also a leader in promoting environmentalism. In 1941, *TIME* magazine dubbed Carver a "Black Leonardo."[199]

---

196   "7 African American Firsts: Black Men and Women Who Broke Barriers." Belief-Net.com, n.d. beliefnet.com/inspiration/galleries/7-african-american-firsts.aspx.

197   Mary Bellis. "Charles Drew, Inventor of the Blood Bank." ThoughtCo.com, April 6, 2017. thoughtco.com/charles-drew-inventor-1991684.

198   Matthew Alexander Henson, and Deirdre C. Stam. *Matthew A. Henson's Historic Arctic Journey: The Classic Account of One of the World's Greatest Black Explorers.* Explorers Club Classics 5. Lyons Press, 2009.

199   Mark D. Hersey. *My Work Is That of Conservation: An Environmental Biography of George Washington Carver.* Environmental History and the American South. University of Georgia Press, 2011.

Booker T. Washington (April 5, 1856–November 14, 1915) was an educator, a visionary, an entrepreneur, and a bridge-builder. The former slave was the founder of Tuskegee University, founder of the first National Business Network, and a conduit of millions of dollars from wealthy White donors for southern Black school development.

Black Wall Street was an early 1900 Tulsa, Oklahoma Black community built on the principles of free market, supply and demand, and financial reward for risk-taking Capitalism. There were reports of over fifty millionaire businessmen with twenty-one churches, twenty-one restaurants, thirty grocery stores, two movie theaters, a hospital, bank, post office, libraries, schools, law offices, a half-dozen private airplanes, and a bus system.[200]

This successful and independent community was the vision of conservative leaders like Booker T. Washington. An article titled *What Happened to Black Wall Street on June 1, 1921?* best described Black Wall Street, or Little Africa as it was also known. It was compared to a mini Beverly Hills and represented the golden door of the Black community during the early 1900s. It proved that African Americans could create a successful infrastructure. [201]

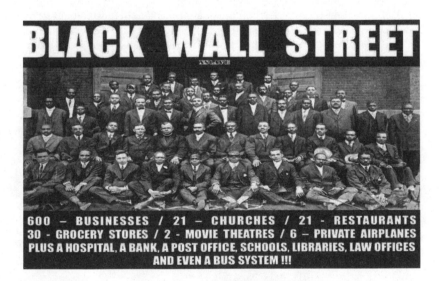

BLACK WALL STREET

600 – BUSINESSES / 21 – CHURCHES / 21 - RESTAURANTS
30 - GROCERY STORES / 2 - MOVIE THEATRES / 6 – PRIVATE AIRPLANES
PLUS A HOSPITAL, A BANK, A POST OFFICE, SCHOOLS, LIBRARIES, LAW OFFICES
AND EVEN A BUS SYSTEM !!!

200   Josie Pickens. "The Destruction of Black Wall Street." Ebony.com, May 31, 2013. ebony.com/Black-history/the-destruction-of-Black-wall-street-405.

201   Mike House. "What Happened to Black Wall Street on June 1, 1921?" *San Francisco Bay View National Black Newspaper*. February 9, 2011, sec. News & Views. sfbayview.com/2011/02/what-happened-to-Black-wall-street-on-june-1-1921.

In the Black community, the dollar circulated thirty-six to one hundred times, sometimes taking up to a year before its currency would leave the community. Comparatively, in modern times a dollar can circulate in Asian communities for a month, Jewish communities for twenty days, and White communities for seventeen, but it leaves the modern-day Black community within six hours.[202] As for resources, there were Black Ph.Ds., attorneys, and doctors residing in Black Wall Street. One physician was Doctor Berry, who owned the bus system. His average income was five hundred dollars a day, hefty pocket change in 1910. It was a time when the entire state of Oklahoma had only two airports, yet six Blacks owned their own planes. It was a fascinating community.

The mainstay of the community was to educate every child. Nepotism was the one word they believed in, a sense of continuity, family prosperity, and inheritance that has been embraced by every successful culture throughout time. The main thoroughfare was Greenwood Avenue, intersected by Archer and Pine Streets. From the first letters in each of those three names you get G.A.P. This is where the renowned R&B music group the GAP Band got its name. They're from Tulsa.[203]

Unfortunately, this Black community success ended in June of 1921 with an attack organized and implemented by the Democratic Party's terrorist arm, the KKK. They worked in consort with ranking city officials and many other envious White sympathizers.[204] The community was bombed from the air and burned to the ground. Within a period of fewer than twelve hours, a once thriving Black business district in northern Tulsa lay smoldering. The night's carnage left some three thousand Black Americans dead and over six hundred successful businesses lost.[205]

Nationwide, the increasingly independent Black community was being rewarded due to its embrace of meritocracy, hard work and risk taking. These segregated communities blossomed with a prosperous Black middle class. As success became more prevalent within this middle class, others were inspired to move forward. This hard working, humble, and empathetic class paved a pathway that allowed hope that the American Dream was indeed accessible.

There were distinct tenets that propelled past generations and that will, in the same manner, serve as pillars for success in the present. Those tenets of independence, industry, patriotism, and pride remain embedded within

202   "Tulsa Race Riot." Wikipedia, August 3, 2018. en.wikipedia.org/wiki/Tulsa_race_riot.

203   Mike House. "What Happened to Black Wall Street on June 1, 1921?"

204   *Ibid.*

205   kristalklear. "Black Wall Street • Tulsa, Oklahoma 1921." The Internet Post (blog), November 19, 2013. theinternetpost.net/2013/11/19/Black-wall-street-%e2%80%a2-tulsa-oklahoma-1921-full-documentary.

the soul of the Black community. Once nourished with the elixir of hope this community will experience a miraculous resurrection. As with the Chinese bamboo tree, it will blossom with men of courage who are willing to stand alone, if necessary, against the elitist groupthink that has infected their community. They will once again stand as examples of loyalty and commitment as fathers and embrace their responsibilities as husbands and community leaders. Black mothers will, as in days of old, prioritize their children's welfare above self-interest and convenience. They will refuse to embrace the message of abortionists who view their children as having no value other than for research or profit. Instead, they will rejoice in motherhood, protect, nurture, and prepare their children to accept their value as envisioned by the God who created them.

As it has been from the founding of our nation upon Judeo-Christian principles and family values, embraced by these Black mothers and fathers will be God's vision of an eternal partnership consummated within the bounds of marriage. It is within this partnership of equity, loyalty, and service where their children will be taught the pillars of happiness...love, discipline, respect for selves and others, service, and submission to moral authority.

Our past generations of Americans flourished in the fertile ground of Judeo-Christian values, an environment that encourages and rewards excellence. As the Black community once again plants its roots deep within this environment it will be ensured results likened to the Chinese bamboo tree metaphor. It will be through this same scenario of tenacity, patience, endurance, and faith that it too will experience its miraculous growth.

CHAPTER 9

IT'S ALL ABOUT TEAM

The ideologies that continue to compete for the heart and soul of the American people—Liberalism, Socialism, Marxism, Communism, Capitalism and conservatism—represent distinctly different world-views of economics, freedom, and man's relationship with God. Based on the acceptance or rejection of these views, a society will embrace varying degrees of individual initiative and accountability in its quest for happiness. Regardless of what era or continent these competing ideologies are found, the foundational premises remain intrinsically unchangeable. Socialism, for example, whether mandated by the Russian dictator Stalin, Germany's Hitler, Cuba's Castro, Venezuela's Hugo Chavez, or American Socialist/Marxist Bernie Sanders, will always result in a predicable outcome. As those of the progressive Left pace themselves, they will ultimately pass laws to prohibit freedom of religion. They will insist on limiting contrary individual thoughts and actions, increase the power of the state, and inevitably resort to stealing property, freedom, rights, and the lives of a rebellious citizenry. This explains the consistent exodus of millions from Socialist/Marxist regimes instead of migration to them.

Regardless of the society where Socialism and Marxism has been instituted, such as the Republic of China, the republic of Cuba, the Socialist Republic of Vietnam, the Republic of Afghanistan, Albania, or America's urban cities and Indian reservations, the end result remains commonly consistent: a population that is angry, uneducated, unemployed, hopeless, poor, and dependent.

Because of the emotional dependency that prevails within a Socialist society, consistent is the fan-like celebration and loyalty of the ideology. This loyalty, witnessed throughout every political election cycle, can best be summarized with my observations of the NFL fan during my ten-year career. In short, "it's all about team."

As a ten-year NFL veteran, I had a unique sideline prospective of the commitment of the NFL fan. Regardless of the consistency of disappointing seasons or the revolving door of unsuccessful coaches, true fan loyalty remained palpable due to the emotion of hope. This loyalty defined the 1970s and early 1980s Oakland Raider fan, whose commitment could be observed through the silver and Black coloring of their cars and homes and with family pets and offspring named after famous Raider all-stars.

It was during a frigid 1981 AFC play-off game in which the temperatures had plunged to -35 degrees that I vividly remember viewing the commitment of a Cleveland Brown fan. As I stared at a dedicated and loyal fan, celebrating in the stands totally bare-chested, I wondered if there would be a price this young man would pay later for his youthful, rambunctious zeal. Would there be in his future some physical accountability for this extreme, fanatical commitment to the team? I've wondered where this willingness to "sell out" at all costs came from. Was it decades of a family tradition, a love of the team colors, a mascot, or did he, while in his youth, play for a high school team with the same name? It was easy for me to conclude that his passion was not driven by the same personal investment of blood, sweat, and tears as the professional athletes on the field. Instead, the catalyst for such blind loyalty must be under the heading *"pure emotion."*

My commitment to the NY Jets team organization was also driven by emotion, but unlike the fan, it was anchored by a weekly paycheck. At the end of my seventh season, it was this logic that allowed me to switch my uncompromised loyalty from one team to another within the first three words of a five-minute conversation: "you've been traded."

This change would remain so for the remainder of my NFL career. It was a reasonable transition in a free market in which financial survival is predicated on the concept of employee loyalty. At that moment, logic trumped all previous emotional investment as my future income and ability to provide for my young family was no longer connected to the Jets organization, but instead to a former adversary.

This self-survival logic was experienced again as I transitioned from the NFL into the marketplace where I would spend the rest of my income-producing career. My transition into my post-NFL chapter came with a clear understanding that my future success was no longer based on my physical prowess and understanding of game plans and strategies. It would now be based on my ability to create a customized game plan for my "real world" personal Super Bowl.

As pointed out in the previous chapter, the beginning of the 1900s represented a renaissance within the Black community. It was a generation committed to send educated, hard-working, young Americans into the marketplace who would build, support, and reinvest into their own communities. And reinvest they did. The talent derived from this education-centric community and its nation-leading percentage of entrepreneurs facilitated an aggressive vertical financial mobility. There was a commitment embedded within this community that overcoming *all* obstacles was a sacred obligation to not only present but future generations. It was understood there was a responsibility to produce great minds, business strategists, visionaries, and leaders who would contribute to their community and nation. These expectations resulted in highly competitive and respected Black colleges throughout our country. These institutions sent into the marketplace who were disciplined, moral, and committed to reflect well on their family's name and their race.

This community responded with a contribution of industrial pioneers who added incalculable value to our nation. This included visionaries such as the founder of Tuskegee Institution, Booker T. Washington; the great agronomist, George Washington Carver, dubbed in 1941 by *Time Magazine* as the Black Leonardo[206]; Garrett Morgan, the inventor of the automatic traffic light, the gas mask, and a hair-strengthening process[207]; the first self-made female American millionaire entrepreneur, Madame CJ Walker; and many, many others.

These Americans reflected opportunities made available once the doorway to education and the free market had opened. Hard work, commitment to race, family, and country bore fruit within this generation of Christians. It was their new country, America, that granted them opportunity found nowhere else on Earth. Their tenacious faith, vision, and work ethic emboldened their progress in the face of repressive Jim Crow laws and racist violence of that era.

Unfortunately, over the more recent decades of indoctrination by the Socialist/Marxist Left, millions of Black Americans lost their belief in the American promise that empowered past generations. We're now living during an era when over ninety percent of the Black community cling with fan-like loyalty to a single party, ideology, and group of Royalty Class Black politicians, all of which have failed them demonstrably for over a century.

It has been this "all about team" mentality on the part of the Black community that has justified the donning of an ideological uniform, leaving its communities, schools, neighborhoods, and families bankrupt. After decades of empty promises and the loss of hopes, dreams, and innocent lives, the only beneficiaries of the urban misery are the Royalty Class Black politicians, the same class of elitist Black people who imposed it. They have become wealthy, popular, and powerful by giving their White Democrat leadership cover and by refusing to uphold their election promises. These political Black coaches have racked up over sixty years of consistent and dismal losing seasons. Unlike the world of sports where fans can simply turn off their widescreen to debate what might have been, these losing seasons have had dire consequences.

Consequences that are now documented in every predominantly Black community where the Democratic Party's policies have dominated. In the once-thriving city of Detroit, the population has dropped by 25 percent over

---

206   "George Washington Carver." Wikipedia, July 24, 2018. en.wikipedia.org/wiki/George_Washington_Carver.

207   "Garrett Morgan." Wikipedia, July 31, 2018. en.wikipedia.org/wiki/Garrett_Morgan.

the last decade, and 47 percent of those who are functionally illiterate.[208] In Oakland, California, the school board attempted to legitimize the debased language of Ebonics[209] as a certified second language. This soft bigotry of low expectation and guaranteed illiteracy would have ensured a life of failure for urban Black children whose unionized teachers and school administers failed to teach them.

As previously noted, a June 2017 CALmatters analysis reported that seventy-five percent of Black boys in the state of California failed to meet the state's reading and writing standard.[210] Noticeably absent has been the public outcry and outrage from the Royalty Class Black politician. They instead use their most passionate political capital and "tears of rage" to ensure that illegal immigrants can remain in this country, compete, and win against the low-skilled workers of their own race, for whom they feign support.

This exhibition of betrayal and representative malfeasance by the Congressional Black Caucus has been on display for decades in Washington, D.C., Chicago, Detroit, and Baltimore, which alternate annually as our country's murder capitals. Their elitist disdain for the poor of their own race is reflective in consistency of education death traps poor Black children are not allowed to leave and the reign of death that White abortionists can pour down on poor Black babies.

These cities reflect the death of manhood, the demeaning of womanhood, and the destruction of our society's innocent children when trapped in government-mandated hopelessness. In this environment is also abnormally high unemployment of Black teenagers, the absence of Black entrepreneurs, a seventy percent abandonment rate of children by Black men, and exceptionally high Black-on-Black crime. Sadly, due to sensitivities dulled by Socialist/ Marxist media's "soft bigotry of low expectations" messaging, these disastrous statistics are now accepted by both Black and White Americans as normal.

Accepted is the disproportionate eighty percent placement of abortion centers in the Black community. Racist targeting has accounted for the deaths of over twenty million Black babies since 1973—approximately forty percent of today's Black American population. In another time and in any other

---

208   "Nearly Half Of Detroit's Adults Are Functionally Illiterate, Report Finds." Business. *Huffpost*, July 8, 2013. huffingtonpost.com/2011/05/07/detroit-illiteracy-nearly-half-education_n_858307.html.

209   "African-American Vernacular English and Education: Oakland Ebonics Resolution." Wikipedia, July 27, 2018. en.wikipedia.org/wiki/African-American_Vernacular_English_and_education#Oakland_Ebonics_resolution.

210   Grace Carr. "Report: 75% of Black California Boys Fail to Meet Reading and Writing Standards." Political news. Dailycaller.com, June 5, 2017. dailycaller.com/2017/06/05/report-75-of-black-california-boys-fail-to-meet-reading-and-writing-standards.

civilized nation, this amounts to genocide. The KKK's 1900s effort to eliminate the Black race pales in comparison to the success of abortion clinics. The founder of Planned Parenthood, elitist Margaret Sanger, was pro-KKK, Pro-Nazi, Pro-eugenics, and a purely evil woman. Today, both White and Black Socialist/Marxists within the Democratic Party lionize her as a liberal savior.

During the KKK's reign of terror, 4,800 Americans were lynched, 1,300 of them White abolitionists and Republicans.[211] The early 1900s Democratic Party of the KKK would indeed be proud of those who make up the Democratic Party today. Pro-life activist and niece of slain civil rights leader Doctor Martin Luther King, Jr., Doctor Alveda King, has stated that abortionists "plant their killing centers in minority neighborhoods and prey upon women who think they have no hope. The great irony," she said, "is that abortion has done what the Klan only dreamed of." The documented deaths and decimation of the Black family over the last fifty years brings truth to this statement.

1925 Democratic Party KKK

In the competitive arena of sports, a record reflecting this magnitude of failure would not be tolerated. Players would be traded, coaches and management replaced. In time, attendance would plummet, and fans would demand a new owner. Broken promises and perpetual potential in the world of sports is simply not tolerated. The number of NFL coaches who are fired annually due to their failure to enter the postseason playoffs or to capture

---

211   William Brannan. 1300 White Republicans Lynched by the KKK. American Heritage Series, 2010. youtu.be/fClzzfMR3ek.

the coveted Super Bowl title attests to this. This demand for accountability by NFL fans reflects their expectations of excellence and low tolerance for incompetence.

How ironic is it that in the world of entertainment, high standards for performance are demanded, yet within the Black community there is tolerance and acceptance for ineptitude? As a team, Black professional elitists are celebrated, enriched, empowered, and excused. Without shame, they forfeit the lives, hopes, and dreams of millions of men, women, and children of their own race. In positions of perpetual royalty these professional Black politicians work incessantly to keep a vise grip on their congressional seats. Only death from old age or prison sentences long enough for their constituents to forget their names end their reigns.

The Playbook

At the beginning of the 20th century, the Black community stood at a crossroads of two diametrically-opposed visions. One was that of Booker T. Washington, who used an analogy to describe his perception of the relationship between the Black and White races in 1900. He stated: "In all things social we can be as separate as the fingers, yet one as the *hand* in all things essential to mutual progress." It was his vision that respect between each race could be obtained with a combination of interdependency for the community's basic needs (the hand) and independency from each other for individual needs (the fingers).

The pathway envisioned by Washington was one of independence, self-sufficiency as a productive race adhering to the concept of meritocracy and Capitalism. As an entrepreneur, academic, and founder of Tuskegee University, Washington's approach was based on the concept of commanding (not demanding) respect. The consequential acceptance by others would be a byproduct of self-worth gained through work ethic, entrepreneurship, and commitment to morality and family. He felt that the delivery of a valued service, product, and association would eventually minimize bigotry due to self-interest on the part of the receiving party. Washington once stated: "Say what you will, there is something in the human nature which makes one man, in the end, recognize and reward merit in another, regardless of race."

Washington's vision was seen in his establishment of Tuskegee College in the deep south of Alabama. In the face of overt southern White bigotry and criticism from northern liberal Blacks, Tuskegee graduates became beacons of Black achievement throughout the agricultural Deep South. Their example was one of applied education; business ownership/trade, personal hygiene, and pride in partaking of manual labor. The culture developed here was centered on principles that led to the valuing of a "good name." It was from this institution, decades later, from where the WWII Tuskegee Airmen would herald.

The Ivy League-educated W.E.B Du Bois articulated a different pathway for the Black community. It was one that envisioned leadership of the Black community as a natural entitlement for its more "talented, educated, higher echelon, and predominantly light-skinned" members. With the self-anointed name of "the Talented Tenth," this group of Black elitists shared the ideology of Socialism and Marxism with their White counterparts. It was with the financial support of wealthy northern White progressives that Du Bois and his fellow "Talented Tenth" were given a platform to hype the benefits of forced integration, or as envisioned by Black and White eugenicists, race neutralization. Based on eugenics beliefs articulated by W.E.B Du Bois in describing his own race, and based on his rule of inequality, "some were fitted to know and some to dig."[212] The priority of the Black "Talented Tenth" to force White acceptance of their class into their neighborhoods, schools, and businesses was, as Du Bois stated, "My own panacea of earlier day was flight of class from mass through the development of the Talented Tenth...."[213]

From behind the façade of the NAACP founded in 1910 by twenty-one White Socialists, Marxists, eugenicists, and atheist Democrats, the *Crisis* publication would be the source of Socialist propaganda. It was this stealth messaging from a trusted source, the NAACP, that would eventually lead the Black community away from its mooring of free enterprise and meritocracy-based competition as their means of mitigating racism. This community instead, for over sixty-five years, followed the leadership of White Socialist NAACP presidents as they "demanded" respect, acceptance, and a forced *entré* into White communities and enterprises. This integrationist pathway commandeered by the NAACP would, in the coming decades, undermine and obscure the vision of Capitalism and meritocracy as a fundamental solution for the Black community. Once established, the NAACP, via *Crisis* magazine, proceeded to attack the motives, character, and Tuskegee University funding efforts of Booker T. Washington.

With the death of Booker T. Washington in 1915, the White Socialist/Marxist NAACP Board of Directors had unfettered access to the Black community. The NAACP's vision of "integration eugenics" led to devaluation of Black property, talent, and businesses, and the loss of millions of Black Americans' jobs. This was a natural consequence of the free market's invisible hand. With higher demand, the "value" of White-owned services, property, and associations increased, while the lower demand for Black-owned businesses, property, education, schools, and neighborhoods declined. As middle class Black Americans succeeded, deriving much of their success from within the Black community, they would "move on up" and out of their community.

---

212   W.E.B. Du Bois. *The Souls of Black Folk*. Chicago: A.C. McClurg and Co., 1903, Chapter V – "Of the Wings of Atalanta." media.pfeiffer.edu/lridener/DSS/Du Bois/sbf5.htm.

213   Jerry Ward. "A Blues Moment in Dusk of Dawn: A Note on Autobiography." Blog. HBW: The Project on the History of Black Writing (blog), January 29, 2013. projecthbw.blogspot.com/2013/01/a-blues-moment-in-dusk-of-dawn-note-on.html.

The integration psychology, envisioned as the ultimate embodiment of Black success, led to the abandonment by its best to a resettlement into hostile all-White neighborhoods and the support of White business establishments. This mindset of "Royalty Class elitism" ultimately resulted in a physical and emotional disconnect between the Black middle and upper class and those who aspired to join them economically. The underlining pull of earlier generations that had supported the vertical movement of the Black race through example, mentoring, and reinvestment by its own middle class, ceased.

Entering the new millennium, we now have the benefit of 20-20 hindsight. We can look back over the last sixty years and tally the billions of tax dollars invested and wasted by elected officials of both the Democratic and Republican parties in their attempt to legislate behavior within the Black community. These "War on Poverty" programs were designed to address and alleviate specific areas of concern such as poverty, low-income housing, family planning, education, and employment. Based on our present reality, the results of these programs show a striking contrast to their lofty intentions. These legislative policies have relegated a once-entrepreneurial, self-reliant, family-centric community to the precise opposite. Now, the Black community leads our nation in every negative indicator denoting failure, ranking highest in illiteracy, rates of unemployment, percentage of single mothers, percentage of deadbeat and irresponsible fathers, communicable diseases, dropout rates, abortion rates, juvenile incarceration, and drug abuse. At a time when technology allows for more opportunities and upward mobility, it is difficult to calculate the human suffering that has infected the Black community like a cancer.

Unfortunately for the trusted modern day "talented tenth" and Black urban poor, the verdict is already in. Consistent with the empathy-free class of Royalty Black politicians, it will always be all about the team. *Their team.*

CHAPTER 10

THE ROYALTY CLASS BLACK MAN

The Purveyor of Urban America's Killing Fields

To understand the impact of the Royalty Class Black man on the urban community, it is necessary to highlight the *anti-Black* policies they have advocated for. Promoted for decades by the White Socialist/Marxist Democratic leadership, these policies are at the core of "urban city misery."

The 115th Congressional Black Caucus

As we look at the consistent lack of accomplishment of the Black Caucus, several trends become apparent. The first is that the Black Caucus does not approve of legislation that improves the value of Black lives. Note that each of their policies places limitation on an individual's life, liberty, and the pursuit of happiness, increased death of Black lives (abortion), limitation of Black education and dreams (Anti-School Choice), limitation of job opportunities/happiness (pro-Union/Davis-Bacon). As a pro-Socialist/Marxist caucus their policies are anti-Black Capitalism. The Black Caucus, for example, supports the Davis-Bacon Act, which directly limits growth of Black business enterprise and labor within the urban Black community.

Anti-Black Policy Advocacy

1. Pro Unlimited Abortion   (Anti-Black Life)

2. Pro Socialism/Marxism Policies   (Anti-Black Capitalism)

3. Pro Davis-Bacon Law   (Anti-Black Enterprise/Labor)

4. Pro Minimum Wage   (Anti-Black Low Skill labor)

5. Pro Gay Marriage   (Anti-Judeo-Christian Values)

6. Pro Unlimited Illegal Immigration   (Anti-Black Low Skill labor/ Education)

7. Pro Education Unionist   (Anti-Black School Choice)

The national failure of the Congressional Black Caucus

- Eighty-three percent of Black teen males are unemployed throughout nation; ninety-two percent of Black teen males are unemployed in Chicago.

The Urban League study indicates that only 17 percent of Black males between the ages of sixteen and nineteen had jobs throughout the US. But in Illinois, that number was twelve percent. And, as stated, the Windy City clocks in with only eight percent of Black male teens with jobs.[214]

Democratic Party controlled State of California

- *Seventy-five percent of Black boys fail to meet the state's reading and writing standard.*

---

214   National Urban League Wire. "Chicago's Black Male Teens' 92 Percent Unemployment Rate Leads Nation." I Am Empowered. January 28, 2014, sec. Newsroom. iamempowered.com/article/2014/01/28/chicagos-black-male-teens-92-percent-unemployment-rate-leads-nation.

Department of Education (June 2017) statistics indicate that out of every four Black boys in California classrooms, three failed to meet reading and writing standards on the most recent round of testing. (California State Department of Education (DOE).[215]

- Seventy-two percent of Black men abandon their children and forsake marriage.

The Black community's seventy-two percent abandonment rate eclipses that of all other groups: seventeen percent of Asians, twenty-nine percent of Whites, fifty-three percent of Hispanics, and sixty-six percent of Native Americans were born to unwed mothers in 2008. The rate for the overall U.S. population was 41 percent. Statistics show that children of unmarried mothers of any race are more likely to perform poorly in school, go to prison, use drugs, be poor as adults, and have their own children out of wedlock.[216]

- Forty-eight percent of Black males fail to graduate from high school in four years.

The Schott Foundation for Public Education released "The Urgency of Now", a study showing that only 52 percent of Black male ninth-graders graduate from high school, compared to 58 percent of Latino male ninth-graders and seventy-eight percent of White, non-Latino male ninth-graders.[217]

- Only thirty-five percent of Black males will graduate from college.

This compares with rates of 59 percent, 46 percent, and 45 percent for White males, Hispanic males, and Black women, respectively. In other words, Black men are a little more than half as likely to finish.[218]

---

215   Grace Carr, "Report: 75% Of Black California Boys Fail to Meet Reading and Writing Standards."

216   Jesse Washington. "72% of Black Babies Born to Unwed Moms; Data Revive Debate." Chron. November 6, 2010, sec. Politics & Policy. chron.com/life/mom-houston/article/72-of-black-babies-born-to-unwed-moms-data-1709669.php.

217   Ugonna Okpalaoka. "Report: Only 52 Percent of Black Males Graduate from High School in 4 Years." The Grio. September 20, 2012, sec. Politics. thegrio.com/2012/09/20/report-only-52-percent-of-black-males-graduate-from-high-school-in-4-years.

218   "Black Student College Graduation Rates Remain Low, But Modest Progress Begins to Show." The Journal of Blacks in Higher Education, November 4, 2013. jbhe.com/features/50_blackstudent_gradrates.html.

- Twenty-five times more reports of Black on Black crime vs White on Black crime.

Both victims and perpetrators are disproportionately minority, by huge margins. New York City is emblematic of the country's gun violence. According to victims and witnesses, Blacks commit eighty percent of all shootings in New York, though they are twenty-three percent of the city's residents. Add Hispanics and this accounts for ninety-eight percent of all shootings. Whites commit a little over one percent of shootings, though they are thirty-five percent of the city's population.[219]

The Congressional Black Caucus

"Black people have no permanent friends, no permanent en-emies...just permanent interests."

The Congressional Black Caucus purports its mission as "positively influencing the course of events pertinent to African Americans and others of similar experience and situation." Based on the policies they have supported for decades, it can be factually stated that they have failed miserably in their mission. If held to the standards that fans hold for their professional teams and stockholders hold for their corporate leaders, they would have *all* been fired long ago. Only within the confines of federal employment can the type of incompetency proven consistent by Black Democratic legislators be rewarded with six-figure incomes and federal retirement security. Also consistent within this group of urban Black representation is the hubris and greed reflected by their actions outside the boundaries of the rule of law. Unfortunately, too many of them, with impunity, have illustrated a complete subversion of the original meaning of the civil rights movement. Rather than representing the best of Doctor Martin Luther King's dream, many of his self-described intellectual heirs are using their public platforms to enrich themselves and those around them.[220]

Columnist Jonah Goldberg hit the nail on the head recently in decrying the claims of racism employed by Black congressmen and their defenders. By their race and unyielding support of their voters, Black representatives are shielded

---

219   Jim Hoft. "Inconvenient Truth...Blacks Commit 25X More Violent Assaults Against Whites Than Whites Against Blacks." Politics. Gateway Pundit (blog), December 12, 2014. thegatewaypundit.com/2014/12/inconvenient-truth-blacks-commit-25x-more-violent-assaults-against-whites-than-whites-against-blacks.

220   Staff. "Congressional Black Caucus Bogged down by New Ethics Scandal." The Grio. August 31, 2010, sec. Politics. thegrio.com/2010/08/31/congressional-black-caucus-bogged-down-by-another-ethics-scandal.

from the consequences of their actions. In most cases, it takes nothing short of an act of God to remove them from office.

For far too long, Black (Democratic) Congressional representatives have entrenched themselves in the Washington establishment. Their elections are often over before they even begin, as constituents overwhelmingly elect them in ways more befitting third world dictators for life than the world's most successful democracy. The wages of this kind of behavior are corruption, cronyism, and decisions that place these congressmen far out of step with the needs of their districts. Their constituents also do themselves no favors by claiming that every attempt to hold these officials accountable are conspiracies to take down successful African American politicians.[221]

Since 2013 there have been over nine felony convictions leading to jail time from this group of politicians. Many others have been charged but not convicted of charges ranging from tax fraud, conspiracy, lying to federal investigators, racketeering, mail fraud, money laundering, and filing false disclosure forms to hide unauthorized income. One of these Congressional Black Caucus members was forced to resign in 1995 after a conviction for statutory rape.

Here are some examples:

Alcee Hastings (D-FL 20th District)

In 1981, Hastings was charged with accepting a 150,000 dollar bribe in exchange for a lenient sentence and a return of seized assets for twenty-one counts of racketeering by Frank and Thomas Romano. In 1988, the Democratic-controlled U.S. House of Representatives took up the case, and Hastings was impeached for bribery and perjury by a vote of 413–3. He was then convicted in 1989 by the United States Senate and removed from office. Hastings was elected to the U.S. House of Representatives in 1992, representing Florida's 23rd district.

In May 2009, the *Wall Street Journal* reported that Hastings spent over twenty-four thousand dollars in taxpayer money in 2008 to lease a luxury Lexus hybrid sedan. In June 2011, a lawsuit filed by one of his staff members, Winsome Packer, alleged that Hastings made repeated unwanted sexual advances and threatened her job when she refused him.

State by state reports on all members of Congress, published by the Citizens for Responsibility and Ethics in Washington, reported Hastings paid his girlfriend Patricia Williams, an attorney who worked as his deputy district director, 622,574 dollars over the four-year period from 2007-2010.[222]

---

221   *Ibid.*
222   "Alcee Hastings." Wikipedia, August 6, 2018. en.wikipedia.org/wiki/Alcee_Hastings.

Maxine Waters (D-CA)

Waters has spent thirty-seven years in office, many of those as head of the Congressional Black Caucus, promising to make life better for constituents in economically ravaged South Central Los Angeles. In 2012, she was charged with multiple ethics violations related to her meddling in minority-owned OneUnited Bank. The banks' executives donated 12,500 dollars to Maxine's congressional campaigns. Her husband, Sidney Williams, was an investor in one of the banks that merged into OneUnited. As stockholders, they profited handsomely from their relationship with the bank. After Waters' office personally intervened and lobbied the Treasury Department in 2008, the financial institution received twelve million dollars in federal TARP bailout money. This was despite another government agency's conclusion that the bank operated "without effective underwriting standards" and engaged in "speculative investment practices."

Top bank executive Kevin Cohee squandered money on a company-financed Porsche and beachfront mansion in Santa Monica, California. After the federal bailout of Fannie and Freddie, OneUnited's stock in the government-sponsored enterprises plunged to a value estimated at less than five million dollars. Only through Waters' intervention was OneUnited able to secure an emergency meeting with the Treasury and its then-secretary, Henry Paulson. Waters' government cronyism earned her a "Most Corrupt Member of Congress" designation from the left-wing Citizens for Responsibility and Ethics in Washington.[223] She was eventually given a pass by the hapless and patronizing Ethics Committee, before which all Republican and Democratic offenders seek an audience to eventually be exonerated.

Sheila Jackson Lee (D-TX)

In 2012, Lee was forced to distance herself from a multi-million dollar Medicare fraud racket by associates regarding a local hospital in her district.[224] The latest Jackson Lee drama came in December 2017 when a United Airlines passenger said she was booted from her first class seat to accommodate the Texas Democrat. Jackson Lee was put in seat 1A, which was originally paid for by a Jean-Marie Simon, a schoolteacher from Washington, D.C., who accused the airline of evicting her from the seat, so they could give it to a member of congress.

Simon claims that after an hour-long weather delay United carelessly tossed her out of her first-class seat to make way for Jackson Lee, saying

223   Michelle Malkin. "Congressional Black Corruption." Ammoland: Shooting Sports News, July 13, 2016. ammoland.com/2016/07/congressional-black-corruption.

224   M. Catharine Evans. "Systemic Medicare Fraud Under Houston's Sheila Jackson Lee." American Thinker. October 10, 2012, sec. Articles. americanthinker.com/articles/2012/10/systemic_medicare_fraud_under_houstons_sheila_jackson_lee.html.

in a Facebook post that she saw a uniformed airline employee pull the congresswoman from the boarding line and escort her to a first-class seat. Then Simon, who was on the second leg of her return flight from Guatemala, said she went to the gate to board and was told her ticket wasn't in the system. When the attendant asked her if she had canceled her ticket, Simon replied, "No. I just want to go home." "It was just so completely humiliating," said Jean-Marie Simon, a sixty-three-year-old attorney and private school teacher who used 140,000 miles to purchase the first-class tickets to take her from Washington, D.C. to Guatemala and back home.[225]

After she was seated, she claims she was told by another passenger that her original seat was occupied by a congresswoman and that he had seen her do it twice before. The airline compensated her with a five-hundred dollar voucher and another ticket for that flight in Economy Plus, again apologizing to her and promising they would reimburse her with a second five-hundred dollar voucher.

Royalty Class Black politician Jackson Lee comments: "Since this was not any fault of mine, the way the individual continued to act appeared to be, upon reflection, because I was an African American woman, seemingly an easy target along with the African American flight attendant who was very, very nice," the sixty-seven-year-old congresswoman tweeted. "But in the spirit of this season and out of the sincerity of my heart, if it is perceived that I had anything to do with this, I am kind enough to simply say sorry. But as an African American, I know there are too many examples like this all over the nation."

Instinctively ready to pull the race card, it should be noted that the woman who Rep. Sheila Jackson Lee accused of being a racist is a celebrated photojournalist who helped document human rights abuses in war-torn Guatemala during the 1980s.

Jean-Marie Simon, a Democrat, had her first-class seat on a United Airlines flight given to Ms. Jackson Lee. Ms. Simon lived and worked in Guatemala during the turbulent decade that saw the military seize control of the government in a coup. Hundreds of thousands of Guatemalans were killed or "disappeared" during the conflict.

Now a teacher, Ms. Simon, age sixty-three, is the author of *Guatemala: Eternal Spring Eternal Tyranny*. A 2012 blog post on Amnesty International said Ms. Simon donated one-thousand copies of her book to schools and universities in Guatemala "to keep the truth of what happened alive."

"I was the last passenger on the plane," Ms. Simon wrote on Facebook. "A Texas congressman, a nice guy, sat down next to me. He said he was glad I had

---

225   Katie Pavlich. "Of Course: Sheila Jackson Lee Cries Racism After Kicking a Teacher Out of First Class." Townhall.Com via Salem Media Group. December 28, 2017, sec. Racism. townhall.com/tipsheet/katiepavlich/2017/12/28/sheila-jackson-lee-united-saga-n2427421.

made it on the flight. I showed him my boarding pass with my seat, 1A, printed on it. He said, 'You know what happened, right? Do you know who's in your seat?' I said no. He told me that it was Jackson Lee, a fellow U.S. congresswoman who regularly does this, that this was the third time he personally had watched her bump a passenger."[226]

Previous reports show that this House member, who was elected in 1994, has had a history of transportation drama, including berating flight attendants on first class flights and making her Congressional staff drive her one block, while waiting on her for hours and disrupting traffic. She's been documented calling her employees "stupid motherf***ers," while referring to herself as Congressional royalty. "You don't understand. I am a queen, and I demand to be treated like a queen," she was quoted saying in 1998, three years into her nearly twenty-three-year tenure on Capitol Hill.

And while Jackson Lee would book coach tickets, the congresswoman was often bumped to first class. In February 1998, while sitting in first class, Jackson Lee famously berated a flight attendant over her meal choice not being available on the plane she chose to fly home on.

"Don't you know who I am?" the congresswoman reportedly said. "I'm Congresswoman Sheila Jackson Lee. Where is my seafood meal? I know it was ordered!" After this incident, the vice president of Continental's government affairs office called Jackson Lee and warned her that her behavior needed to improve, or she would not be flying the airline again, sources told the *Weekly Standard*.[227]

Greg Meeks (D-NY)

Meeks earmarked 400,000 dollars for a fake health clinic in New York City and Caribbean resort jaunts underwritten by convicted financier Allen Stanford. Citizens for Responsibility and Ethics in Washington (CREW) named Meeks one of the most corrupt members of Congress in 2011. It was subsequently reported that Meeks' continuing ethical and criminal probes would cause his premature exit from Congress, however, he won the Democratic primary and was re-elected with 89.7 percent of the general election vote in November 2012.[228] No doubt a benefit to Meeks is a constituency of which a

226   Bradford Richardson. "Woman Accused of Racism by Rep. Sheila Jackson Lee Is Human-Rights Activist." *The Washington Times.* December 27, 2017, Online edition, sec. Politics. washingtontimes.com/news/2017/dec/27/woman-accused-racism-dem-rep-human-rights-activist/.

227   Nikki Schwab, Abigail Miller, and Ariel Zilber. "'I'm a Queen and I Demand to Be Treated like a Queen!' How Congresswoman Involved in Race Row on Plane Was Chauffeured a Block to Congress and Was Nearly Banished from an Airline Before." DailyMail.com. December 27, 2017, sec. News. dailymail.co.uk/news/article-5216023/Rep-United-flight-fight-history-bad-behavior.html.

228   Michelle Malkin. "Congressional Black Corruption."

large percentage cannot read of his legal mishaps. This is a good reason for him to withhold support for school choice of quality education.[229]

Gwen Moore (D-WI)

The abortionist who once stated, "I don't think we do children a favor by forcing women to give birth." Close your eyes and imagine a White supremacist eugenicist saying the exact same thing as this Royalty Class Black elitist politician.

Translation: "It is a much bigger favor to valueless poor Black children to kill them than to clutter our neighborhood with them. By the way, Planned Parenthood pays well for their body parts."

Moore had her sister Brenda on the campaign payroll to the tune of nearly 40,000 dollars annually and has brought on her twenty-seven-year-old son, Sowande Omokunde, also known as Supreme Solar Allah. Moore paid her son fifteen-hundred dollars for political consulting. Omokunde told others that he was the campaign's deputy field director. Omokunde was one of four Democratic staffers who pleaded guilty to misdemeanors for slashing tires on twenty-five vans hours before Republican Party officials were to use them to drive voters to the polls on election day in 2004. In April 2006, Omokunde was sentenced to four months in jail and fined one-thousand dollars for his role in the much-publicized caper.[230]

Eddie Bernice Johnson (D-TX)

This twelve-term Democrat from Dallas similarly helped steer thousands of dollars in Congressional Black Caucus Foundation college scholarships to four family members and two of her top aide's children, in violation of the nonprofit's rules. During the 2010 scandal, Johnson was found to have awarded twenty-three scholarships over five years to two of her grandsons, two sons of her nephew, and the children of her top congressional aide in Dallas. It was a clear violation of the scholarship fund's anti-nepotism and residency rules. Johnson eventually repaid the foundation more than 31,000 dollars for the misappropriated scholarships.[231] Interesting is the consistent hypocrisy of the Royalty Class Black politician, as this Democratic Congresswoman joins the remaining CBC members in voting against granting poor Black Americans access to school choice scholarships.

229   "Gregory Meeks." Wikipedia, August 4, 2018. en.wikipedia.org/wiki/Gregory_Meeks.

230   Michelle. "Culture Of Corruption, Milwaukee Edition." HotAir.Com via Salem Media Group, November 14, 2006, sec. Archive. hotair.com/archives/2006/11/14/culture-of-corruption-milwaukee-edition.

231   Tim Sampson. "Someone Keeps Erasing This Texas Political Scandal from Wikipedia." DailyDot.Com. May 15, 2013, sec. Layer 8. dailydot.com/layer8/texas-wikipedia-scandal-eddie-bernice-johnson.

Rep. Charlie Rangel (D-NY)

Rangel was once one of the House's most powerful members, was found guilty in November 2010 of breaking eleven separate congressional rules related to his personal finances and his fundraising efforts for a New York college. The charges pointed to a collection of infractions: that Rangel improperly used his congressional staff and official letterhead to raise seven-figure donations from corporate charities and chief executives for a college wing named in his honor; violated New York City rules by housing his political committees in his rent-controlled apartments in Harlem; did not pay taxes on a villa he owns in the Dominican Republic; and did not properly disclose hundreds of thousands of dollars in personal financial assets.

Rep. John Conyers (D-MI)

The eighty-eight-year old Congressman Conyers with a fifty-four year career in the House of Representatives allegedly paid 27,000 dollars in public funds to a female employee. She had filed a claim against him with the secretive Office of Compliance in 2014. Also alleged is that he repeatedly made sexual advances to several women that included requests for sexual favors and contacted and transported other women with whom Conyers was believed to be having affairs.[232]

Melanie Sloan, a well-known Washington lawyer who for three years in the 1990s worked as Democratic counsel on the House Judiciary Committee where Conyers remains the ranking Democrat, told the *Free Press* that Conyers constantly berated her, screamed at her, and fired her, rehiring her several times, and once showed up to a meeting in his underwear. She said he criticized her for not wearing stockings on at least one occasion. On another occasion, in a committee field hearing on crime she had organized in New York City, she said he ordered her backstage to babysit one of his children. Sloan made clear that she did not feel she had ever been sexually harassed, but that she felt "mistreated" by Conyers. Conyers has denied all the allegations. His lawyer, Arnold Reed, told CNN that Conyers has no plans to resign even with an Ethics Committee investigation into his behavior underway.[233]

---

232 John Bresnahan, and Heather Caygle. "John Conyers Sexual Harassment Scandal Rocks House Democrats, Congressional Black Caucus." Black Christian News Network One (BCNN1). November 21, 2017, sec. Politics. blackchristiannews.com/2017/11/john-conyers-sexual-harassment-scandal-rocks-house-democrats-congressional-black-caucus.

233 Todd Spangler. "New John Conyers Accuser: He Showed up to a Meeting in His Underwear." *Detroit Free Press.* November 23, 2017, Online edition, sec. Politics. freep.com/story/news/politics/2017/11/23/john-conyers-accuser-harssment/891335001.

Typical of the circle the wagon mentality, morally corrupt Royalty Class Black politician and fellow CBC member Rep. James Clyburn (D-SC) stated for the record "these women accusing Conyers could be lying."

Rep Cedric Richmond (D-LA)

Richmond, another Black career politician, has a long history of playing fast and loose with the law. He was running for and later successfully earned the seat vacated with the imprisonment of Congressional Black Caucus Congressman Jefferson in 2008. Jefferson was convicted of bribery and is currently serving a thirteen-year prison sentence.

According to the Louisiana Truth PAC, Cedric Richmond (D-LA):[234]
- Misdemeanor charge arising from a violent Baton Rouge bar fight in 2007
- Suspension of law license in 2008 for using a false address to run for City Council in 2005
- Accused of profiting from a charity after he pushed for multiple grants
- Threatened girl in Baton Rouge bar, claiming: "I don't work for the state. The state works for me."[235]

"Go Directly to Jail" Notables

Columnist Star Parker reported, "This is par for the course for the so-called leaders in the Black community. Like Black-overseers on a slave plantation, members of the Congressional Black Caucus have been complicit in keeping Blacks dependent on government, while enriching themselves on the engorged teat of that same government."

"Today's twenty-nine count indictment (Chaka Fattah) is a testament to the corruption manifested in the CBC. Here we have a member who represents a congressional district with twice the poverty rate of the national average, while using campaign funds to pay personal debts. It is time to break the shackles that the CBC has over our Black communities and enable the poor to get off the government dole. We can do this through creating opportunity, dismantling our ghettos, and providing educational choice. The time is now."[236]

---

234   NRCC. "Clyburn to Campaign for Scandal-Plagued Career Politician in Louisiana." Political news. NRCC.org, September 2, 2010. nrcc.org/2010/09/02/clyburn-to-campaign-for-scandal-plagued-career-politician-in-louisiana.

235   *Ibid.*

236   Martin Barillas. "Congressional Black Caucus Chair Indicted on Racketeering Charges." Spero News. July 29, 2015, sec. Politics. speroforum.com/a/WMHKHVANKK2/76222-Congressional-Black-Caucus-chair-indicted-on-racketeering-charges.

William "Bill" Jennings Jefferson (D-LA)

Jefferson served as a member of the U.S. House of Representatives from Louisiana for nine terms, from 1991 to 2009. He represented Louisiana's 2nd congressional district, which includes much of the greater New Orleans area. He was elected as Louisiana's first Black congressman since the end of Reconstruction.

On November 13, 2009, Jefferson was sentenced to thirteen years in federal prison for bribery after a corruption investigation[2], the longest sentence ever given to a congressman. He began serving that sentence in May 2012 at a Federal Bureau of Prisons facility in Beaumont, Texas. He appealed his case after a U.S. Supreme Court ruling on similar issues. Considering these findings, on October 5, 2017, Jefferson was ordered released, pending sentencing or other action, after a U.S. District judge threw out seven of ten charges against him.[3] On December 1, 2017, Judge T. S. Ellis III accepted his plea deal and sentenced Jefferson to time served.[237]

Corrine Brown (D-FL)

This twelve-term Democrat from Florida received a twenty-four-count federal indictment in May 2017 while her Congressional Black Caucus colleagues tried to drown out the news with diversionary gun-control theatrics. Brown and her chief of staff are charged with creating a fraudulent education charity to collect over 800,000 dollars in donations from major corporations and philanthropies for their own private slush fund between 2012 and early 2016.

As director of the hoax group, dubbed One Door for Education, Inc., Brown pleaded guilty to fraud and conspiracy. Prosecutors say that two relatives of Brown and her chief of staff steered tens of thousands of dollars in cash deposits to their accounts. The charitable contributions paid for lavish galas, NFL tickets, luxury box concert seats, golf tournaments, and apparently Brown's tax bills.[238] Brown could, in theory, be sentenced to decades in prison.

Chaka Fattah (D-PA)

This eleven-term Pennsylvania Democrat was convicted in late June 2016 on twenty-three charges of racketeering, money laundering, and fraud, along with four other co-defendants. His son was sentenced to a five-year prison term after being found guilty of twenty-two separate counts of federal bank and tax fraud charges related to his misuse of business loans and federal education contracts to pay for designer clothes, massive bar tabs, and luxury cars. The elder Fattah's crimes are tied to schemes to repay an illegal one million dollar campaign loan. Fattah siphoned off federal grant money and

237　"William J. Jefferson." Wikipedia, May 16, 2018. en.wikipedia.org/wiki/William_J._Jefferson.

238　Michelle Malkin. "Congressional Black Corruption."

nonprofit funds (including donations to his educational foundation) to pay off political consultants.[239]

Jesse Jackson, Jr. (D-IL)

In 2013, Jackson faced up to five years in prison for diverting 750,000 dollars in campaign funds and a conspiracy to commit wire fraud, mail fraud, and making false statements. His wife Sandi agreed to plead guilty to providing false information to the IRS.[81]

Mel Reynolds (D-IL)

This former lawmaker, community activist, and Rhodes Scholar was convicted in 1995 on sexual assault and sexual abuse charges against a sixteen-year-old campaign volunteer who worked on his 1992 campaign. He was sentenced to five years in prison and was forced to resign his position weeks after his conviction. While serving his sentence, Reynolds was convicted on a series of charges including bank fraud, misusing campaign funds, and making false statements to the Federal Election Commission. Those charges resulted in an additional seventy-eight-month federal prison sentence. He served forty-two months in prison on those charges before President Bill Clinton commuted the sentence. He was arrested in 2014 while traveling in Zimbabwe for overstaying his visa. In 2012, he launched an unsuccessful campaign to win back a seat in Congress.

In September 2017, a federal judge found the former U.S Representative guilty on additional misdemeanor charges that he failed to file income tax returns for four years, despite earning hundreds of thousands of dollars. Reynolds was found guilty of knowingly failing to file tax returns for about 400,000 dollars in income he made while consulting for Chicago businessmen in Africa.[240]

---

239   *Ibid.*

240   "William J. Jefferson." Wikipedia.

CHAPTER 11

FOR THE RECORD:
THE CONGRESSIONAL BLACK CAUCUS VOTE

"Because of the house slave's close proximity to his owner, he often identified with his master and looked out for his well-being. Their misguided allegiance caused them to imitate their owner's deportment and adopt his political ideology as their own." [241]

CHOICE

The Education of Poor Black Children

School choice describes a wide array of programs aimed at giving families the opportunity to choose the school their children will attend. As a matter of form, school choice does not give preference to one form of schooling or another. Rather, it manifests itself whenever a student attends school outside of the one they would have been assigned by geographic default. The most common options offered by school choice programs are open enrollment laws that allow students to attend other public schools, private schools, and charter schools. Tax credits and deductions for expenses related to schooling, vouchers, and homeschooling are also part of the package.

The Black Community vs The Congressional Black Caucus
- Black Americans: 72 percent *agree School Choice for poor*

---

241   John Simkin. "House Slaves." Education. Spartacus Educational, January 2018. spartacus-educational.com/USASdomestic.htm.

- NAACP: 100 percent *oppose School Choice for poor*
- Congressional Black Caucus: 100 percent *oppose School Choice for poor*
- Labor Unions: 100 percent *oppose School Choice for poor*

The polling question: "How much are you in favor of or against allowing poor parents to be given the tax dollars allotted for their child's education and permitting them to use those dollars in the form of a scholarship to attend a private, public, or parochial school of their choosing?"[242]

As indicated above, seventy-two percent of African Americans polled affirmative for supporting poor children. It is the other side of the polling within the Black community that reflects the deeply embedded ills within. A disturbingly high number, 37 percent, of Black people polled elect to *deny* poor Black children an opportunity for a quality education.

If we are to see the insidious decade undermining our community, we need look no further. This is not the action of '60s segregationists, but the polling of the self-centered among us who have already gotten theirs.

Look to the NAACP and the Congressional Black Caucus for an answer as to the type of Black adult who would, for their own self-interest, block opportunity for our community's most vulnerable.

Look to the Black union teachers who, while teaching at failing schools, send their own children to successful public or private schools and then vote against opportunities for the poor children they teach.

This poll is representative of the mentality of the Talented Tenth, who consistently and unanimously stand against the progress of Black families with whom they no longer empathize.

ABORTION

The protection of poor Black babies

In a 2009 poll, Black Americans opposed *Roe v. Wade* by a 58–35 percent margin, and Hispanics opposed it by a 58–40 percent margin.[243]

The Black Community vs. The Congressional Black Caucus
- Black Americans: 58 percent *opposed* to abortion
- NAACP: 100 percent for unlimited abortion (Including Live-Birth)
- Congressional Black Caucus: 100 percent *for unlimited abortion (Including Live-Birth)*

---

242   "Resource Hub: School Choice FAQs." **Education. edCHOICE.org**, n.d. edchoice. org/resource-hub/school-choice-faqs.

243   Steven Ertelt. "Harris Poll Shows Strong Shift to Pro-Life Position on Abortion, Roe v. Wade." *Advocacy. LifeNews.com*, August 11, 2009. lifenews. com/2009/08/11/nat-5347.

- Planned Parenthood: 100 percent for unlimited abortion (Including Live-Birth)

When Live Action uncovered Planned Parenthood clinics willingly accepting donations from donors who specifically asked that their funds go to help "lower the number of Blacks in America," the NAACP's silence was deafening. That largely unreported scandal inspired Rep. Mike Pence (R-IN) to introduce legislation to deny Title X funding to Planned Parenthood. The NAACP sided with Planned Parenthood over Pence.[244]

The question asked by Jerome Hudson, a member of the Project 21 Black leadership network, is noted: "It's a bad sign when the NAACP, America's oldest civil rights group, finds itself on the same side of the abortion debate as Margaret Sanger. The NAACP's leadership is putting political expediency and ideology before the interests of the people the organization supposedly represents. Why else would so-called advocates for the Black community tacitly support the holocaust of unborn Black babies?"[245]

Each member of the Congressional Black Caucus, other than Republican Congresswoman Mia Love, was given a rating of one-hundred percent by the National Abortion Rights Action League (NARAL), indicating a pro-abortion voting record. *Not once* have Royalty Class Black Democratic politicians voted against their White eugenics leadership. Georgia is among the states leading in abortions performed on Black women. One-hundred percent of Georgia's abortion clinics are in urban areas where Blacks reside.[246]

Traditional Marriage (One Man and One Woman)

The protection of the Judeo-Christian marriage

The larger element consists of African American voters, who are solidly opposed to gay marriage. California's Proposition 8 ban on same-sex marriage passed in 2008 thanks to overwhelming support by Black people. Seventy percent backed it, according to exit polls. Recent gay marriage legislation in Maryland drew opposition from leading Democratic African American

---

244 Jerome Hudson. "Why Does the NAACP Support Abortion, Oppose Pro-Life Bill?" Advocacy. LifeNews.com, December 27, 2011. lifenews.com/2011/12/27/why-does-the-naacp-support-abortion-oppose-pro-life-bill.

245 *Ibid.*

246 "Abortion in the Hood." Advocacy. The Restoration Project, n.d. the-restoration-project.org/abortion-in-the-hood.html.

legislators in the state. The same ministers who organized "get-out-the-vote" efforts in Black churches for Obama also railed against gay marriage.[247]

The Black Community vs. Congressional Black Caucus
- Blacks: 70 percent *for Traditional Marriage*
- NAACP: 100 percent against Traditional Marriage
- Congressional Black Caucus: 100 percent *against Traditional Marriage*

NAACP Chairman Julian Bond and NAACP President Ben Jealous publicly spoke out Against Prop. 8, which defined marriage as between a man and a woman.[248] One-hundred-sixty members of a Black clergy group came from twenty-six states as far away as Texas, Colorado, and California to meet with the Congressional Black Caucus. They invited the Caucus to their Monday morning news conference in the Rayburn House Office Building, where they affirmed: "Gay marriage is not a civil right," and asked for caucus support in their opposition to same-sex marriage. The members of the Black Caucus were no-shows, except one, who arrived late.[249]

Illegal Immigration

Protection of low-skilled Black jobs
The U.S. Commission on Civil Rights concluded in a 2010 study that, "Illegal immigration to the United States in recent decades has tended to depress both wages and employment rates for low-skilled American citizens, a disproportionate number of whom are Black men."[9]

A joint paper by professors at the University of California, University of Chicago, and Harvard for the National Bureau of Economic Research concluded that immigration has measurably lowered wages for Black workers. One author, Doctor Gordon H. Hanson of UC San Diego, said, "Our study suggests that a ten percent immigrant-induced increase in the supply of a skill group is associated with a reduction in the Black wage of 4 percent, a reduction in the

---

247 Zandar. "Splitting The Coalition: Fractured Facts On Blacks And Same-Sex Marriage." Angry Black Lady Chronicles (blog), March 25, 2012. angryblacklady.com/2012/03/25/splitting-the-coalition-fractured-facts-on-blacks-and-same-sex-marriage.

248 Adam Serwer. "The NAACP Takes a Stance Against Prop. 8." Politics. The American Prospect, March 3, 2009. prospect.org/article/naacp-takes-stance-against-prop-8.

249 "Congressional Black Caucus Disses Black Clergy (Rant of Fire!!!)." Black Informant (blog), September 9, 2004. blackinformant.wordpress.com/2004/09/09/congressional-black-caucus-disses-black-clergy-rant-of-fire.

Black employment rate of 3.5 percentage points, and an increase in the Black institutionalization [incarceration] rate of 0.8 percentage points."[250]

Vernon M. Briggs, Jr., professor emeritus in labor economics at Cornell, has noted that both illegal immigrant and Black workers tend to "cluster in metropolitan areas," thus increasing the likelihood they will compete for the same jobs. Doctor Briggs adds, "There is little doubt that there is significant overlap in competition for jobs in this sector of the labor market. Given the inordinately high unemployment rates for low-skilled Black workers (the highest for all racial and ethnic groups for whom data is collected), it is obvious that the major loser in this competition are low-skilled Black workers. This is not surprising since, if employers have an opportunity to hire illegal immigrant workers, they will always give them preference over legal workers of any race or ethnic background. This is because illegal immigrant workers view low-skilled jobs in the American economy as being highly preferable to the job opportunities in their homelands..."

The Black American Leadership Alliance (BALA) stated: "Many studies have shown that Black Americans are disproportionately harmed by mass immigration and amnesty. Even though these figures are readily available and have been reported by the U.S. Commission on Civil Rights, many lawmakers have chosen to do nothing, putting politics over the well-being of constituents."[251]

Doctor Briggs concludes, "The continued reluctance by our national government to get illegal immigrants out of the labor force—and to keep them out—by enforcing the existing sanctions at the worksite against employers of illegal immigrants is itself a massive violation of the civil rights of all low-skilled workers in the United States and of low-skilled Black American workers in particular".[252] The Democratic Party continues to favor illegal immigration because of its benefits for the Democratic Party.

The Black Community vs. Congressional Black Caucus

According to data from the Pew Research Center, Hispanic illegal immigrants identified themselves as Democrats fifty-four percent to nineteen percent when those who leaned toward either party were included. In Pew's 2012 National Survey of Latinos, 31 percent of illegal immigrants described

---

250   National Center. "Obama Amnesty Would Hurt Black Americans." Project 21 Black Leadership Network, August 11, 2014. nationalcenter.org/2014/08/11/obama-amnesty-would-hurt-black-americans.

251   Andrew Stiles. "Black Leaders Urge Congress to Oppose 'Irresponsible' Gang of Eight Legislation." *National Review*, June 3, 2013. nationalreview.com/corner/black-leaders-urge-congress-oppose-irresponsible-gang-eight-legislation-an-drew-stiles.

252   National Center. "Obama Amnesty Would Hurt Black Americans."

themselves as Democrats, while only 4 percent said they were Republicans.[253] Eighty percent of American adults endorse "stricter border control to... reduce illegal immigration." This includes 93 percent Republicans, 76 percent Democrats, 83 percent Independents, 74 percent Blacks, 61 percent Hispanics, and 75 percent of Americans eighteen to thirty-nine years old.[254]

The data below gives the breakdown:
- Black Americans: 74 percent *against* Illegal Immigration
- NAACP: 100 percent *for* unlimited Illegal Immigration
- Congressional Black Caucus: 100 percent *for* unlimited Illegal Immigration
- Labor Unions: 100 percent *for* unlimited Illegal Immigration

The Davis-Bacon Act

Protection of the Black Laborer and Entrepreneur

The 1932 anti-Black Davis-Bacon Act also added power to the labor unions. The NAACP, the Black Caucus, and the labor unions support this act in its fullness. It was passed as a racial deterrent to prevent non-unionized Black and immigrant laborers from competing with unionized White workers. The discriminatory effects continue, as even today minorities tend to be vastly underrepresented in highly unionized skilled trades and over-represented in the pool of unskilled workers.

The Black Community vs. Congressional Black Caucus
- NAACP: 100 percent *for Davis-Bacon*
- Congressional Black Caucus: 100 percent *for Davis-Bacon*
- Labor Unions: 100 percent *for Davis-Bacon*

For decades, institutional racism existed on both state and the federal levels of government. While great strides have been made since the Jim Crow era, some of these relics remain. One of them is the Davis-Bacon Act, legislation passed in 1932 with a specific goal to stop the flow of Black laborers and entrepreneurs from competing for Federal construction dollars against segregated White labor unions. It continues to suppress Black trades and the hiring of Black laborers. This anti-Black law continues to be protected by the Congressional Black Caucus at the behest of White Democratic leaders.

---

253   Courtney Coren. "Pew Poll: Illegal Immigrants Heavily Favor Democratic Party." *Newsmax.* July 22, 2013, sec. Newsfront. newsmax.com/Newsfront/illegals-favor-democrats-immigration/2013/07/22/id/516417.

254   "Illegal Immigration and Amnesty Polls." FAIR, October 22, 2013. fairus.org/issue/illegal-immigration-and-amnesty-polls.

CHAPTER 12

THE DAVIS-BACON ACT

Pro-Union/Anti-Black-Cause and Effect

Tyrone Dash of Seattle owned and operated his own company, T&S Construction, from 1984 to 1990. He was forced into bankruptcy because of a law passed in 1931 that required him to pay his workers a set amount, the "prevailing wage," on nearly all federally funded construction projects, regardless of the workers' individual skill levels or the nature of the job. Most often, the "prevailing wage" corresponds directly to the union wage, giving large union shops an inherent advantage over small entrepreneurial start-ups.[255]

Davis-Bacon: Jim Crow's Last Stand
The Davis-Bacon Act Imposes Tremendous Social and Economic Costs [256]

This article by John Frantz was originally published in 1994 on FEE.org:

The ugliest and most disturbing events in American history have usually been linked with state-sponsored or sanctioned racism: Incidents of police brutality, symbolized by the Rod-

---

255   "Davis Bacon Act: Removing Barriers to Opportunity." Case Study. Institute for Justice, 2018. ij.org/case/brazier-construction-co-inc-v-reich.

256   John Frantz. "Davis-Bacon: Jim Crow's Last Stand." Politics. Foundation for Economic Education, February 1, 1994. fee.org/articles/davis-bacon-jim-crows-last-stand.

ney King trials; slavery; the Dred Scott decision; the post-Civil War Jim Crow laws; school segregation.

Today, however, most people like to believe that their government fairly represents the interests of everyone, regardless of race. Unfortunately, the states and the federal government still discriminate against Blacks, but this state-sponsored racism has taken on more subtle forms. Thus while great strides have been made since the Jim Crow era, some relics remain. One of them is the Davis-Bacon Act.

Passed in 1931, Davis-Bacon requires private contractors to pay "prevailing wages" to employees on all construction projects receiving more than $2,000 in federal funding. The Secretary of Labor is charged with conducting surveys of a region's wages and setting rates for up to one hundred various classifications of workers. Most often, the "prevailing wage" corresponds to the union wage, especially in urban areas, where union membership tends to be higher. The Davis-Bacon Act covers approximately twenty percent of all construction projects in the United States and affects more than twenty-five percent of all construction workers in the nation at any given time.

The Act was passed to prevent non-unionized Black and immigrant laborers from competing with unionized White workers. The discriminatory effects continue, as even today minorities tend to be vastly under-represented in highly unionized skilled trades and over-represented in the pool of unskilled workers. Davis-Bacon restricts the economic opportunities of low income individuals in several ways. Minority contracting firms are often small and non-unionized and cannot afford to pay the "prevailing wage." The Act also requires contractors to pay unskilled laborers the prevailing wage for any job they perform, essentially forcing contractors to hire skilled tradesmen, selecting workers from a pool dominated by Whites.[257]

Thus, the Davis-Bacon Act constitutes a formidable barrier to entry into the construction industry for unskilled or low-skilled workers. This is especially harmful to minorities, be-

---

257   Johnson, "Negro Workers and the Unions," *The Survey*, April 15, 1928.

cause work in the construction industry pays extraordinarily well compared to that for other entry-level positions and could otherwise provide plentiful opportunities for low-income individuals to enter the economic mainstream.[258]*

In November 1993, the Institute for Justice, a Washington, D.C. based public-interest law firm, filed suit challenging Davis-Bacon constitutionality, as part of the Institute's litigation program to help restore judicial protection of "economic liberty," the basic right to pursue a business or profession free from arbitrary government regulation.

The History of the Davis-Bacon Act

Prior to the enactment of the Davis-Bacon Act, the construction industry afforded tremendous opportunities to Blacks, especially in the South. In at least six southern cities, more than eighty percent of unskilled construction workers were Black. Blacks also represented a disproportionate number of unskilled construction workers in the North and constituted a sizable portion of the skilled labor force in both parts of the country. This was even though most of the major construction unions excluded Blacks, and that Blacks faced widespread discrimination in occupational licensing and vocational training. These unions felt seriously threatened by competition from Blacks and favored any attempt to restrict it.

The co-author of the Act, Representative Robert Bacon, represented Long Island. Bacon was a racist who was concerned lest immigration upset the nation's "racial status quo." In 1927, he introduced H.R. 17069, "A Bill to Require Contractors and Subcontractors Engaged on Public Works of the United States to Comply With State Laws Relating to Hours of Labor and Wages of Employees on State Public Works." This action was a response to the building of a Veterans' Bureau Hospital in Bacon's district by an Alabama contractor that employed only Black laborers.[259]

Representative William Upshaw, understanding the racial implications of Bacon's proposal, stated: "You will not think that a southern man is more than human if he smiles over the fact of your reaction to that real problem you are confronted with in any community with a superabundance or large aggregation of Negro labor." Over the next four years, Bacon submitted

---

258   *Ibid.*

259   Employment of Labor on Federal Construction Work, Hearings on H.R. 7995 and H.R. 9232 Before the House Committee on Labor, 71st Congress, 2nd Session, March 6, 1930, p. 26- 27.

thirteen more bills to regulate labor on federal public works contracts. Finally, the bill submitted by Bacon and Senator James Davis was passed in 1931, at the height of the Depression, with the support of the American Federation of Labor. The Act required that contractors working on federally funded projects over 5,000 dollars pay their employees the "prevailing wage." The law was amended in 1935, reducing the minimum to 2,000 dollars and delegating the power of determining the "prevailing wage" to the Department of Labor. The Department's regulations governing the determination of wages remained basically unchanged for five decades and equated the prevailing wage with the union wage in any area that was at least thirty percent unionized. In practice, the "prevailing wage" was almost universally determined to be the same as the union wage.

The debate over Bacon's bills betrayed the racial animus that motivated passage of the law. Representative John Cochran stated, "I have received numerous complaints in recent months about southern contractors employing low-paid colored mechanics getting work and bringing the employees from the South."

Representative Clayton Algood similarly complained, "That contractor has cheap colored labor that he transports, and he puts them in cabins, and it is labor of that sort that is in competition with White labor throughout the country." Other derogatory comments were made about the use of "cheap labor," "cheap, imported labor," "transient labor," and "unattached migratory workmen." While supporters of the Act intended to disadvantage immigrant workers of all races, they were particularly concerned with inhibiting Black employment.

Supporters of Davis-Bacon were also full of anti-Capitalist rhetoric. Representative McCormack said of Davis-Bacon, "It will force the contractor who heretofore has used cheap, imported labor to submit bids based upon the 'prevailing wage scale' to those employed. It compels the unfair competitor to enter into the field of fair competition." This rhetoric of "fairness" dominates much of the contemporary debate over Davis-Bacon as well.

Two important modifications have recently been made in the way that the Davis-Bacon Act is enforced. In 1982, the Department of Labor altered the basis for determining the prevailing wage, deciding to equate the union wage with the "prevailing wage" only in places where the construction industry was fifty percent unionized. This change has had little effect on minority-owned firms' ability to secure contracts because union membership tends to be much higher in urban areas, where large minority populations reside.

The Department of Labor has also attempted to alter its regulations to allow contractors to hire a limited number of unskilled "helpers" to work on Davis-Bacon projects for less than the prevailing wage. This change, which was to go into effect on February 4, 1991, would help to diminish some of the discriminatory effects of the Act, but Congress has so far prevented the DOL from enforcing it. Moreover, labor unions pressured Congress and the Clinton Administration to repeal the changes. Similarly, while President Bush suspended the Act in South Florida, coastal Louisiana, and Hawaii in October of 1992 following hurricanes Andrew and Iniki, President Clinton reversed course upon entering office.

In the Senate Senator Hank Brown (R-CO) sponsored a bill to repeal the Davis-Bacon Act. A similar bill was introduced in the House by Representative Tom DeLay (R-TX). Both proposals have attracted congressional co-sponsors, but not surprisingly, have failed to attain majority support.

Effects of the Davis-Bacon Act

The Davis-Bacon Act imposes tremendous economic and social costs, at least one billion dollars in extra federal construction costs and one hundred million dollars in administrative expenses each year. Industry compliance costs total nearly one hundred ninety million dollars per year. Repeal of the Act would also create an estimated thirty-one thousand new construction jobs, most of which would go to members of minority groups.

Davis-Bacon's impact on the ability of minorities to find work in the construction industry has been particularly devastating. The Department of Labor's initial set of regulations did not recognize categories of unskilled workers except for union apprentices. As a result, contractors had to pay an unskilled worker who was not part of a union apprenticeship program as much as a skilled laborer, which almost completely excluded Blacks from working on Davis-Bacon projects.[260] This effectively foreclosed the only means by which unskilled Black workers could learn the necessary skills to become skilled workers.

While Black and White unemployment rates were similar prior to passage of the Davis-Bacon Act, they began to diverge afterwards. This problem persists today. In the first quarter of 1992, the Black unemployment rate was 14.2 percent, even though the overall national rate was only 7.9 percent.

The racial difference in unemployment rates is especially pronounced in the construction industry. According to a recent study by the National Urban League, in the fourth quarter of 1992, 26.8 percent of all Blacks involved in the construction industry were jobless compared to only 12.6 percent of White construction workers.[261]

Despite recent racial progress, Davis-Bacon continues to inhibit minority economic progress in several ways. For instance, union apprenticeship programs, even if they no longer discriminate, still strictly limit the number

---

260   National Urban League, *Quarterly Economic Report on the African American Worker*, Fourth Quarter, 1992, Table 7 (presently unpublished).
261   John Gould and George Billingmayer, *The Economics of the Davis-Bacon Act*, Washington, D.C.: American Enterprise Institute, 1980, p. 62.

of enrollees and impose arbitrary educational requirements on potential applicants, thereby excluding the most disadvantaged workers.[262]

Moreover, unskilled workers must be paid the same wage as a skilled worker, forcing the contractor to pay laborers considerably more than the market value of their work. For example, in Philadelphia, electricians working on projects covered by the Davis-Bacon Act must be paid 37.97 dollars per hour in wages and fringe benefits. The average wage of electricians working for private contractors on non-Davis-Bacon projects is 15.76 dollars per hour, with some laborers working for as little as 10.50 dollars per hour.[263]

Since unskilled workers are required to be paid the same as a skilled worker, Thus, even minority, open-shop contractors have no incentive to hire unskilled workers. Ralph C. Thomas, former executive director of the National Association of Minority Contractors, stated that a minority contractor who acquires a Davis-Bacon contract has "no choice but to hire skilled tradesmen, the majority of which are of the majority." As a result, Thomas said, "Davis-Bacon closes the door on such activity in an industry most capable of employing the largest numbers of minorities."[264]

The paperwork a contractor must fill out pursuant to Davis-Bacon contracts also discriminates against small, minority-owned firms. Many do not have personnel with the necessary expertise to complete the myriad forms and reports required.

Because of all these factors, the Davis-Bacon Act prevents rural and inner-city laborers and contractors from working on projects in their own communities.[265] Ironically, this is one problem Davis-Bacon was intended to prevent. Bacon said during debate over the Act, "Members of Congress have been flooded with protests from all over the country that certain Federal contractors on current jobs are bringing into local communities outside labor," and "...the government is in league with contract practices that make it possible to further demoralize local labor conditions."[266]

Such a claim could easily be made today by inner-city and rural contractors. Yale Brozen, an economist at the University of Chicago, found that the "prevailing wage" for the Appalachian region of Western Pennsylvania is set at the same level as that of Pittsburgh, even though the wages normally

262 Testimony by National Association of Minority Contractors before House Subcommittee on Labor Standards of the Committee on Education and Labor, Sept. 30, 1986, p. 3.
263 Rates of Wages for Laborers and Mechanics on Public Buildings of the United States, 74 Congressional Record 6504, 6513, (1931).
264 Employment of Labor on Federal Construction Work, p. 6511.
265 Ibid., p. 4.
266 Patrick Barry, "Congress's Deconstruction Theory," The Washington Monthly, January, 1990, p. 11

paid by the rural contractors are only half the levels of union contractors in Pittsburgh. The same is true of inner cities, where small, minority-owned, open-shop firms are forced to pay union wages when working on Davis-Bacon projects, because of the high concentration of unionized workers in other parts of the city.

As a result, rural and inner-city contractors are deterred from seeking Davis-Bacon contracts because they cannot afford to pay the higher wages to their employees and larger, more highly unionized firms are encouraged to seek out such contracts. The result makes it clear that the government is in fact "in league with contract practices" that "demoralize local labor conditions," only now at the expense of minorities rather than Whites.

The results of this practice were clearly demonstrated in Los Angeles. In the parts of the city where the riots occurred, the rate of unemployment for Black workers is 27.6 percent. Despite an ample supply of local labor to help rebuild the city, Davis-Bacon has and continues to freeze out local unskilled minority workers from those available jobs. In contrast is the situation in South Florida and coastal Louisiana, where the suspension of Davis-Bacon created 5,000 to 11,000 jobs.

In addition to this statistical evidence, individuals involved in the construction and renovation of low-cost public housing have testified as to the disastrous effects of the Act. When Ralph L. Jones, president of a company that manages housing projects for the Department of Housing and Urban Development, gained control of a pair of dilapidated 200-unit buildings in Tulsa, Oklahoma, he intended to hire many of the building's unemployed residents to help restore the property. However, the Davis-Bacon Act required him to pay everyone working on the project union wages, forcing him to hire only skilled laborers, very few of whom were minorities.

Mary Nelson, director of Bethel New Life, Inc., a social service organization located in Chicago, has found that Davis-Bacon adds up to twenty-five percent to her total costs and frequently prevents her from hiring unskilled, low income workers to work on projects renovating the public housing that they themselves live in. Elzie Higginbottom, builder of low income housing in Chicago's South Side, has had similar problems. Davis-Bacon requires him to pay carpenters (defined by the Act as someone who hammers in a nail) twenty-three dollars per hour. As a result, he complained, "I've got to start out a guy at $16 per hour to find out if he knows how to dig a hole. I can't do that."

Conclusion

The constitutional challenge to Davis-Bacon is a cornerstone of the Institute for Justice's program to restore economic liberty as a fundamental civil right. The Institute is challenging Davis-Bacon claiming it is racially discriminatory, since it was passed to discriminate against Blacks and immigrants, and as a result, violates the equal protection guarantee of the Fifth Amendment. The courts need only look to the legislative and administrative history of the law to determine that racial discrimination was among its purposes. The courts could also void the Davis-Bacon Act for impinging on the right of individuals to pursue employment opportunities, thereby violating the Fifth Amendment's due process clause. The Institute for Justice has brought together a unique coalition of plaintiffs to challenge the law. Complainants range from individual minority contractors, who have either lost opportunities to successfully acquire government contracts or who have gone out of business altogether because of the application of Davis-Bacon, to resident-management corporations who because of the law have been unsuccessful in their attempts to involve public-housing residents in rebuilding programs at their own developments.

Borne of racial animus, the Davis-Bacon Act has undermined the efforts of economic outsiders to find employment in the construction industry for more than six decades. Given the influence of organized labor over Congress and the extent to which the Clinton administration's support of NAFTA alienated this key constituency, it is highly unlikely that either branch will risk further undermining union support by pursuing reform or repeal of the Davis-Bacon Act. Thus, the only avenue that remains open is the judiciary. The courts should bury this relic of the Jim Crow era.

Congressional Black Caucus

Official Statement Supporting the Davis-Bacon Act

From the Response to decades of Black job-killing–Pro-White Union Davis-Bacon by Congressional Black Caucus (December 13, 1995):

> *"Prior to the enactment of Davis-Bacon in 1931, there were many shocking examples of abusive labor practices and wholesale exploitation of female and minority workers on construction sites. For the last sixty years, the Davis-Bacon Act has protected wages of all construction workers, including minorities and women, who are particularly vulnerable to exploitation. We believe the Davis-Bacon has been instrumental in bridging the wage gap for historically disadvantaged sectors of our society. In the face of decaying social and economic opportunities this measure provides women and minorities with an important tool to achieving greater parity with their mainstream counterparts."*

CHAPTER 13

THE BIG LIE

Washington, D.C. Capitol Steps

For the last fifty years the Black community has been engaged in a fight with an enemy more tenacious, insidious, and destructive than any other threat in its history. Unlike the physical chains of slavery, the intimidation of the KKK or the legislative barriers of Jim Crow segregationists, this enemy has been a metastasizing cancer attacking its soul and essence, its manhood, womanhood, family, and its dreams and vision. It is an evil ideology that bans God and replaces Him with a spiritual addiction and dependency on others. It is an extremely seductive ideology that can grant only one promise: *misery.* It is the ideology of Socialism and Marxism. It is in the mist of this ferocious decades-long battle that we become aware of the absence of political defenders for the defenseless. Missing in action are those most trusted by the urban Black community: John Lewis, Elijah Cummings, Maxine Waters, Sheila Jackson Lee, and their Democratic Congressional Black Congress comrades. To this group of legislators, who themselves can be safely be defined as Socialist and Marxist, there is another quote that is applicable: "The deepest betrayal begins with ultimate trust."

An educated, informed, employed, and job-providing electorate is an "empowered" electorate. Consistently, the Democratic Congressional Black Caucus has voted 100 percent as a united body, *against them being so empowered.* They have voted 100 percent *against* school choice for their poor Black constituents. They have voted 100 percent *against* the elimination of federal regulations that hinder job opportunities for poor Black teenagers, considered unskilled labor. They have voted 100 percent *against* the elimination of the racist Davis-Bacon Act. This law was passed in 1932 to erect barriers preventing Black entrepreneurs from competing against White owned/controlled trade Labor Unions. Instead, it has been the Democratic Congressional Black Caucus that has voted 100 percent *for* policies statistically proven to expand an environment of misery, hopelessness, frustration, and anger. This type of environment represents dry kindle for the Left, allowing them to stoke the racial fire of divisiveness when needed.

By keeping alive an environment of distrust, anger, and hatred, the Democratic Party has discovered an effective way to energize its voting base: resistance, riot, and retaliation. The strategy of fomenting urban anger is witnessed on the evening news in every urban city and during every election cycle. It culminates into demonstrations, rioting, looting, attacks on law enforcement, and unfortunately in 2016, the assassination of five Dallas police officers. This stratagem is effective only in the presence of human misery, anger, and hopelessness. And as human misery increases, so does the Democratic urban voter turnout.

The stoking of anger to energize its base was seen on full display on the Washington, D.C. Capitol steps on May 2010, a day before the congressional vote on President Obama's Health Care bill. Reported in the liberal *Huffington Post* as follows:

> Tea Party Protests: 'Ni**er,' 'Fa**ot' Shouted at Members of Congress
>
> *Huffington Post (05/20/2010):*
>
> *"...Abusive, derogatory, and even racist behavior directed at House Democrats by Tea Party protesters on Saturday left several lawmakers in shock. Preceding the president's speech to a gathering of House Democrats, thousands of protesters descended around the Capitol to protest the passage of health care reform. The gathering quickly turned into abusive heckling, as members of Congress passing through Longworth House office building were subjected to epithets and even mild physical abuse."[267]*
>
> *A staffer for Rep. James Clyburn (D-SC) told reporters that a protestor had spit on Rep. Emanuel Cleaver (D-MO).*
>
> *Rep. John Lewis (D-GA), a hero of the civil rights movement, was called a "ni**er."*
>
> *Rep. Barney Frank (D-MA) was called a "faggot," as protestors shouted at him in a deliberately "lisp-y" fashion.*

---

267   Sam Stein. "Tea Party Protests: 'Ni**er,' 'Fa**ot' Shouted At Members Of Congress." *The Huffington Post*. May 25, 2011, sec. Politics. huffingtonpost. com/2010/03/20/tea-party-protests-nier-f_n_507116.html.

Approached in the halls after the president's speech, Frank shrugged off the incident; however, Congressional Black Caucus member, Clyburn, stated he had not witnessed such treatment since he was leading civil rights protests in South Carolina in the 1960s. "It was absolutely shocking to me," Clyburn said in response to a question from the *Huffington Post*. "I stayed home to meet on the campus of Claflin University where fifty years ago as of last Monday...I led the first demonstrations in South Carolina, the sit-ins...and quite frankly I heard some things today I have not heard since that day. I heard people saying things that I have not heard since March 15, 1960 when I was marching to try and get off the back of the bus."

"It doesn't make me nervous at all," the congressman said, when asked how the mob-like atmosphere made him feel. "In fact, as I said to one heckler, I am the hardest person in the world to intimidate, so they better go somewhere else."

Asked if he wanted an apology from the group of Republican lawmakers who had addressed the crowd and, in many ways, played on their worst fears of health care legislation, the Democratic Party, and the president, Clyburn replied: "A lot of us have been saying for a long time that much of this...is not about healthcare at all. And I think a lot of those people today demonstrated that this is not about healthcare...it is about trying to extend a basic fundamental right to people who are less powerful."

Black Congressman, Rep. Andre Carson (D-IN), told a reporter as he left the Cannon House Office Building with Rep. John Lewis that they "heard the crowd chant 'the N-word' fifteen times." Both Carson and Lewis are Black, and Lewis spokeswoman Brenda Jones corroborated that it occurred. "It was like going into the time machine with John Lewis," said Carson, a former police officer who said he wasn't frightened but worried about the seventy-year-old Lewis, who is twice his age. "He said it reminded him of another time."

Rep. Emanuel Cleaver II (D-MO), Statement in *The NY Times*:

> *"For many of the members of the CBC, like John Lewis and Emanuel Cleaver, who worked in the civil rights movement, and for Mr. Frank, who has struggled in the cause of equality, this is not the first time they have been spit on during turbulent times.*
>
> *"This afternoon, the congressman was walking into the Capitol to vote when one protester spat on him. The Congressman would like to thank the U.S. Capitol Police officer who quickly escorted the other members and him into the Capitol and defused the tense situation with professionalism and care. After all the members were safe, a full report was taken, and the U.S. Capitol Police handled the matter. The man who spat on the congressman was arrested, but the congressman has*

chosen not to press charges. He has left the matter with the Capitol Police."

"This is not the first time the congressman has been called the 'n' word and certainly not the worst assault he has endured in his years fighting for equal rights for all Americans. He is disappointed that in the 21st century our national discourse has devolved to the point of name calling and spitting. He looks forward to taking a historic vote on health care reform legislation tomorrow, for the residents of the Fifth District of Missouri and for all Americans. He believes deeply that tomorrow's vote is, in fact, a vote for equality and to secure health care as a right for all. Our nation has a history of struggling each time we expand rights. Today's protests are no different, but the congressman believes this is worth fighting for."[268]

The 'BIG LIE'

The only problem with this reported episode of racist epithets, spitting on Black members of the Democratic Party and racial threats reminiscent of the days of the 1960s KKK is that ""it never happened." It was all strategically fabricated. A racist lie.

The entire midday walk by House Democrats to the Capitol building was purposely taken through thousands of Tea Party Americans who had gathered for a peaceful demonstration, which was recorded by the national media and private citizens. When their efforts to antagonize and get a negative response from this conservative crowd didn't work, they simply made up and reported a story designed to antagonize their own trusting Black base.

The New York Times correction

Three months after a thorough investigation of viewing many recordings of that walk, *The New York Times* ran a correction to this recollection by noted members of the Congressional Black Caucus. They noted *"There is no proof that Tea Party supporters shouted racial epithets at Congressman John Lewis."* [269]

---

268   *Ibid.*

269   Frances Martel. "NYT's Apology For Tea Party Racism Accusation Not Enough For Breitbart." Mediaite, August 3, 2010. mediaite.com/online/nyts-apology-for-tea-party-racism-accusation-not-enough-for-andrew-breitbart.

These aggrieved Black Congressmen did have an opportunity for this incident to be a financial benefit to Black college students nationwide. Within days of the accusation of racism there was a 10,000-dollar reward to anyone who could offer any evidence of one racial epithet being used. If proven, the 10,000 dollars would be donated to the United Negro College Fund. When there was no response to this offer, this reward was increased to 100,000 dollars.[270]

With this very generous offer for evidence and proof of *one* "N word," what was the response of the Royalty Class Black Politicians? Total silence.

A Recap

Very detailed, inflammatory, racist accusations were charged against peaceful Blacks with the collusion of the national media a day before an historic Democratic vote on Obamacare. With the opportunity of 100,000 dollars that would benefit the Black community with *one word* of proof, how did these aggrieved Royalty Class Black men respond? With *silence.*

Who are the cowardly race hustlers who purposely lie to inflame their uninformed constituents? Who are these paid government servants who use the emotions of their own race, purposely incite the raw emotions of anger, hopelessness, and racism to pass a legislative bill demanded of them by their White Democratic leaders?

- **Rep Emanuel Cleaver** (D-MO) - "For many of the members of the CBC, like John Lewis and Emanuel Cleaver who worked in the civil rights movement, and for Mr. Frank who has struggled in the cause of equality, this is not the first time they have been spit on during turbulent times."
- **Rep. James E. Clyburn**, (D-SC) - "I heard people saying things today that I have not heard since March 15, 1960, when I was marching to try to get off the back of the bus."
- Rep Clyburn's staffer reminded national reporters that Rep. Cleaver had been spat on, Rep. John Lewis had been called a "nigger," and Rep. Barney Frank had been called a "faggot."
- **Rep. Andre Carson** (D-IN) - "It was like going into the time machine with John Lewis," said Carson, a large former police officer who said he wasn't frightened but worried about

270 AP staff. "Tea Party, Dems Row Over N-Word Video 'Evidence.'" CBS News. April 13, 2010, sec. News. cbsnews.com/news/tea-party-dems-row-over-n-word-video-evidence.

the seventy-year-old Lewis, who is twice his age. "He said it reminded him of another time."

- Carson did respond to the 100,000-dollar reward. "In many regards I think [the challenges are] a veiled attempt to justify actions that are simply unjustifiable. I think we need to move toward a dialogue that explores why this kind of divisive and reprehensible language is still making it into our political debate."

Carson has still not offered any proof of this explosive charge of what many would consider a racially-motivated crime. He recommends we should "move to a dialogue to explore," yet he has not offered video or recording.

I imagine something like this:

Rep. Andre Carson: "Hey guys, I've gotten my propaganda sound bite which I've targeted for my poor and uneducated constituents via the Black Entertainment TV channel, so let's move on. We don't want to take this too far and get ourselves in trouble by having to repeat a lie of racism under oath so...let's move on. Since my poor urban constituents trust our Black Socialist/Marxist President Obama when he tells them to never, ever look beyond the curtains of BET, MSNBC, and CNN for truth, let's move on. Finally, since most of my constituents are not readers—and I'll do my level best to keep it that way—I'm confident they'll never read The NY Times 'correction' that we were lying through our teeth."

There was a report by the Associated Press that Cleaver's office initially claimed a protester was arrested after spitting on him, but the congressman decided not to press charges. It later offered an update from the U.S. Capitol Police that the protester was never arrested—he was only detained and put in handcuffs, and then released.

Sgt. Kimberly Schneider, spokeswoman for the Capitol Police, told Fox News the individual was released because Cleaver couldn't identify him. "There were no elements of a crime, and the individual wasn't able to be positively identified," she said. As for the initial claim that the individual was arrested, Petrovic said staff members mistakenly presumed he had been arrested because he was temporarily in handcuffs.[271]

Though a true accounting of this incident has been corrected and reported by national publications like The NY Times, it is important to remember the real target of these charges of racism. It must be noted that Royalty Class Black politicians never corrected their initial charges, they simply went silent. This

---

271   "Tea Party Protesters Dispute Reports of Slurs, Spitting Against Dem Lawmakers." Fox News. March 22, 2010, sec. News. foxnews.com/story/2010/03/22/tea-party-protesters-dispute-reports-slurs-spitting-against-dem-lawmakers.html.

un-collaborated racist attack on civil rights legend John Lewis has remained uncorrected by the Democrats' Black propaganda arm, BET. Very similar to the Nazi Goebbels' propaganda strategy, this false narrative has been continually repeated and referenced. It has therefore remained real and relevant to those who it was meant to influence: uninformed, trusting, and emotional Black citizens within the urban community.

Silencing and Targeting

With talking points that are uncannily similar, the Democratic Party Leadership, the Congressional Black Caucus, Black Entertainment TV, and the national mainstream media had successfully branded the Tea Party as White supremacists. Comprised of peaceful, respectful, family friendly, inclusive, and patriotic Americans, this group was silenced by the left after President Obama's first term. This stealth strategy of rebranding or bullying others has now been observed in other Federal agencies. In 2017 the Trump administration DOJ, after years of litigation, reached an awarded settlement with Tea Party and other conservative groups for millions of dollars for unfair targeting by the IRS under the Obama administration.[272]

The Congressional Black Caucus' "big lie" helped the Democratic Party, in the short term, to sell Obama's medical reform as an "anti-racist" Republican policy. In the long term the "big lie" messaging would be used in future election cycles as a strategically "Demonstrate, Riot, Loot, and Steal to Get Out the Urban Black Vote" campaign.

Over one hundred years ago, Booker T. Washington warned us about this group of Royalty Class Black elitists. He called them the "problem profiteers."

"There is a class of colored people who make a business of keeping the troubles, the wrongs, and the hardships of the Negro race before the public. Having learned that they are able to make a living out of their troubles, they have grown into the settled habit of advertising their wrongs—partly because they want sympathy and partly because it pays."

—*Booker T. Washington*

---

272   Brooke Singman. "Trump DOJ Settles Lawsuits over Tea Party Targeting by Obama IRS." Fox News. October 26, 2017, sec. Law. foxnews.com/politics/2017/10/26/trump-doj-settles-lawsuits-over-tea-party-targeting-by-obama-irs.html.

At a time when our country had proven its progress by electing for two terms a Black president and with wealthy Black men and women within every segment of our society, what kind of party and people would *purposely* use the divisiveness of hate as a political strategy? What kind of party and people would invest, for decades, propaganda to indoctrinate an American community to become anti-White and anti-American?

> *"Evil is the purposeful stealing of someone's hopes, dreams, and future. Pure Evil is the purposeful targeting of an entire race, for generations."*
>
> —Burgess Owens

There are millions of Black Americans today in Democratic controlled urban communities who still believe the "big lie" Tea Party scheme. They believe that America is a place where most White citizens stand by and condone the hurling of racial epithets at a respected seventy-year-old civil rights legend. They still believe the "Hands Up Don't Shoot" narrative of an innocent Black teenager pleading to a police officer and being gunned down in this act. They are clueless of the proven Department of Justice facts, that this young man attacked the officer while he was seated in his patrol vehicle; that he attempted to take the officer's holstered pistol from him, resulting in the firing of a shot inside the vehicle. When the officer demanded that the teenager stop in his retreat, he refused, turned, and "bull rushed" the officer.

Pushing the long-debunked narrative of a White police officer gunning down an innocent, unarmed, non-dangerous Black teen, the collective of elected Black political representatives, White Democratic pundits, academic intellectuals, Black entertainers and athletes' message through the urban American portal, BET, is that America is an innately racist and oppressive country, a place of racist White oppressors in dire need of "Social Justice."

Though these accusations of a racist police execution and taunting racist epithets toward a celebrated civil rights politician have been proven untrue (within months), they are still used years later by the Democratic Party for their racist rhetoric. Painted by the Democratic Party operatives as the true heart of Americans, such images have been emotionally internalized. Once internalized to generate and justify anger, these emotions effectively close doors to opportunities.

These "big lie" moments have, for many others, substituted feelings of optimism with a power-draining pessimism and deep anger toward White Americans. It is guaranteed, regardless of race, creed, or color, that a soul of pessimism and anger is one destined to failure. This destination has been purposely navigated by a heartless ideology that prospers and profits from the failure of others. Behind the false façade of a compassionate Democratic Party is the narcissistic Royalty Class Black man colluding with their White Socialist/

Marxist counterparts to spread misery to those who are less fortunate and not of their class.

> *"The first battlefield is the rewriting of history."*
>
> —*Socialist founder Karl Marx*

Regarding the Congressional Black Caucus, it is time we grant to this group of politicians a name more fitting with their history and priorities. For decades, they have proven their abject loyalty to the Democratic Party. Since skin color is secondary, it should no longer represent a unique designation for this Black Caucus.

Time has proven these Black politicians will never have the inclination or courage to vote against their White Democratic leaders. Regardless of the negative impact their White leaders' policies have on Black men, women, and children, they have shown themselves incapable of independent action.

With their predictable voting history of placing ideology over the good of their own race, there should be a different designation to reflect this. It should be a designation that allows this Caucus to continue to represent their ideology of choice and allow the dispersion of confusion within the Black community—those whom they inevitably betray, for "the deepest betrayal begins with ultimate trust."

So, let them be renamed...The Congressional "Socialist/Marxist" Caucus.

CHAPTER 14

JOHN LEWIS:
THE MAN, THE BRIDGE, THE
SOCIALIST HERO

The words of Tina Trent, a former liberal Democrat activist and former resident in John Lewis's district...

> While John Lewis spent the last fifty years growing rich and influential by repeating the same speech about being beat up on the Edmund Pettus Bridge in Selma, Alabama in 1965, the people living in the crime-ridden parts of his district have spent the fifty years since then being subjected daily to violent crimes and threats of crime at least as bad and frequently far worse than what Lewis experienced, day after day, week after week, year after year, decade after decade, unabated.

> In his years in Congress, Lewis has done little for the district in southeast Atlanta he represents. For all his years in Congress, Lewis has opposed every piece of criminal justice or welfare reform legislation that would make the people of his district safer, more self-reliant, and more prosperous. I'd go farther. Nearly every time John Lewis has "acted" legislatively, life for the poorest in his district has become more dangerous, more destabilized, and more tragic.

> John Lewis grew more rich and influential with each repetition of his Edmund Pettus Bridge speech, yet the people of his district watched the value of their homes, their communities, and their schools—their life's work—disintegrate because of crime and multigenerational family dysfunction. There are

*no federal monuments to the crime victims of John Lewis'
district. These victims are barely acknowledged by Lewis
himself.*[273]

In the arena of athletics, some have difficulty closing out the chapter of their years of glory. Some continue to rehash those years by spending hours looking at old films and fading news clips. It has been so with Rep. John Lewis, whose time of glory, i.e., "The Bridge," came amid the civil rights era of the '60s.

At the age of twelve, I marched with a busload of Florida A&M students in front of the White-only segregated Florida State Theater, expressing our opposition to Jim Crow racism. I remember racial epithets shouted at us from White drivers passing by and the ever-present tension due to the potential of violence. During this era, millions of Americans, Blacks, Whites, men, women, Christians, and Jews took part in this nation changing movement. They did so for racial equality, many adding their contributions away from cameras and microphones with no thought or desire for fame and fortune.

These were the true heroes of the civil rights era. Some would pay the ultimate sacrifice. Their efforts resulted in a paradigm shift in race relations and drove forward the passage of legislation that would grant equal opportunity to all. The effort included nameless FAMU college students in front of the Tallahassee Florida State Theater, hundreds of marchers walking across the Edmund Pettus Bridge in Selma, and hundreds of thousands of diverse Americans in multiple ways doing what they could to move our nation forward. They stood courageously and non-violently in whichever venue was selected by civil rights leadership and, in the process, earned the respect of their fellow Americans, the votes of their politicians, and equal rights for the Black race. They continued building, knowing that their efforts, large and small, had made a difference for the future of our country. Never was there a thought by these everyday Americans that their efforts could potentially be used to catapult them into a life of personal wealth and fame. Never was there a consideration that their mid-1960s effort that resulted in progress, opportunities, and the tearing down of physical and emotional walls would be used for ideological divisiveness. Instead of highlighting an era of turning points and unified efforts that paid off dividends in race relations, it is a piece of history used by the Left and compliant Royalty Class Black elitists to inform those they have made hopeless, that "nothing has changed."

How did the actions of these thousands of American heroes in 1965 differ from those of nineteen-year-old John Lewis? Simple. John Lewis had media face time, the remaining multitude did not—and had not sought. Like the old

---

273   Tina Trent. "Trump Is 100 Percent Right about Congressman John Lewis." Political blog. Bombthrowers (blog), January 16, 2017. bombthrowers.com/article/trump-is-100-percent-right-about-congressman-john-lewis.

NFL receiver whose "catch" has been immortalized for all time, Lewis is able to review, relive, and share his past season of courageous acts. Simultaneously, he has worked in lockstep compliance to party policies and strategies to place impediments in the way of others who, if granted the opportunity, would like to experience their own monumental "catch." For over three decades, John Lewis, as a member of the Royalty Class Congressional Black Caucus, has come to represent the empathy-free heart and soul of a select club of elitist Black politicians. Granted the opportunity to give voice and power to the urban powerless, instead they opt to ingratiate themselves with fame, fortune... and a fantastic retirement pension. As they've taken on the role of eternal professional politicians, their journey has taken them the humble urban communities they purportedly represented to a destination of wealth and hero-worshiping cable TV time.

As in the 1970s TV show *The Jeffersons*, they've "moved on up" and out of their poor neighborhoods, leaving behind those who, regardless of their chronic failure of leasdership,, can't help but trust them. Unfortunately for these trusting poor urban Black Americans, the bridge of opportunity that granted Lewis an escape route from poverty was drawn behind him with a plethora of anti-Black policies. Welcomed with open arms by the White Democratic leadership, what is *not* expected of these Congressional Black Caucus members is courage, backbone, or independent critical thinking. Instead, demands are simple compliance and a creativity to toe the party line, regardless of the consequences (to their own race). In return, an enticing promise none of them have turned down: power, prestige, profit, pension, a great upper middle class lifestyle, a lifetime of government perks, all wrapped with a beautiful bow. They are granted lifetime Royalty Class treatment as mini kings and queens.

During his younger days, as he joined hundreds of others in the Selma March, John Lewis was respected for his courage. It was on this occasion that the racist White Democrat sheriff Bull Conner released his vicious police dogs and turned pressured fire hoses on the demonstrators. Unfortunately, since that time, Lewis has not found the same courage to stand for the poor constituents of his district against the Socialist/Marxist White leadership of his own Democratic party. He has, on the other hand, become powerful, wealthy, and famous as a facilitator of their destructive policies. This lack of willingness to stand for the powerless is a statistical fact. His party's ideological policies have decimated every urban Black community throughout our country. It will be the legacy of thirty years of failure to address the increased Black misery and hopelessness of the poor and powerless that will eventually condemn John Lewis's legacy of courage on the Edmund Pettus Bridge. History will, in time, expose his lifelong commitment to Socialist/Marxist polices as antithetical to Martin Luther King's vision of freedom, racial harmony, and progress.

As we enter a new millennium, the fight for civil rights equality needs to continue to be a priority of nation. It is no longer the fight of the 1900s against physical barriers, denying access to jobs and opportunities based on the color of one's skin. It is rather the right for equal access to quality education regardless of an individual's zip code.

Vicious police dogs, pressured fire hoses, and the racist intimidation of the KKK guarded the 1960s Democratic Jim Crow barriers. This same culpable Democratic Party has made today's barriers to poverty-breaking education impenetrable. Supported by the educational labor union, its politicians have, through their policies, facilitated rampant illiteracy and peddled brainwashing Marxist propaganda to every public school system they control. It is in the most populist state in the union, the Democratic-run state of California, where three-quarters of the population of Black boys are, due to progressive education, illiterate. It has been the same Democratic Party's anti-Black policies that have condemned poor children within John Lewis's district, strictly because of their zip codes, to wither in failing schools. His policy will lead to yet another generation of Black children denied the opportunity to break the poverty cycle. Every caring parent understands the life changing impact of education, and they desire it for their children; yes, even the poor and powerless. Indicative of a parent's innate desire for their child's best interest can be seen with the education options John Lewis proudly gave his own son. He was granted access to the best education taxpayer dollars could buy. He simply used the income of his job, granted to him by the voters of his 5th District, and moved to another zip code where quality education was guaranteed.

For the poor urban Black Americans who live in the 5th District, John Lewis' thirty years of "Black leadership" is guaranteed *not* to grant them what they, with their taxes and votes, gave him and his son. Instead, for them will be a continuation of high unemployment and welfare among Black adults, a continuation of high incarceration rates of Black male teens, and a continuation of low Black entrepreneurship (3.8 percent). The percentage rate of Black men abandoning their own children (70 percent) will continue its national high rate, and his district will continue to lead all other Georgia counties in the abortion rates of Black babies.

When not busy reflecting on his glory days of the 1965 "march across the bridge," Lewis seems willing to take the lead when his White Democratic leaders feel a need to stoke the emotions of racial divide. When a White Republican politician begins to get too much attention with alternative solutions from the status quo, i.e., school choice, lowering Black on Black crime, or unemployment, he is predictably among the first to utter the word "racist." Noted is Lewis's absence in the arena of debates where ideas and policies are put forth for scrutiny. Absent is any sense of accountability for the failure within the poor urban parts of his own District. Chronic anger, illiteracy, lawlessness, and hopelessness for a major portion of the citizenry who live in Atlanta's 5th District should be a reflection of its leadership. For over three decades, that has resided in one person. John Lewis.

As we're asked to revisit the march across the Selma bridge, now over sixty years ago, it's important to remember the collective efforts of others. Forgotten by the Left are efforts of many thousands of selfless and courageous foot soldiers who, with non-violent restraint, fought against institutional racism and won. Because of the actions of these Americans of every color, religion, and creed, there is no longer a need for minority demands for access to lunch counters, movie theaters, and restaurants. With Black millionaires represented in every business sector of our society, we no longer must accept the false narrative of exclusion. Americans now, regardless of background, have been empowered by the efforts of hundreds of thousands during the 1960s to work, risk, invest, and *to own*. More important, the cornerstone of freedom was reinforced for every citizen: the opportunity to dream, to attempt, to fail, to man-up, to stand up, and to start anew if need be. No longer is there fear in our nation of rogue police releasing attack dogs or using fire hoses on innocent demonstrators. In positions of power throughout our country are Black police, Black sheriffs, Black mayors, and Black politicians who have been, for the most part, elected or appointed by non-Black Americans. These leaders have been put in positions to lead, delegate, direct, and dictate the success or failure of their organizations. If they fail to produce, as per the valued standard of meritocracy, they should be fired, the color of their skin inconsequential.

Annually, our nation comes together to commemorate the life and vision of an American hero, Martin Luther King, Jr. At one or more of these major celebrations, John Lewis will be scheduled as a keynote speaker. Unfortunately, he forgets to mention that due to the courageous and unselfish acts of thousands from our previous generation, over sixty years ago, *we've won*. Predictably, he will put on his most somber, angry face and shed a tear at the mention of Martin Luther King, Jr.'s name. It would be appropriate if those tears represented his empathy for the poor and suffering constituents in his district, but they do not.

John Lewis will not shed a tear for the 1,800 Black babies aborted every day, targeted by White abortionists, because for over thirty years he has supported them. It does not concern him that because of his policies since 1973 over twenty million Black babies have been killed, representing forty percent of today's Black American population. He remains unfazed by the fact that Planned Parenthood places eighty percent of its abortion clinics nationwide in the Black community, or that under his watch most of Georgia's abortion clinics are located within the two counties he represents, Fulton and DeKalb. These two counties account for seventy-nine percent of all abortions in Georgia.[274]

John Lewis will not shed a tear for the eighty-three percent of Black urban teen males nationwide who are chronically unemployed. It has, after all, been his Socialist/Marxist policies for the last thirty years that have guaranteed these results. As these Black teen males become rebellious, unemployable

---

274   "The Impact on Georgia." Statistical. The Radiance Foundation, n.d. toomanyaborted.com/georgia.

and/or incarcerated, they have no idea that their exalted Black Congressional leader has voted 100 percent for pro-union/anti-Black labor policies that purposely price low-skilled labors, like themselves, out of the job market. They will never know that it was he and his fellow Democratic Congressional Caucus members who have voted for "minimum wage" laws and prevailing wage mandates. As unskilled/low-skilled laborers, such policies guarantee their unemployment.

They'll never know John Lewis has voted 100 percent with the labor union *against* poor urban Black children being granted freedom to leave failing unionized public schools. With lack of training of imperative critical thinking skills, they will never know it was his policies that have negated their opportunity to achieve the American Dream.

No, John Lewis will not shed a tear for today's Black entrepreneur and independent contractors who, because of the Davis-Bacon Act, do not have the opportunity to bid on federal/state building contracts. This 1932 law, mockingly labeled the "Negro Removal Act," was passed specifically to protect "White Only" labor unions from competitive Black entrepreneurs and laborers.[275] It is the only law ever passed by our federal legislative body specifically targeting a minority race, and today, thanks to Black and White Democratic Socialist/Marxists, it remains the law of the land. The results over the decades have been *billions* of Federal tax dollars pouring into poor urban communities with legitimate Black-owned businesses barred from bidding on contracts and the absolute minimum number of Black laborers being employed. The result of this closed door to the trades travesty has been a nation-low percentage of Black entrepreneurs (3.8 percent), nation-high rate in Black unemployment, and the dollars granted to urban community projects, leaving the community immediately as White union laborers go home to spend in their own neighborhoods. Absent for decades has been the presence of Black entrepreneurs in positions to hire, train, inspire, mentor, and teach Capitalism. Thus, the Democratic controlled urban community has become the perfect environment for the planting of the seeds of Socialism, Marxism, and atheism.

John Lewis will not shed a tear as he brags to the rest of the nation about the prosperous downtown Atlanta community. Through the last decade of gentrification, this portion of his district has become a convenient oasis for upscale successful professions. Here they can purchase increasingly expensive property snuggled safely behind gated, police-patrolled communities with the best quality school systems the taxpayer dollar can buy. Deep down though, these Black professionals must know that the real reason their property values are rising is because the Feds and John Lewis continue to quietly ship the

---

275 Horace Cooper. "The Untold, Racist Origins Of 'Progressive' Labor Laws." Conservative issues. Illinois Review (blog), June 25, 2014. illinoisreview.typepad.com/il-
linoisreview/2014/06/the-untold-racist-origins-of-progressive-labor-laws.html.

troubled families and crime-blighted projects out of their increasingly valuable real estate into neighboring Clayton County. A once-White, middle-class, stable rural community, Clayton County has devolved into a crime-ridden hellhole within just a few years of wholesale deportation. *Out of sight, out of mind.* What John Lewis has done is create a playground for hipsters of all races by shunting Atlanta's social problems down to neighboring Clayton County.[276]

The Royalty Class Black professional politician John Lewis represents a segment of elitist Americans who enjoy the sweet savor of the American Dream, and then work to convince others that they are incapable of accomplishing the same. Poor Black Americans have suffered for generations under the leadership of the Congressional Black Caucus. *Not one* urban community represented by a member of the Congressional Black Caucus has experienced an improvement in their standard of living, i.e., education, job opportunities, increase of entrepreneurs, decrease in crime rates, or child abandonment/abuse. Instead, *every urban community* represented by Black Socialist/Marxist legislators has in common the growth of Black misery: poverty, unemployment, distrust/disdain for law enforcement, and a decreasing love for God and country.

At the core of Capitalism is the concept of financial reward in return for adding value, whether it is tangible, intangible, a service, or a product. Members of the Congressional Black Caucus have become very wealthy during their tenure of public service. Some, like Maxine Waters, John Lewis, and Elijah Cummings, have become multi-millionaires. They rent out their property in the poor and crime-ridden districts where they used to live and still represent. Meanwhile, their permanent residence is on the other side of town or in a different district, nestled within a plush, gated community and protected by armed security in integrated neighborhoods of the rich and famous. The question based one of the key pillars of Capitalism—that wealth creation is predicated on the value of the services rendered—begs to be asked: What product or service has the Congressional Black Caucus provided in exchange for their multi-million dollar homes and first class lifestyle? Since poor people are not in position to create wealth for others, is it possible it has been wealthy White Democratic Socialist/Marxists who represent the source of wealth for these formerly poor Black politicians?

The universal spiritual law called the Law of Seed and Harvest may provide an answer to the source of chronic urban failure. It states, "We reap what we sow." A planted apple seed is only capable of germinating into an apple tree, nothing more, nothing less. This is a simple but undisputable truth. Given this, the harvest of misery within the urban community can only begin with the planting of misery seeds. In this case, the sowers are the sharecroppers responsible for planting and harvesting within the urban community for over sixty years, the Democratic Congressional Black Caucus. Their votes and

---

276 Tina Trent. "Trump Is 100 Percent Right about Congressman John Lewis."

policies have impacted the lives of millions of Black Americans. However, the genesis of power rests with those who can afford to purchase the seeds, pay for sharecroppers to plant them, and then wait a season for a return on their investment. The payoff for the owner of this plantation is profit, power, and prestige as the poor, hopeless, and dependent view them as political saviors and demigods and the source of their deliverance.

The success and wealth creation for the Royalty Black Class Politician is therefore not predicated on the improvements of the Black lives they represent, but on the amount of power they transfer to the White Socialist/Marxists who pay them.

Let's look at the seeds of misery planted by John Lewis over the decades. Whether it is legislation on education, minimum wage, Davis-Bacon, or abortion, every vote by John Lewis over his thirty years as a Congressman has had one of two results: they have either added to the misery or, like his "Selma to Montgomery National Trail Study Act of 1989," added *no* value at all to the lives of those at risk within his district.

Thirty-Four Years of *Liberal* Policies

The voting record of Rep. John Lewis, Representative for Georgia's 5th District[277]

- **Voted YES** on federal health coverage to abortion. (May 2011)
- **Voted YES** to allow interstate transport of minors to get abortions. (April 2005)
- **Voted YES** on partial-birth abortion with no exception (October 2003)
- **Voted YES** for expanding abortion funding in US aid abroad. (May 2001)
- **Voted NO** to allow poor DC children education vouchers scholarships (March 2011)
- **Voted NO** on allowing school prayer during the War on Terror. (November 2001)
- **Voted NO** on allowing vouchers in DC schools. (August 1998)
- **Voted NO** on education vouchers for private and parochial schools. (November 1997)
- **Voted NO** on establishing nationwide AMBER alert system for missing kids. (April 2003)
- **Voted NO** on reducing Marriage Tax by three hundred ninety-nine billion dollars over ten years. (March 2001)

---

277   "Rep. John Lewis: Representative for Georgia's 5th District." Metrics. GovTrack, July 2018. govtrack.us/congress/members/john_lewis/400240.

- **Voted YES** to Davis-Bacon Act (February 2011)
- **Voted YES** on increasing the minimum wage (2007)

Top pressing issues within the Urban Black community:
- High Black adult unemployment (double that of national rate)
- High Black teen male unemployment: 83 percent
- Child abandonment by Black fathers: 70 percent
- Child abuse
- Targeting: Big Abortion Industry: 80 percent within Black communities
- High Black on Black crime
- High Black juvenile incarceration
- High education failure, illiteracy and Black teen dropout
- Lack of Black entrepreneurs: 3.8 percent

John Lewis' bill sponsoring priority: Seventeen Congressional Bills during his thirty-four years in the Democratic House of Representatives[278]
- H.R. 5067 (114th): Emmett Till Unsolved Civil Rights Crimes Reauthorization Act of 2016
- H.R. 4488 (113th): Gold Medal Technical Corrections Act of 2014
- H.R. 3899 (112th): To provide for rollover treatment to traditional IRAs of amounts received in airline carrier bankruptcy.
- H.R. 4994 (111th): Medicare and Medicaid Extenders Act of 2010
- H.R. 4275 (111th): To designate the annex building under construction for the Elbert P. Tuttle United States Court of Appeals Building in Atlanta, Georgia, as the "John C. Godbold Federal Building".
- H.R. 2040 (110th): Civil Rights Act of 1964 Commemorative Coin Act
- H.R. 923 (110th): Emmett Till Unsolved Civil Rights Crime Act of 2007
- H.R. 3491 (108th): National Museum of African American History and Culture Act
- H.R. 1616 (108th): Martin Luther King, Junior, National Historic Site Land Exchange Act
- H.R. 3442 (107th): National Museum of African American History and Culture Plan for Action Presidential Commission Act of 2001

---

278   *Ibid.*

- H.R. 613 (105th): To designate the Federal building located at 100 Alabama Street NW, in Atlanta, Georgia, as the "Sam Nunn Federal Center"
- H.R. 1933 (103rd): King Holiday and Service Act of 1994
- H.R. 904 (102nd): African American History Landmark Theme Study Act
- H.R. 690 (102nd): To authorize the National Park Service to acquire and manage the Mary McLeod Bethune Council House National Historic Site, and for other purposes.
- H.R. 3834 (101st): Selma to Montgomery National Trail Study Act of 1989
- H.R. 801 (101st): To designate the United States Court of Appeals Building at 56 Forsyth Street in Atlanta, Georgia, as the "Elbert P. Tuttle Court of Appeals Building"
- H.R. 3811 (100th): A bill to designate the Federal building located at 50 Spring Street, Southwest, Atlanta, Georgia, as the "Martin Luther King, Jr. Federal Building"

For John Lewis, the Man, the Bridge, the Socialist Hero, his public service to the poor urban Black community that has elected him for three decades to serve can best be summarized as: "Why work, why dream, why find solutions, why even care...when you're paid more not to?"

CHAPTER 15

JAMES MEREDITH:
THE FORGOTTEN/IGNORED CIVIL
RIGHTS PIONEER

During my ten-year career in the NFL, I was honored to play with two Super Bowl Champion MVP's, Jim Plunkett and NFL Hall of Famer Joe Namath. They were both "game changers" in their era, and once at the crossroads when they concluded they could no longer be, they both retired and moved on to their next life chapter. In time, every athlete, business owner, and employee, regardless of profession, comes to this same crossroads. Only in the world of American politics is this not always the case. In this arena, a class of professionals who can, with long-term strategy and name recognition, conceivably keep their elected position until they die of old age.

My former teammates continue to be well-compensated by fans from that era that seek to relive the memories of World Championship organizations. They are credited as tenacious overcomers and have a sports room full of trophies and lines of autograph seeking fans who confirm their past value. They continue to command the respect of their former teammates not only for their contributions on the field, but also for their grace in leaving it. It would be an embarrassment and case of misplaced ego for either Joe or Jim to attempt to compete in today's game.

So it is with the eternal reliving of crossing the 1968 Birmingham Bridge by John Lewis. Today's battle for success in the urban community is no longer one that needs judicature against institutional racism or protection from the night-riding KKK. There are no schools, businesses, communities, or opportunities that are off-limits to Black Americans due to his or her skin color, proving that institutional racism has indeed been eradicated from our nation. Is there still individual racism? Yes, and there will always be, for it is within the nature of everyone to love and hate. This power of choice results in both good and evil being selected. Neither can be demanded nor legislated away

Addressing today's problems within the Black community with strategies that were effective sixty years ago would be akin to today's NFL World Champion running the 1960s Green Bay Sweep and thinking they could win. This approach to an offensive game plan would end in embarrassment for both the coaching staff and players forced to use it.

Today's failure within the Black community requires a new strategy. The act of walking across the Selma, Alabama bridge in 2017 to invoke sentiments of institutional racism that were real and palatable during the 1960s is a misplaced effort. It is a strategy that is embarrassing to both Lewis and the Democratic Party. The reality is that most racists of the '50s and '60s are long dead, while the real enemy gnawing at the heart and soul of our nation, Socialism/Marxism, is alive and well. The first step to victory for our nation is identifying this enemy, one that is color blind and portrays itself as compassionate through stealth and deceit.

This raises the question. What does a march across the Edmund Pettus Bridge sixty years ago have to do with addressing the misery prevalent in today's Black community, i.e., lack of jobs, education, abandonment of one's own children, and hope? In this light, I'm tempted to rehash a play I made as a former Jet many decades ago:

Question: What does an eighty-two-yard touchdown return my 1973 rookie year in the NFL have to do with today's NY Jets' attempts to get to the Super Bowl Championship?

Answer: Absolutely NOTHING!

At the age of twelve-years old, I participated in a demonstration in front of the segregated Florida State Theater. During the civil rights era my parents were pioneers, often being the first, with my four siblings, to enter formerly segregated parks, lakes, and schools. I've often wondered why John Lewis has been singularly chosen to represent the courage of the civil rights movement. If the 1965 crossing of the Edmund Pettus Bridge was the act that serves as a benchmark for civil rights courage, shouldn't the NAACP, the Democratic Party, and other civil rights leaders also honor the civil rights freedom fighter James Meredith? Meredith, after all, attacked the evils of the Jim Crow segregation on several fronts, *solo*, and nearly lost his life in the process. The courage of this American hero is left unspoken by those who exalt Lewis (who did less for the cause).

After serving his country in the Air Force in the late '50s, James Meredith was the first Black American student admitted to the segregated University of Mississippi in 1962. This event was a flashpoint in the civil rights movement. He graduated years later, enduring daily racism, verbal taunts, and intimidation tactics that few Americans today, Black or White, have the courage or discipline to endure.

Speaking in a 2002 interview with CNN, Meredith explained the purpose for his solo effort to integrate Ol' Miss: "I was engaged in a war. I considered myself engaged in a war from day one. And my objective was to force the federal government—the Kennedy administration at that time—into a position where they would have to use the United States military force to enforce my rights as a citizen."[279]

It was James Meredith who, in 1966, began a solo 220-mile "March Against Fear" from Memphis, Tennessee to Jackson, Mississippi. He wanted to highlight racism in the South and to encourage voter registration after passage of the Voting Rights Act of 1965. He also did not want any involvement by the NAACP. He saw himself as an individual citizen demanding the same constitutional rights held by other Americans, not as a participant in the civil rights movement. In a CNN interview, Meredith said, "Nothing could be more insulting to me than the concept of civil rights. It means perpetual second-class citizenship for me and my kind."[280]

During the second day of his march, Meredith was shot by a White gunman and suffered numerous wounds. Leaders of major organizations vowed to complete the march in his name after he was taken to the hospital. While Meredith was recovering, more people from across the country joined the marchers. He later rejoined the march and with other leaders entered Jackson, Mississippi on June 26, 1966. There were an estimated 15,000 marchers, making it the largest civil rights march in Mississippi. As a result, more than 4,000 African Americans registered to vote. The march was a catalyst to continued community organizing and additional registration.[281]

To put Meredith's efforts in perspective, he singularly ended the segregation barriers in one of our country's most racist and violent regions. Meredith's 1962 University of Mississippi registration required the Kennedy administration to nationalize the Mississippi National Guard and send in federal troops. During a riot the day before his admission, two men were killed, and the White mob burned cars, pelted federal marshals with rocks, bricks, and small arms fire, and damaged university property.[282] Not only did Meredith enter this hostile environment alone, he remained and succeeded in earning his degree.

After these remarkable acts of courage, why hasn't James Meredith received the annual hero-worshipping granted John Lewis? If the goal is to exemplify the grit, tenacity, and courage of the civil rights era, why hasn't

279 CNN staff. "Mississippi and Meredith Remember." CNN.Com. October 1, 2002, On-line edition, sec. U.S. news. edition.cnn.com/2002/US/South/09/30/meredith/index.html.

280 Sheila Byrd Hardwell. "Meredith Ready to Move On." Athens Banner-Herald. September 21, 2002, sec. Local.

281 "James Meredith." Wikipedia. Wikimedia Foundation, Inc., July 20, 2018. en.wikipedia.org/wiki/James_Meredith.

282 "1962: Mississippi Race Riots over First Black Student." BBC News. October 1, 2005, Online edition, sec. On This Day. news.bbc.co.uk/onthisday/hi/dates/stories/october/1/newsid_2538000/2538169.stm.

Meredith been granted a Presidential Award, had a Navy destroyer named after him, have a prominent statue in the Washington, D.C. African American Museum, or the annual commemoration of the "Bridge Crossing" by BET, MSNBC, NBC, CBS, ABC, CNN, *The New York Times*, or *Washington Post*? Is it possible that the lack of acknowledgement of Meredith's contributions has to do with the fact that he is a Republican? Or is it possible that, unlike Lewis, Meredith would never conceive of writing for the Communist publication, the *People's Weekly World* and others? It was, after all, John Lewis, and not James Meredith, who received an endorsement from the Democratic Socialists of America Political Action Committee.[283]

Civil rights icon James Meredith represents a model for Black manhood lacking in our communities today. He represents the men of generations past who commanded the respect of their fellow Americans, not begged for or demanded it. He is a Black man who is courageous, educated, articulate, self-respecting, patriotic, God-fearing, visionary, and, most of all, fiercely independent. These attributes pose a threat to the Socialist/Marxist Left; therefore, he is purposely ignored by their propaganda arm, Black Entertainment TV (BET).

It is within this media environment of *indoctrination* that successful conservative Black Americans like Condi Rice, Clarence Thomas, Ben Carson, Star Parker, Col. Allen West, Sherriff David Clarke, Harris Faulkner, Deneen Borelli, David Webb, Lonnie Poindexter, Jason Riley, Jennifer Carroll, and many, many others are "hidden in plain sight" from Black youth.

The following statements highlight why a true American civil rights hero, James Meredith, remains a small footnote in the history books written by the Socialist/Marxist progressives.

Quotes by 1960s Civil Rights Pioneer James Meredith

> *"Nothing could be more insulting to me than the concept of civil rights. It means perpetual second-class citizenship for me and my kind."*

> *"White Liberals are the greatest enemy of African Americans."*

> *"My answer to the racial problem in America is to not deal with it at all. The founding fathers dealt with it when they made the Constitution."*

---

283   Steve Byas. "Who Is John Lewis, the Rep. Who Calls Trump Illegitimate?" *The New American.* January 17, 2017, sec. Politics. thenewamerican.com/usnews/politics/item/25154-who-is-john-lewis-the-rep-who-calls-trump-illegitimate.

CHAPTER 16

THE ROYALTY CLASS BLACK MAN: WHO'S WHO

Where is the Black leadership voice for decency and self-respect?

Black Atlanta Councilman, C. T. Martin sponsored an amendment to the city's indecency laws to ban sagging pants, which he called an epidemic. "We are trying to craft a remedy," said Mr. Martin, who sees the problem as "a prison mentality."[284]

According to Black American Judge Greg Mathis if hip-hop is the voice of a generation, ass-sagging pants is the uniform. And both are rooted in a rebellion so entrenched that many Black men proudly regurgitate, through words and attire, the telltale sign of psychological ownership. If we could delve beneath the often exploitative lyrics of poverty, violence, drug consumption, and slangin', we might recognize that the price tags on our youth's sagging jeans are nothing more than potential inmate numbers in disguise.

"In prison you aren't allowed to wear belts to prevent self-hanging or the hanging of others," Judge Greg Mathis said in a 2007 interview for *Jet Magazine*. "They take the belt and sometimes your pants hang down. Many cultures of the prison have overflowed into the community unfortunately," continued Mathis, who spent time in Detroit's Wayne County Jail as a youth. "Those who pulled their pants down the lowest and showed their behind a little more raw, that was an invitation. [The youth] don't know this part about it."

Homophobic and unsubstantiated scare tactics aside, Judge Mathis' panoramic perspective as former gangbanger-turned-judge and prison

---

284   Niko Koppel. "Are Your Jeans Sagging? Go Directly to Jail." *The New York Times*. August 31, 2007, Online edition, sec. Teacher Connections. nytimes.com/learning/teachers/featured_articles/20070831friday.html.

advocate suggest that the sagging trend is nothing more than a prison uniform encapsulating the wreckage of our communities. In urban warzones of the late '80s and early '90s, as Black men returned from lengthy crack-induced prison-bids, sagging pants were being worn on street corners simmering with freestyle cyphers and riddled with dirty needles. The beltless, low-riding style worn by "thugs" and "hustlers" became the symbolism of manhood, victimhood, and the "hood."[285]

The Royalty Class Black Man

> *"There is a class of colored people who make a business of keeping the troubles, the wrongs, and the hardships of the Negro race before the public. Having learned that they are able to make a living out of their troubles, they have grown into the settled habit of advertising their wrongs—partly because they want sympathy, and partly because it pays. Some of these people do not want the Negro to lose his grievances, because they do not want to lose their jobs."*
>
> —Booker T. Washington

Among this Elitist Royalty Class are:
- The Royalty Class Black *Politician*
- The Royalty Class Black *college Academic/Intellectual/Theorist*
- The Royalty Class Black *Entertainer*
- The Royalty Class Black *Media Pundit*

Anti-Black Policies of the Elitist Royalty Class Black Man
- **Pro-Abortion** (unlimited): Responsible for deaths since 1973 of twenty-million Black babies representing a loss of forty percent of today's Black American population.
- **Anti-School Choice** for poor Blacks: resulting in seventy-five percent of Black boys in the No-Choice State of California are unable to pass standard reading and writing tests.
- **Pro-Illegal Immigrants**: Immigration impact makes poor and working-class African-Americans the "major loser" in the workforce. A study of the New York area by Howell and Mueller found a ten-percentage-point increase in the immigrant share

---

285 Kirsten West Savali. "Sagging Pants: Prison Uniform Represents Wreckage of Black Communities?" Alternet. July 17, 2012, Online edition, sec. Human Rights. alternet.org/story/156354/sagging_pants:_prison_uniform_represents_wreckage_of_black_communities.

of an occupation's reduced wages of Black men to about five percentage points.[286]

- **Pro-Socialist/Marxist**: Anti-Black Capitalism.
- **Pro-Davis-Bacon**: A racist 1932 law designed to protect White unions against competitive Black entrepreneurs and laborers. Davis-Bacon directs all Federal construction revenue, even within the urban community, to White unions. Black entrepreneurship, at forty percent during the mid-1900s, is at race-low rate of 3.8 percent.
- **Anti-Black Family**: Pro-Welfare that destroys manhood and incentive.

The greatest destruction to the once family-centric Black community over the last fifty years has not been due to the actions of White supremacists. Despite the oppressive Jim Crow segregation laws and the presence of the terrorist group the KKK, the Black community still prospered. During the '40s, '50s, and early '60s, this community led our nation in the growth of its middle-class, of which over 40 percent of Black Americans belonged. They led our nation in the percentage of entrepreneurs, over 40 percent, and its men led all other races in the percentage committed to marriage and to higher education.

The demise of this competitive community lies at the feet of a segment of Black Americans who facilitated the "Trojan Horse" entrée of an anti-American ideology. The payment for this betrayal has been power, wealth, prestige, and media hero-worshiping. It has been this class of the Royalty Class Black man who lives the American Dream and tells those who trust them it is beyond their reach. As they kneel at the altar of Socialism/Marxism, they predictably acquiesce, granting their loyalty and support for every anti-Black policy that the Democratic Party implements. These policies have ensured hopelessness, failure, and death. This is indeed a unique class of Black folk, empathy-free with no shame.

It has been within the two-hundred-year American DNA that each generation's commitment to the following generation is that the inheriting generation will stand on higher ground. This envisioned future is not just for their children, but for the millions of others who share the future with them.

America's founding on Judeo-Christian values and principles has, as a society, separated it from every other society throughout history. This is because of the intrinsic value placed on the power of an individual's dream. It is this dream of a better life, more liberty, increased opportunity, and the pursuit of happiness that gives promise to every American. It is this promise

---

286   John Binder. "Evaluating the Damage: Immigration's Impact on Black Americans." Breitbart, January 15, 2018. breitbart.com/big-government/2018/01/15/evaluating-the-damage-immigrations-impact-black-americans.

that has been stolen and pawned by a Royalty Class of Black Americans who have shown they simply don't care.

Hip-Hop Culture and the Angry Black Man

The Black community has continued to devolve from its financial heyday of the '50s and '60s segregated communities. The introduction of the "angry Black man" gave additional speed to its downward trajectory. This was the era of the subgenre of hip-hop and gangster ("gangsta") rap beginning in the 1980s and truly gaining a foothold in the urban community in the '90s. The music genre reflected an often-violent lifestyle within American inner cities afflicted with poverty, drug use, and dealing. This destructive, stereotypical depiction of urban Black America has since been glorified in every aspect of Black entertainment and news since 2001. This was the year of the purchase of BET (Black Entertainment TV) and promotion of the rap lifestyle "on steroids" by the White liberal billion-dollar media giant, Viacom.

Though concerns from within the Black community have been raised about the increase criminality and anti-social behavior of Black boys due to the influence of the rap culture, it has been the Royalty Class Black man who has consistently praised this new destructive voice of expression. They have encouraged our Black urban youth to embrace the messaging of misogamy, self-centered and failing manhood, denigrating of womanhood, thuggery, and anger depicted by a gangster sub-culture of music and videos. Its seductive programming has even been promoted by appearances on BET by the first Black president of the United States, Barack Obama.

Royalty Class Black Academic Cornel West

Philosopher, political activist, social critic, author, public intellectual, and prominent member of the Democratic Socialists of America, academic theorist (one who comes up with abstract ideas and then spends their lives debating and trying to prove them.[287]) and elitist Cornel West describes rap music with wordy incoherence as "...the musical expression of the paradoxical cry of desperation and celebration of the Black underclass and working poor class, a cry that openly acknowledges and confronts the wave of personal cold-heartedness, criminal cruelty, and existential hopelessness in the Black ghettos."[288]

After returning from WWII, my dad left the Jim Crow South of Texas, where the pursuit of a post graduate degree was prohibited, to earn his Ph.D. in agronomy from Ohio State University in Columbus, Ohio. His older

---

287   "Theorist." Vocabulary.Com, n.d. vocabulary.com/dictionary/theorist.
288   "The Origins of Hip Hop and Rap." Research. eCheat.com, n.d. echeat.com/free-essay/The-Origins-of-Hip-Hop-and-Rap-26516.aspx.

brother also received his Ph.D. in economics from Ohio State. Their academic disciplines would serve them both well for the remainder of their lives as college professors, researchers, entrepreneurs, and mentors. Unlike in the safe world of academia where intellectuals/theorists/elitists spend their lives debating the hypothetical and demanding that impressionable teenage students see life as they do, my dad and uncle spent their lives in the real world pursuing their dreams via risk-taking Capitalism. As full time college professors and part-time entrepreneurs, they risked time and resources to give their families more financial options. They invested time and income into "at risk" children, sharing with them the pathway to success. They mentored the fatherless, exposing them to travel, people, new ideas, experiences, and more importantly, to hope. Always the underlining message of their efforts: "If I can do it, you can do it. Simply do what I have done: dream, work, serve, risk, man-up, and stand up when you fail." Unlike the Royalty Class academia, who thrive in the safe intellectual bubble of theory, my dad and his siblings established an environment of application, action, and real life consequences. In this environment was found an invaluable life-changing serendipity called *Common Sense.*

My dad spent thirty-eight years as a professor at Florida A&M University. He was raised by a generation whose mission was to empower inquisitive minds with critical thinking. He and others of this era were driven by a passion to see their students prepared to compete, contribute, and represent their race proudly. Typical of the educators of his day, his success was gauged by the success of his students to bring added value to their community.

During the last ten years of his profession, my dad often expressed a deep frustration at the increasing number of students entering college unprepared to work and learn. Without understanding the source, what he saw was the product of present day academic theorists posing as educators. These young people were graduating from high school and entering his college classroom with no critical thinking skills, no study skills, no respect for authority, and a belief that they were entitled to promotion based on time spent in class, not grades earned. Added to his frustration were college deans who demanded that these unprepared and entitled students were summarily passed through the system. Their predictable failure in the real world of competition and accountability were of no concern.

As a fitting example of the Royalty Class Black academia, Cornel West is perfectly aligned with the emotionally-charged entertainment "groupthink" mentality. Within these two worlds, academia and entertainment, traditional American success ethics—honest hard work, delayed gratification, risk taking, respect for God, country, family, and the free market—are looked upon with disdain. If Black Americans dare show any sense of independence from Black "groupthink" they are labeled as Uncle Toms and coons. White Americans, on the other hand, who dare challenge these Royalty Class Black elitists are not debated in the arena of thoughts or policies but rather are called racists and White supremacists.

The ideology of Socialism/Marxism is all-inclusive, embracing all colors, creeds, and religions, if the priority is their ideology, their class, and themselves above all else. This loyalty can be seen within the collusive nature of Black academia elitists and the wealthy White media elitist. It is here within the petri dish of Socialism/Marxism where the demeaning and racist Black stereotypes are fostered. It is with this combined effort of Black and White Socialist theorists that the most vulnerable within are targeted behind a craftily disguised Black façade. For it is behind the facade of Black employees, a Black website, promoted Black faces, and morally decrepit Black entertainers where the cowardly Wizard of Oz hides. The wizard, a wholly White-owned media giant, Viacom, has for two decades owned and controlled the messaging of Black Entertainment TV (BET) network. It is behind this trusted curtain of Blackness where the indoctrination of millions of Black urban children occurs daily. It is through this entertainment cesspool, in the homes of fatherless and uneducated children, where strategically the worst images of Black manhood and womanhood are portrayed.

Through the stealth of wealthy White Socialist/Marxists and the betrayal by Black elitists like West, generations of Black Americans have accepted a degraded view of themselves and of their country. The history of the media giant Viacom and its racist stereotypical messaging through its BET portal, which will be discussed in another chapter, as will be a noted characteristic of this elitist Black American, regardless of the industry, their shameless hypocrisy. Consistent with this class is their predictable "*do as I say, not as I do*" decree.

The empathy-free elitist Black can be counted on to deliver a different message to those they envision differently. It is the Royalty Class who *demands* of their own children that they comport themselves respectfully. They expect their own children to learn people skills and social etiquette that will allow them to compete within their interracial circle of movers and shakers. They expect nothing less than the best education for their own children in the most successful school system available—if unavailable, they will do what "No School Choice" advocate, President Obama, did for his two daughters and pony up to make sure their choice happens. It was worth the investment of 64,000 dollars a year to President Obama to ensure a quality education in an upscale private school for his two daughters.

This is the same group of Royalty Class Black politicians, educators, Socialists, theorists, political pundits, and activists who reject the same quality school choice for the "at risk" poor urban Black child. This class of "anti-school choice for poor children" represents approximately thirty percent of the Black community.

It is within this upper/middle class sector of Black Americans where we see a true betrayal of Black progress. These education obstructionists are not the 1960s White segregationists standing in the doorway; instead, they are today's empathy-free Black Socialist/Marxists. Representative of this segment of Black Americans are Democratic members of the Congressional Black Caucus. As they consistently vote against school choice for their own poor constituents, twenty-nine percent of them send their own dear children to private schools.[289] A guarantee among the Royalty Class Black politician would be more of them choosing private education for their own children if they lived in the same community as their district's poor constituents.

West and his fellow Royalty Class members are aware of the failure of the national public school system; yet, to their shame, there is absolutely *no* outcry. Faced with California's statistical data of overwhelming Black youth illiteracy, what was the response from the informed intellectual theorist West and his ilk? *Silence.* No comment, no rebuke, and no concern from this group of Black people. As the lives of millions of Black youth, past and present, are destroyed by the Democratic Party's anti-education policies, there will continue to be *no* outcry and *no* shame. It is, after all, an ideology that prioritizes "class over race / class over country" and, for the Royalty Black Class, it is their passionate loyalty to their class of elitists that only truly matters.

Choice represents free market options, empowering the customer—in this case, Black children. It ensures the customer a better product, a better experience, and a better outcome at the best cost. It is founded on the concept of competition. Choice represents a threat to the educational labor union's monopoly. It represents the potential loss of revenue and children whose parents would leave seeking better educational options if available. Our founders understood the fundamental link of our nation's freedom to an educated populace. It was Thomas Jefferson who spoke: "Ignorant and free, has not and never will be."

As Cornel West prioritizes his loyalty for labor-unionized public school's continued monopoly over the future of millions of Black children, he summarizes school choice in the following manner:

> *School choice...the stamina of the conservative ideology to privatize public education as part of its measure to eliminate many other social institutions in order to 'cut the budget.'*

Mind you they never advocate to cut spending that may affect them or their million-dollar golden parachutes. A rose by any other name still spells privatizing education.[290] The corporate reformers, er, uh, I mean the 'choice' advocates at the very top, the ones turning the wheels and playing on the fears

---

289 Grace Chen. "How Many Politicians Send Their Kids to Public Schools?" Public School Review, April 30, 2017. publicschoolreview.com/blog/how-many-politi-cians-send-their-kids-to-public-schools.

290 "School Choice? A Rose by Any Other Name Still Spells Privatizing Education." Seattle Education, n.d. seattleeducation.com/school-choice-2.

and hopes of parents who want nothing more than the best for their children, have been digging away at the pillars of public education to turn a profit, and to turn the socio-political tides of American power relationships between the one percent and the remaining ninety-nine.[291]

Note that this elitist Socialist theorist does not speak of the wellbeing of the urban child. He does not speak of alternative solutions he would seek if it were his own daughter trapped in a systemically failing educational system. For the true Socialist, it is his disdain for the private market that matters most. It is this "class over race" priority that allows an empathy-free heart to sacrifice OPC (other people's children), who are not his own and not of his class, to a life of failure. For the Royalty Black Class politician, academic intellectual/theorist, entertainer, and media talking head, the need for school choice is not a personal concern for them. Their upper/middle class income has secured them a nice home in a zip code surrounded by others with upper/middle class income. Factored into the purchase was the understanding that their dear children were assured a quality education. Having achieved this normal parental priority, they attempt to achieve what is not normal...to convince poor Black mothers their children do not have a great potential future. They *must* remain in progressive public schools, regardless of how bad they are, until their children are trained to be good Socialist/Marxists.

Anti-School Choice Socialism

As West highlights the conservative organizations that support the Black parents' educational choices, note that his animus for an organization, ALEC, supersedes the concern and wellbeing for millions of underserved Black children. These are organizations that support poor Black parents attempting to flee failing schools. By the tens of thousands, mostly single mothers are signing up their children on a list with hopes of randomly being selected for an annual school lottery.

Cornel West comments: "This takes me to an examination of other partners listed as supporters of School Choice Week. The organizations listed below have direct connections with, or strong ties to, a right-wing agenda to privatize many American institutions, including education."[292]

1. **Goldwater Institute:** Is a member of ALEC. Founded in 1988 with the blessing of the late Senator Barry Goldwater, the Goldwater Institute's mission is to advance freedom and protect the Constitution.

---

291   *Ibid.*
292   *Ibid.*

2. **Friedman Foundation**: Is a member of ALEC and funds Michelle Rhee's brainchild, Students First. Additionally, Friedman Foundation is an Indiana-based nonprofit devoted to the privatization of schools through the promotion of an educational voucher system. It is regarded as one of the most influential proponents of neo-liberal market economics.

3. **Heartland Institute**: According to ALEC Exposed, it "is a nonprofit 'think tank' that questions the reality and import of climate change, secondhand smoke health hazards, and a host of other issues that might seem to require government regulation."

4. **Connections Academy**: An online charter school company that serves as the current co-chair for the ALEC Educational Taskforce.

5. **The Heritage Foundation**: Founded in 1973, its stated mission is to formulate and promote conservative public policies based on the principles of "free enterprise, limited government, individual freedom, traditional American values, and a strong national defense." It is widely considered one of the world's most influential public policy research institutes. Heritage is also a member of ALEC.

6. **Freedom Foundation**: A non-profit organization that is member of ALEC. Media Transparency, as cited in ALEC Exposed states: "In fact, foundation tax records show that more than one-third of Evergreen's support comes from out-of-state foundations—most of them financed by advocates of anti-public education efforts, including school vouchers, or anti-labor activity including 'paycheck protection.' Several Evergreen contributors have strong ties to the State Policy Network, the national string of smaller think tanks that promote conservative agendas in their respective states."

7. **Institute for Justice**: A member of ALEC. According to its website, "The Institute for Justice has a long history of successfully defending school choice from legal attacks."

8. **Atlas Network**: "Atlas is coordinating essay contests and summer schools to encourage students to go beyond the anti-market biases of their professors and grapple with the moral issues surrounding respect for property, achievement, and free exchange."

Royalty Class Black Entertainer, Jay-Z, Prominent Elitist Democrat

"I think that hip-hop has done more for racial relations than most cultural icons save Martin Luther King, because his dream speech we realized when President Obama got elected. Racism...is a learned behavior that becomes difficult to teach in a home where hip-hop artists are respected and

celebrated. Racism is taught in the home. It's very difficult to teach racism when your kid looks up to Snoop Doggy Dogg."[293]

—Jay Z

The Burgess Owens Translation:

"Hey, my posse! I, Jay-Z, represent the quintessential Royalty Class Black man, the absolute perfect blend of the professional elitist, the professional profiteer, the wealthy Socialist entertainer, and the passionate eugenicist advocate for unlimited abortion of Black babies. I also claim a title that most of my Socialist Black brethren secretly harbor but will not share. After all, I'm wealthy enough to do so. I'm a proud Communist-sympathizing Royalty Class Black man. I couldn't wait for the opportunity to fly my private jet to Cuba and embrace the oppressive, freedom-denying, anti-Christian, murderous dictators, the Castro brothers. I'll discuss further in a minute.

"As for my adulation of my man Snoop Dogg, who I mentioned above, here's a brief sample of his genius. As I mentioned, it's very difficult to teach racism as you listen to my homie:

> *"It's off the limbo with Timbo, you m.....f... bimbo,*
> *So quit knockin' at my window, you nympho."*

[A description of the lyrics to this solo was described in 2008's *Rolling Stone*:

> *"The album's lyrics caused some controversy, as the subject matter included homophobia and violent representations. It was noted that the album was a 'frightening amalgam of inner-city street gangs that includes misogynist sexual politics and violent revenge scenarios.'" [294]]*

"Yo, enough about Snoop Dog, let's talk about me. My real luck was that I was able to begin a very profitable career as a full scale, unabashed narcissist and misogamist and had the full backing of a 100 percent White-owned record

---

293   OWN. "Jay-Z: 'Hip Hop Has Done More for Racial Relations Than Most Cultural Icons' (VIDEO)." *The Huffington Post.* January 5, 2015, sec. Politics. huffingtonpost.com/2015/01/05/jay-z-hip-hop-impact_n_6391274.html.

294   Havelock Nelson. "The Chronic." *Rolling Stone Magazine,* March 18, 1993. 6/21/2008. rollingstone.com/music/music-album-reviews/the-chronic-250626.

label. Imagine belittling, degrading, and using Black women at my whim and getting paid millions of dollars to do it!

"I was also fortunate that instead of condemnation from my Royalty Class Black brethren, I received praise as I pushed Black-denigrating album after album into my own community with such names as *Jigga That Nigga* or *Ain't No Nigga*. And who can forget my linguistic masterpiece, *Jigga What, Jigga Who (Originator 99)*, a song whose title was changed to avoid airing the word nigga?

"Hey, good marketing strategy, because as a bestseller, my young audience heard it instead over and over in their own homes and at my sold-out performances. As you read the lyrics to my big hit *Big Pimpin'*, do you wonder why pre-teen and teenage Black boys who grew up listening to my message now endearingly call each other niggas, and now have such utter disrespect and disdain for Black women? I can proudly say that was me. I did that!

"Here's a tame taste of my genius. As you see, I've proven to those who view me as a role model that there is no need for education, a grasp of the English language, respect, or classiness in the world of rap:

Nigga what, nigga who?
Nigga what, nigga who?
Switcha flow, getcha dough
Can't f...with this Roc-a-Fella s...doe
Switcha flow, getcha dough
Can't f...with this Roc-a-Fella s...doe

"In my ascension to mega-wealth, I am now worth over five-hundred-million dollars! As an entrepreneur and investor, I co-own the 40/40 Club, and I am the co-creator of the clothing line Rocawear.[295] I am the former president of Def Jam Recordings, co-founder of Roc-A-Fella Records,[296] and the founder of Roc Nation. I once had a small share in the Brooklyn Nets, founded the sports agency Roc Nation Sports, and am now a certified NBA, MLB, and NFL sports agent.

"Now, you might think this ironic, but I take every opportunity afforded me to state for the record and to my fans who adore me that though free enterprise has given me wealth, power, and influence over so many of my hopeless peeps, I absolutely *love* the oppressive Communist regimes. I'm just saying!

"I've been very 'lucky' to be paid with enormous fame and fortune just for filling my community with degrading, misogynous, filth, i.e., my rap music. By the way, luck is the word I use as false humility to hide the self-acceptance of

295 "Jay Z." Wikipedia. Wikimedia Foundation, Inc., July 31, 2018. en.wikipedia.org/wiki/Jay_Z.

296 "Roc-A-Fella Records." Wikipedia. Wikimedia Foundation, Inc., August 7, 2018. en.wikipedia.org/wiki/Roc-A-Fella_Records.

my superior intelligence, genius, and talent! I'm *lucky* that as I began my career as a drug dealer, I'm now a quintessential member of the Royalty Black Class and I can totally dodge all responsibility for my past words, actions, and deeds.

"I'm *lucky* to be in an industry that grants people like me an opportunity to re-define truth by simply repeating untruths over and over through my very successful records and concerts. For example, I have the platform to now blame my actions as a self-serving, narcissistic, woman-demeaning drug dealer in my '80s NY hood on President Reagan, Oliver North, and Iran-Contra. I know, I know. I realize it might be hard to accept that I'm a victim of those rascally Republicans when I'm so willing to take full credit for my lucky decisions in becoming a mega multi-millionaire. You see, my history of past criminal actions wasn't my fault, but the fault of an evil White president who I never met, one of his White generals who I never met, and a group of brown Nicaraguans ('rebels') who were fighting against a Communist regime, supported by my Cuban friends.

"Look. I understand that to the 'common man' this logic might not make sense, but you got to remember two important points. First, my audience has never been the common man, but the poor, hopeless, uneducated, and angry Black man. And, second, as a perfect blend of the Royalty Class Black entertainer and problem profiteer, logic is not expected of me, not when I can redefine truth by repeating anything over and over again, regardless of how ludicrous it is. *Hmmmm...Ludacris...*that's the name of one of my other multi-millionaire rapper peeps! But I digress. Here is an example of this line of thinking that is now the 'gospel truth' in the hood. After all, I've been in their heads since '99. Yo, bro...pretty remarkable power I got! Check it."

> *Blame Reagan for making me into a monster*
> *Blame Oliver North and Iran-Contra*
> *I ran contraband that they sponsored*
> *Before this rhyming stuff we was in concert.*[297]

"I was lucky that the more my records and videos sold, the wealthier me and my homies got. Imagine the power and influence I have on thousands upon thousands of young Black boys mimicking my angry performances, disrespecting women, disrespecting authority, and wanting to grow up to be just like me. Because of me and my gangsta rap posse, young Black men now embrace the sub-culture of 'prison wear,' beltless pants over their butts, even before they can do real jail time.

"For the cause, I'd appreciate if you don't mention that I have an education that allows me to read, speak proper English, and do math. Let's keep as our

---

297   "Blue Magic (Song)." Wikipedia. Wikimedia Foundation, Inc., September 17, 2017. en.wikipedia.org/wiki/Blue_Magic_(song).

little secret I believe it was beneficial to *my* family to give my wife and children the respect of my name through marriage. And please don't let our angry anti-White Black boys back home know I surround myself 24/7 with my White liberal friends.

"Lookit, it's good publicity to claim I was part of an all-Black start-up enterprise, but we began as broke Black brothers. If it weren't for early financial backing from the White owners of the record labels, Payday Records[298] and Universal Music Group,[299] I'd still be hustling in New York or probably in jail. It was good for me that these rich White liberals saw a way to a *big* payoff by paying me to push degrading and misogynous filth into my own community. It's more respectable than selling hard drugs, right?

"Our White financial backer (UMG), headquartered in Santa Monica, California, has reported revenue of over 6.5 billion dollars. They made a good bet to back my rapper posse and me as we push our decadent gangster rap genre into the Black neighborhood. I'll never have to worry about another payday after investing a couple of decades into fun, drugs, an assortment of women, and coming off as an angry, put upon, and discriminated-against Black man. I must admit there was a lot of smiling going on away from the stage with my White financial backers as we all watched our bank accounts blossom!

"You see, I've made mad bucks tapping into and rapping about hopelessness and the abuse of the Black race by the racist White system. Between you and me, it was the liberal White music industry that gave me my break to deliver my message of hopelessness.[300] I have proven through my 'yo man' cursing/rapping example of filthy Ebonics language that urban Black boys can find happiness within a misogamist and decadent lifestyle. I've proven that they don't have to seek success in the traditional manner of acting White but instead do it the way I did...*rapping your way to stardom*. I discovered the angrier I was and the more disrespectful I was toward my peeps and to our Black sisters, the more my White backers loved and promoted my work.

"As an all-star rapper and entertainment mogul, one of my most remarkable triumphs over the span of two decades has been the impact I've had on our country's most respected industry brand, the National Football League. NFL players in earlier decades were revered as role models for America's youth. Today, teams are forced to deal with chronic behavioral issues that require

---

298   "Payday Records." Wikipedia. Wikimedia Foundation, Inc., July 9, 2018. en.wikipedia.org/wiki/Payday_Records.

299   "Universal Music Group." Wikipedia. Wikimedia Foundation, Inc., August 5, 2018. en.wikipedia.org/wiki/Universal_Music_Group.

300   Bandini. "Jay Z's First Record Ever Was in 1986...And It Was Not Hawaiian Sophie. Take a Listen (Audio)." Music news. Ambrosia for Heads, June 18, 2015. ambrosiaforheads.com/2015/06/most-heads-dont-know-that-jay-zs-first-record-was-in-1986-audio.

hiring full-time staff whose sole responsibility is to control, hide, or cover up criminal behavior of some of our nation's wealthiest young Black men. Though they be worth millions and achieved the American Dream, they have not been trained to respect authority and lack both soft skills and critical thinking skills.

"Ever wonder why these wealthy Black athletes who 'finally arrive' continue to act-out as criminals? It is important to understand that the ingrained self-perception doesn't simply change because the bank account is stacked with cash. Has anyone considered the irony that I, as a former gangster rapper and drug dealer with a criminal record linked to a nightclub stabbing, could also become a successful certified sports agent in baseball, basketball, and football? Consider my audience. These athletes are now the same fatherless Black boys who listened to my music years ago. It was my message that molded their lives, their self-identities, man. Their racial identities and their perception of what it takes to be a man. So, come on, it's only natural I use that connection for my successful entrée into their sports world.

"Of course, the consequences of the anti-social behavior they've learned through my peeps and me will impact them far past their productive athletic years. As a Royalty Class Black entertainer, though, that's got nothing to do with me. Once I get my commissioned percentage from their contract, I'm done. Unless, of course, they become superstars, at which time they're invited to come hang in my spacious, wealthy, White-integrated community full of other liberal superstars. I'll even encourage these former urban city superstars to put their children in the same schools with my precious children. They qualify for my offer, of course, since they can afford to live in my zip code, know what I mean?

"As a member of the Royalty Class, my hope is I never lose the influence I have over those who still adore me, the hopeless segment of the Black community. For them only will I suggest that my acquired superior business intelligence, work ethic, and strategy is pure luck. And, as one of America's wealthiest men, I will point to my accumulation of wealth to remind everyone I am truly one of America's greatest Royalty Class Black men.

"My elitist standing allows me to boldly embrace my anti-America ideology and show my love and respect for my oppressive Communist comrades. It really does not matter to me that Human Rights Watch has accused the Cuban government of systematic human rights abuses, including arbitrary imprisonment, unfair trials, and extrajudicial execution. It doesn't matter that, as an officially atheist country since 1992, Cuba limits freedom of expression, association, assembly, movement, and the press. It doesn't matter that I would not have had an iota of a chance to become wealthy in Cuba like I did in America. And it doesn't matter how many thousands upon thousands of Cubans have lost their lives attempting to escape its oppression, or that the seeking of civil rights as a Black Cuban is not tolerated."

*[If you're a Black Cuban and dare to raise race as an is-
sue, you go to jail. Jorge Luis García Pérez, a well-known
Afro-Cuban human rights and democracy activist who was
locked up in prison for seventeen years, in an interview with
the Florida-based Directorio Democratico Cubano, said,
"...authorities in my country have never tolerated...a Black
person [to] oppose the revolution. During the trial, the color
of my skin aggravated the situation. Later, when I was mistreated in prison by guards, they always referred to me as
being Black."[301]]*

"Oppression under Communist regimes means nothing to me and my
fellow Royalty Class Black men. Since we share the same ethos, I share a love
for my Communist Cuban comrades. Our atheist Marxist dictators, the Castro
brothers, treated my wife and me very well. That is the bottom line. As everyone
should remember when thinking about me and my awesome success, at the
end of the day, it truly has always been ALL ABOUT ME!"

Royalty Class Black Intellectual, Michael Eric Dyson, Prominent Elitist Democrat

Michael Eric Dyson is a renowned scholar, ordained Baptist minister,
and public intellectual.[302] Suggestion, always pause when elitists refer to
themselves as "intellectuals" or "academic theorists;" it's a confirmation of
their self-acceptance as an elitist Royalty Class Socialist.

*"Before we discard the genre, we should understand that
gangster rap often reaches higher than its ugliest, lowest
common denominator. Misogyny, violence, materialism, and
sexual transgression are not its exclusive domain. At its best,
this music draws attention to 'complex dimensions of ghetto
life' ignored by many Americans."*

—Michael Eric Dyson

It is very unlikely that the Royalty Class Black intellectual, Dyson, from the
comforts of his mixed middle-class environment, would tolerate his wife and
daughters being referred to as he justifies hip-hop artists addressing young

---

301   "Human Rights in Cuba." Wikipedia. Wikimedia Foundation, Inc., August 6, 2018.
       en.wikipedia.org/wiki/Human_rights_in_Cuba.
302   "Michael Eric Dyson." African American Literature Book Club, March 29, 2018.
       aalbc.com/authors/author.php?author_name=Michael+Eric+Dyson.

girls and women in the 'complex dimensions of the ghetto.' As he expresses his low expectations for urban manhood, it is guaranteed that his own son would not be excused for disrespect that foreshadows failure. Dyson exemplifies the empathy-free disdain of the Royalty Black Class elitists for those deemed below their exalted class.

It is the Royalty Class Black intellectual who colludes with the Royalty Class Black entertainer and Royalty Class Black politician as they show their unrelenting loyalty to White Socialist political leaders. As they watch the misery of their own race, mandated to remain ignorant, illiterate, and hopeless due to anti-Black legislation, they feel no shame. It is this class, not the racist Southern Democratic of the 1960s, who will continue to stand, at the bidding of White Socialist labor unions, in the doorway of school choice for our poor. As he encourages the proliferation of the demeaning gangster rap genre into these same poor households, Dyson's statement does ring true...it is indeed *his* Royalty Black Class that has "ignored" the complex dimensions of ghetto life.

> *"Proponents have bought the myth that sagging pants represents an offensive lifestyle which leads to destructive behavior."*
>
> —Michael Eric Dyson in The New York Times[303]

The Burgess Owens Translation

"Listen, my young Black brothers. Feel free to do whatever you want as long as you don't do it around me and my family. I love your 'in the hood' expressiveness and raunchy anti-establishment attitude, but because of the *'complex dimensions of ghetto life'* I've referred to in my writings, I can't afford to have you or your kind in the same schools with my dear children. I sincerely appreciate your gangster anti-social sub-culture and your willingness to rally, register, and 'Rap to Vote' for my Royalty Class Black political friends every election cycle when we need you. For that I will defend your freedom of expression to pull your pants down as far as you want, speak in public with as much filth as you want, have as many baby mommas as you want, and do as many drugs as you want. I'll even work with my Royalty Class politician friends to legalize marijuana and make the entire hood 'drug-friendly' for you. After all, who needs a clear head and cognizant thinking where you're going?

"On a side note, I'm teaching my son to pull up his pants, to speak proper English without cursing, and to always make a good impression around the White people responsible for my paychecks. I expect my kids to have an even better economic future than me, so I can't afford to have you mess them up with your gangster culture. On that note, I hope you understand that I will

---

303   Niko Koppel. "Are Your Jeans Sagging? Go Directly to Jail."

guarantee you big time problems if you ever attempt to communicate with my daughter. I simply can't have you bring your 'complex dimensions' of ghetto life around my children. Love you, my poor Black people, but sorry, can't have you messing up my good thing."

Dutiful Silence

As Royalty Class Black professionals continue to promote anti-social, anti-authority, anti-White, anti-American, anti-flag sentiment subculture into the urban community, it's important to track their motivation. Follow the money, power, and fame, and you'll uncover their true beliefs. You'll find at the roots of the Royalty Class Black man remnants of 1900s eugenicist W.E.B Boise's Talented Tenth. It is the low expectations and disdain for those who are not smart, connected, talented, or wealthy enough to enter their elite circle.

The financial exploitation of this most "at-risk" segment of the Black community is where the Royalty Class Black entertainer stepped up to the plate. He specifically targets his message to poor, uneducated, hopeless young Black audiences, delivering his sub-culture message through music, video, and cable TV.

BET Black owner Robert Johnson, and others like him, has joined the mega-wealthy club of the rich and famous. All that was asked of him was to sell to White Socialist Leftists the future of millions upon millions of his own race. He is the prototype of the Royalty Class Black billionaire who, without any concern for the welfare of generations to come, willingly facilitates the message of hip-hop, gangster rap, and the misogynistic, self-deprecating messages that accompany it. Angry but popular Black artists such as Ice-T, LL Cool J, Sister Souljah, and others show off their rich and famous lifestyles, as the White-owned entertainment media has promoted them as true Black role models. Devoid of character and morality, the influence of these role models, as could be predicted, eventually took root. Young Black boys looking for direction, acceptance, and respect, began to act on the violence and narcissistic lifestyle highlighted by their Royalty Black Class entertainment heroes. The poisonous influence of gangster rap will be imprinted for generations on the soul of the Black community and will be seen in the lives of millions of Black boys who will fail to grow up to be productive men. The pay-off to the now-rich and famous Royalty Black Class entertainer, whose personal wealth can be counted in the tens and hundreds of millions of dollars, will never justify the sacrifice of destroyed lives they're accountable for.

For millions of Black boys and girls, the messengers have betrayed them. As they die by the thousands in the streets of America's urban cities, the Royalty Black Class entertainers are protesting at the Emmy Awards about the lack of appreciation the White liberal entertainment industry. After all, Affirmative Action was passed to guarantee them a rationed number of Emmys, correct? In the meantime, Black men continue to abandon their children at rates unimaginable in another ethnicity, and the Black Royalty Class entertainers remain dutifully silent.

Within a single generation, the Royalty Black Class entertainer has facilitated a change within the Black community that the KKK of the 1900s, the denigrating laws of Jim Crow, and the murderous eugenic policies of Margaret Sanger failed to do over a one-hundred-year effort. They have overseen and successfully facilitated the devaluation of Black manhood. As can be seen throughout its long and sordid history of the ideology of Socialism/Marxism, when there is a void of manhood, the destruction of society follows.

What is Gangsta Rap?

Gangsta rap,[304] or gangster rap, is a subgenre of hip-hop music[305] street gangs[306] and the 'thug' or *'gangsta'* lifestyle. The genre evolved from *hardcore hip-hop* into a distinct form, pioneered in the mid-1980s by rappers such as Schoolly D[307] and Ice-T,[308] and was popularized in the latter part of the 1980s by groups like N.W.A.[309] After the national attention that Ice-T and N.W.A attracted in the late '80s and early '90s, gangsta rap became the most commercially lucrative subgenre of hip-hop. Many (if not most) gangsta rap artists openly boast of their associations with various active street gangs as part of their artistic image, with the Bloods[310] and Crips[311] being the most commonly represented. Gangsta rap is closely related to other indigenous gang and crime-oriented forms of music, such as the narcocorrido genre of northern Mexico.

304   Henry Adaso. "Gangsta Rap: What Is Gangsta Rap?" Learning. ThoughtCo.com, March 18, 2017. thoughtco.com/what-is-gangsta-rap-2857307.

305   "Hip Hop Music." Wikipedia. Wikimedia Foundation, Inc., August 5, 2018. en.wikipedia.org/wiki/Hip_hop_music.

306   "Gang." Wikipedia. Wikimedia Foundation, Inc., July 30, 2018. en.wikipedia.org/wiki/Gang.

307   "Schoolly D." Wikipedia. Wikimedia Foundation, Inc., January 10, 2018. en.wikipedia.org/wiki/Schoolly_D.

308   "Ice-T." Wikipedia. Wikimedia Foundation, Inc., August 8, 2018. en.wikipedia.org/wiki/Ice-T.

309   "N.W.A." Wikipedia. Wikimedia Foundation, Inc., August 7, 2018. en.wikipedia.org/wiki/N.W.A.

310   "Bloods." Wikipedia. Wikimedia Foundation, Inc., August 7, 2018. en.wikipedia.org/wiki/Bloods.

311   "Crips." Wikipedia. Wikimedia Foundation, Inc., July 11, 2018. en.wikipedia.org/wiki/Crips.

After decades of gangsta rap and subculture propaganda from Royalty Black Class entertainers, the young Black male now lacks the most basic skills required for success. They lack social skills, cognizant thinking skills, communication skills, and a mindset open to education.

As stated in Jason Riley's book, *Please Stop Helping Us: How Liberals Make It Harder for Blacks to Succeed,* we now have allowed a culture within the Black community that our Black boys have embraced with zeal. A culture that takes pride in ignorance and mocks learning. And with the acceptance of a culture of ignorance comes a chronic lack of self-esteem.

Meanwhile, young Black females run circles around them in every category that requires initiative and gumption. The new generation of young Black males expects their girlfriends to get a good education, have their babies, then "man-up" and provide them with a secure life. Nowhere have they been trained to accept the responsibility of self-improvement and of a commitment to marriage and family. Yet, as they continue to define these actions as "manly," the Royalty Class remains dutifully silent.

To successfully resurrect the Black community, there must be a clear and succinct message to the young men. The message must be direct and measured with high expectations that tap into their greatness within. They must be helped to once again appreciate their opportunities and to envision even greater ones.

Royalty Class Black Politician, President Barack Obama

Within the urban Black community, the status of the Royal Class Black man/woman is one of presence, promises, power, and prominence. This class has grown exponentially within the Democratic Party over the last sixty years, yet the promise of increased race prosperity and opportunity has not materialized. Between 1970 and 2012, the number of Black elected officials rose from fewer than 1,500 to more than ten thousand. Conventional wisdom would suggest that these political gains would lead to economic gains. However, that has not proven to be the case. What can be surmised over the last six decades is that with the increase in Black political power has *not* come the reciprocal increase of empowerment for the common Black American.[312] The empirical data shows rather that with the increase in number and power of the Black elite political class, there has been an exponential decrease in the life, liberty, and pursuit of happiness for the poor they oversee.

There is no better example of the wide destructive path left behind by the Royalty Class Black Man on the urban community than by chronicling the journey of Barack Hussein Obama. It is a journey of an obscure community

---

312   Jason Riley. "Blacks in Power Don't Empower Blacks." Education. PragerU, March 26, 2018. prageru.com/videos/Blacks-power-dont-empower-Blacks.

organizer who rose within twelve years through the Democratic ranks to become the 44th President of the United States. It is now through hindsight and empirical data that Americans can measure the difference in his rhetorical promises of hope and change to the reality and impact of his policies on the lives and future of millions of Americans.

For many Black and White Americans, President Barack Obama was perceived as a savior whose election to the nation's highest office would be the dawn of the Earthly paradise Shangri-La, a mythical Himalayan utopia—a permanently happy land.[313] This vision was given credence with his prophecy in 2008, as President-elect, that his victory marked "the moment when the rise of the oceans began to slow and our planet began to heal."[314] Unfortunately for the poor urban neighborhoods throughout this country, Chicago, Detroit, Ferguson, Newark, Baltimore, Philadelphia, Dallas, and every other predominantly Black community, the only noticeable rise was within the hearts of urban Black Americans. A rise in anger, frustration, hopelessness, bitterness, anti-Americanism, and anti-White racism.

As we review President Obama's policies as a senator and president, his impact on those who trusted him most can be evaluated with statistical data. What is a constant over his twelve years as a politician, once stripped of its rhetorical hyperbole, is the prioritization of presence, promises, power, and prominence of the elitist class over the good of the rest of his own race. Also consistent was the advocacy for policies that were statistically detrimental to his race and guaranteed to never impact the lives of his own dear children.

Within this segment of this book will be policies that highlight the empathy free heart of the Royalty Class Black Man when given power to impact for good or ill the lives of the most vulnerable and at risk. Policies that drive the opportunities for life, liberty, and the pursuit of happiness can be captured in simple decisions. Should there be protection for a baby girl or boy who has been born alive after the mother chose to abort it? Should there be a guarantee for the best possible education for the children of caring but poor parents, who dream that their child will break out of the poverty cycle that they were not able to? And should poor families and "at risk" children be granted an opportunity to live in environments that are safe not only from criminals, but also from profit-seeking Black elitist slumlords?

Within this chapter will be witnessed the misery wrought upon the poor and dependent Black Americans by a Black politician they trusted.

---

313   "Shangri-La." Wikipedia. Wikimedia Foundation, Inc., August 6, 2018. en.wikipedia.org/wiki/Shangri-La.

314   Michael Bastasch. "Has Obama Fulfilled His Promise to Slow Sea-Level Rise?" Political news. Dailycaller.com, April 22, 2015. dailycaller.com/2015/04/21/has-obama-fulfilled-his-promise-to-slow-sea-level-rise.

Royalty Class Black Politician

Anti-Poor Black Policies

1. Pro Unlimited Abortion	(Anti-Poor Black Life)*
2. Pro Socialism/Marxism Policies	(Anti-Black Capitalism)
3. Pro Davis-Bacon Law	(Anti-Poor Black Enterprise/Labor)
4. Pro Minimum Wage	(Anti-Poor Black Low Skill labor)
5. Pro Gay Marriage	(Anti-Judeo-Christian Values)
6. Pro "Illegal" Immigration	(Anti-Poor Black Low-Skill Jobs)
7. Pro Education Labor Union	(Anti- Poor Black School Choice)

The Born-Alive Infants Protection Act (BAIPA)

Illinois and Federal legislature eventually passed the BAIPA, making illegal the abortion industry's practice of killing babies born alive but unwanted by their mother "by neglect." Three attempts were made in the Illinois legislation in 2001, 2002, and 2003, to provide legal protection for "babies born alive." All three attempts to grant these babies protection was voted *against* by then-Illinois Senator Obama.[315] Predominantly Black American baby girls and boys born alive after an abortion attempt were often put inside a janitorial closet, refused medical attention and nutrients, and died alone.

These bills were opposed by the majority of the Democrat Party because the original bills could have been construed to say that a pre-birth fetus was a "person protected by law." So the bill in Congress was altered to address that concern by adding a neutrality clause that made it clear the bill would not protect a fetus *in utero*.[316]

Senator Obama stated that he voted against the Illinois bill because the Federal neutrality clause was not included and that therefore he could not support the bill. Turns out he is not telling the truth about this fact. Even worse, he knows better because he was part of the legislative committee that added that clause to the very bill he voted against in 2003. Obama not only was part of that committee adding the Federal neutrality clause to the Illinois bill, he was the chairman of that committee.

The documents prove that in March 2003, Senator Obama, then chairman of the Illinois state Senate Health and Human Services Committee, presided

---

315 Warner Todd Huston. "Obama Lied About Vote Against Live-Birth Abortion Ban, Media Mum." Conservative issues. NewsBusters (blog), August 13, 2008. newsbusters.org/blogs/nb/warner-todd-huston/2008/08/13/obama-lied-about-vote-against-live-birth-abortion-ban-media.

316 *Ibid.*

over a meeting in which the neutrality clause, copied verbatim from the federal bill, was added to the state BAIPA, with Obama voting in support of adding the revision. Yet, immediately afterwards, Obama led the committee Democrats in voting against the amended bill, and it was killed, 6-4.

Less than two years after this meeting, Obama publicly claimed that he opposed the state BAIPA because it lacked the neutrality clause, and that had he been a member of Congress he would have supported the federal version because it contained the clause.[317]

The D.C. Opportunity Scholarship Program: Anti- Poor Black School Choice and President Obama

The view of elitist class over race was best summarized in 1900 by eugenicist, abortionist, and Black Socialist/Marxist W.E.B. Du Bois. He confirmed his belief in "the rule of inequality, that inborn genetic fitness (intelligence) was the basis for educating some and not others," and echoed the sentiments of Margaret Sanger that "millions of Black youth were fitted to know and some to dig."[318]

The D.C. Opportunity Scholarship Program provided scholarships to low-income children in Washington, D.C. for tuition and other fees at participating private schools. The program was the first federally-funded school voucher program in the United States. It was first approved in 2003 and allowed to expire in 2009.[319] A U.S. Department of Education report found that students in the nation's capital provided with vouchers through the D.C. Opportunity Scholarship program had made statistically significant gains in reading achievement.[320]

A 2010 study published by Patrick Wolf of the University of Arkansas found that the scholarship recipients had graduation rates of 91 percent. The graduation rate for D.C. public schools was 56 percent, and it was 70 percent for students who entered the lottery for a voucher but didn't win.[321]

---

317   *Ibid.*

318   Tanya L. Green. "The Negro Project: Margaret Sanger's Eugenic Plan for Black Americans." Citizen Review Online, May 10, 2001. citizenreviewonline.org/special_issues/population/the_negro_project.htm.

319   "D.C. Opportunity Scholarship Program." Wikimedia Foundation, Inc., August 26, 2017. en.wikipedia.org/wiki/D.C._Opportunity_Scholarship_Program.

320   Peter Roff. "Obama Wrong on D.C. School Vouchers and Hypocritical, Just Like Congress." *U.S. News & World Report.* April 22, 2009, Online edition, sec. Opinion. usnews.com/opinion/blogs/peter-roff/2009/04/22/obama-wrong-on-dc-school-vouchers-and-hypocritical-just-like-congress.

321   Jason L. Riley. "Obama's War on School Vouchers." *The Wall Street Journal.* February 14, 2012, sec. Opinion. wsj.com/articles/SB10001424052970204883304577223290975405900.

Barack Obama was inaugurated as the 44th President of the United States on Tuesday, January 20, 2009. In less than six weeks of lifting his hand to take the oath of office, the Democratic party had passed a new 3.8 trillion dollar budget eliminating all funding for a school voucher program in Washington, D.C., even though they were producing *significantly* higher graduation rates than the D.C. public school average.

Though local Democrats, independents, and Republican politicians supported the program due to its overwhelming graduation success rates at the behest of the National Education Association and civil liberty groups including People for the American Way, Senate Majority Whip Richard Durbin (D-Ill.) inserted language into the 410 billion dollar omnibus spending bill effectively terminating the program unless Congress reauthorized it. The Democratic-controlled House and Senate did not. There were 216 Black students who had their scholarship revoked for the 2009-2010 school year.[322] At the same time, President Obama was willing to shell out 64,000 dollars annually to give his two daughters opportunities for quality educations.

Columnist Juan Williams called the decision to end the program, "Obama's outrageous sin against our kids." He also stated: "The cause of my upset is watching the key civil rights issue of this generation—improving big city public school education—get tossed overboard by political gamesmanship.... If there is one goal that deserves to be held above day-to-day partisanship and pettiness of ordinary politics, it is the effort to end the scandalous poor level of academic achievement and abysmally high drop-out rates for America's Black and Hispanic students."[323]

The D.C. voucher program provided District parents desperate to find a quality education for their children a much-needed lifeline. Unfortunately, as Williams pointed out, the program has fallen victim to the education politics. "With no living, breathing students profiting from the program to give it a face and stand and defend it, the Congress has little political pressure to put new money into the program," Williams wrote. The political pressure will be coming exclusively from the teachers' unions who oppose the vouchers, just as they oppose No Child Left Behind, charter schools, and every other effort at reforming public schools that continue to fail the nation's most vulnerable young people, low-income Blacks and Hispanics.

"The National Education Association and other teachers' unions have put millions into Democrats' congressional campaigns," Williams continued, "because they oppose Republican efforts to challenge unions on their

---

322 Sheryl Blunt. "Not Free to Choose." *The Weekly Standard*. October 7, 2009. week-lystandard.com/not-free-to-choose/article/270807.

323 Juan Williams. "Obama's Outrageous Sin Against Our Kids." Fox News. April 20, 2009, sec. Opinion. foxnews.com/opinion/2009/04/20/obamas-outrageous-sin-kids.html.

resistance to school reform and specifically their refusal to support ideas such as performance-based pay for teachers who raise students' test scores."

Education politics are big business in America, often pitting institutionalized interests like the NEA against parents and kids. Unfortunately, in today's environment, far too many parents can take a principled stance, righting the wrongs, but simply don't; instead, they "opt out" of these controversial discussions/debates. After all, their children's education, due to their personal income, will never be in jeopardy.

A report from The Heritage Foundation, a conservative thinktank that supports education reform, found that forty four percent of current United States senators and thirty-six percent of current members of the U.S. House of Representatives "had at one time sent their children to private schools."

"Among the general public," the report says, "only eleven percent of American students attend private schools." What's more, the Heritage report found that one-fifth of members of the 11th Congress attended private high schools themselves, which is nearly twice the rate of the public at large.[324]

The concept of freedom has been the keystone of the American Way since its founding. Therefore, deeply ensconced within our nation's core and highlighted by the opening words of the US Constitution that "all men are created equal" is the belief that the American Dream remains available to all, regardless of race, creed, or color. All who seek it must be willing to dream, work, and overcome all barriers to prosperity, reached only through the doorway of an active and engaged mind. An educated mind is the greatest weapon against the forces and ideologies that seek to enslave. A mind granted the training and blessings of critical thinking cannot be shackled. Once capable of dreaming outside of its present limits, the critical thinking, seeking mind will dream its way beyond its present limitations. To paraphrase the warning of American Founder, Thomas Jefferson, "If a nation expected to be ignorant and free...it expects what never was and never will be."

Ignorance, on the other hand, is the cornerstone of the Socialist/ Marxist Left; this is the source of their unfettered and evil power. As was in the antebellum south, Democratic slave masters ensured themselves a peaceful and prosperous existence by demanding ignorance and a compliant groupthink mentality among their slaves. Almost one-third of all Southern families owned slaves—in Mississippi and South Carolina, this approached more like one-half. The total number of slave owners was 385,000 (including, in Louisiana, some free Negroes).[325] The number of slaves in America in 1850 numbered 1,775,515 in the North and 3,950,511 in the South. In 1860, slaves

---

324   Peter Roff. "Obama Wrong on D.C. School Vouchers and Hypocritical, Just Like Congress."
325   "Selected Statistics on Slavery in the United States." Metrics. Civil War Causes, n.d. civilwarcauses.org/stat.htm.

represented about thirty-three percent of the Southern population. Slaves worked in industry, did domestic work, and grew a variety of food crops.[326]

By controlling a population that outnumbered it fifteen to one, the minority of slave owners wrought unconscionable evil and misery upon a population of six million. Laws were legislated to punish with harsh beatings or death those who dared educate and empower slaves. Blacks and Whites throughout this era continued to risk and circumvent these laws, teaching them anyway.

This post-slavery, anti-poor education scheme was witnessed with the 2008 attack on Washington, D.C.'s poor. At that time, an extremely successful voucher program for two-thousand poor Black children per year was defunded by the Democratic party, led by our first Black president. The Democratic anti-Black education scheme was seen again in 2017 with the DOE report that seventy-five percent of Black boys in California were deemed illiterate.

Though the methods since the 1800s have evolved to high-tech neglect, the endgame of the Democratic Royalty Class has remained the same for over 150 years to ensure those who live within the urban plantation boundaries remain ignorant, hopeless, and mentally and spiritually enslaved.

The Royalty Class Black "Slum Lords"

> When faced with the choice of supporting his well-connected developer friends making millions in Chicago's Plan for Transformation, or his district's poorest public housing residents, Senator Obama, former community organizer, was an expedient politician. He followed the money.[327]
>
> —*Chicago History: From the New Deal to the Plan for Transformation*[328]

In 1937, the Chicago Housing Authority (CHA) became the municipal corporation that administered the city's public housing. Its first project, Cabrini-Green,[329] was built in 1942. The huge Robert Taylor Homes complex was completed in 1962.

---

326 "Number of Slaves in America in 1850." Politics. Infomory, September 23, 2013. infomory.com/numbers/number-of-slaves-in-america-in-1850.

327 Lee Cary. "Obama and Daley's Public Housing Plan." American Thinker. September 23, 2008, sec. Articles. americanthinker.com/articles/2008/09/obama_and_daleys_public_housin.html.

328 *Ibid.*

329 "Cabrini-Green Homes." Wikipedia. Wikimedia Foundation, Inc., August 5, 2018. en.wikipedia.org/wiki/Cabrini%E2%80%93Green_Homes.

In 1966, in *Gautreaux v. Chicago Housing Authority*, Dorothy Gautreaux and a group of African-American CHA residents filed suits against the CHA and the Secretary of Housing and Urban Development (HUD), claiming that the CHA, with HUD support, violated the equal protection clause and Title VI of the 1964 Civil Rights Act by locating all of its public housing properties in African-American communities. The case would move in and out of the courts for the next thirty years.[330]

In 1987, U.S. District Judge Marvin Aspen appointed the Habitat Corp. to oversee new CHA construction to assure the housing was integrated. Until 2008, Barack Obama's senior advisor, Valerie Jarrett, was CEO of Habitat.

In 1999, Chicago launched its Plan for Transformation—the biggest project for reconstruction of public housing in the history of the United States. The old New Deal approach had failed miserably, and the promise was that the new plan would fix things.

The Chicago Housing Authority's (CHA) Plan for Transformation, launched in 1999, sought to accomplish several goals over a ten-year period. It aimed to destroy 18,000 "severely distressed" housing units and help thousands of public housing families become employed, independent citizens. Its relocation efforts promised to integrate them into the wider city; and its redevelopment strategy promised to rebuild the lands into "mixed-income" tracts suitable for both public housing and private market families. It was a grand vision for a public housing authority and a historically novel role for city, state, and federal governments.

The term "mixed income" should have been a clue of what the plans of the Royalty Class Black elitists were for many of the CHA's poorest residents. When Columbia researchers evaluated the progress of the plan, they found that "CHA families relocated from public housing in 2003 continued to move to predominantly African-American, poor communities in Chicago."

Overview of Plan for Transformation

Old vertical high-rises would be coming down, replaced by horizontal complexes renovated, built, and managed by private sector entities. "Mixed income" residents were the targeted clientele. A portion of the units were reserved for the lowest income CHA residents eligible to move back into renovated or new units, usually after lengthy delays. Many more would have no place to which to return.

Chicago Tribune (July 2008):

> "Under the Plan for Transformation, the city has lost more than 13,000 housing units for the poor at a time when low-

---

330 "The Gatreaux Lawsuit." Public interests. BPI (blog), n.d. bpichicago.org/pro-grams/housing-community-development/public-housing/gautreaux-lawsuit.

income families face one of the worst housing crises in recent history. After years of neglect and abandonment, many residents doubt that Jarrett [Habitat CEO] and CHA officials have their interests at heart."

The *Tribune* also found that almost nine years into what was billed as a ten-year program, the city had completed only thirty percent of the plan's most ambitious element—tearing down entire housing projects and replacing them with new neighborhoods where poor, working-class, and wealthier families would live side-by-side.

Obama's Forgotten Poor

"June 27, 2008, three-year-old Curtis Cooper was killed while riding his tricycle when a tall, rusted, steel gate came off its hinges and crushed him to death at the Chicago Housing Authority's (CHA) Cabrini-Green complex. Davis' company, wealthy Black American and Urban Property Advisor (UPA), manages the complex. Davis and his partners have made at least four million dollars in development fees over the last decade"[331]

Cabrini-Green Housing Complex:

Cullen Davis - Son of Obama's former boss: Wealthy Black American lawyer and HUD Developer, Davis Miner Barnhill & Galland.

Barack Obama served on the board of directors of Woods Fund of Chicago from 1993 to 2001. During that time, the tax exempt foundation gave grants to Obama's church, Trinity United Church of Christ, headed by Rev. Jeremiah Wright, and ACORN, a Left Wing voter registration group defunded by congress in 2010 for voter fraud. The fund also used Northern Trust for financial services, which is the same company that provided Obama his 2005 mortgage. The board of directors included Barack Obama; William Ayers, the former Weather Underground terrorist; Howard J. Stanback, who headed New Kenwood, LLC, a limited liability company founded by Tony Rezko; and Allison Davis, Obama's former boss at the law firm of Davis Miner Barnhill & Galland.

Curtis Cooper was three years old and living in the squalor of a slum low-income apartment, Cabrini-Green housing complex. Curtis rode his tricycle and, as his mother watched, he grabbed an old rusty steel gate that fell on

---

331 Lee Cary. "Obama's Friends and Chicago's New Slums." American Thinker. September 16, 2008, sec. Articles. americanthinker.com/articles/2008/09/ obama_and_south_chicago_slum_d_1.html.

top of him and crushed him to death. The housing project was run by Obama contributor Cullen Davis, whose family received huge government subsidies as well as a one-million-dollar grant for the properties from the Woods Fund's board, intended to rehabilitate more than 1,500 apartments and homes, primarily for the poor. Davis and his partners have made at least four million dollars in development fees over the last decade.

The death of the three-year-old prompted a crowd to gather and hurl accusations of mismanagement at property managers. "How many accidents happen over here because of failed inspections?" screamed Willie J.R. Fleming, a resident and a director with the Coalition to Protect Public Housing. "There's no accountability, there's no oversight of this!"

Neighborhood Rejuvenation Partners

Allison Davis - Wealthy Black American Lawyer and Developer; Barack Obama's former boss at Davis Miner Barnhill & Galland.

In 2000, Allison Davis, a Black American, asked the nonprofit Woods Fund of Chicago for a one million dollar investment in a new development partnership, Neighborhood Rejuvenation Partners. Barack Obama, a member of the board, voted in favor, helping Davis secure the investment.

New Evergreen/Sedgwick

Allison Davis - Democratic Black American Barack Obama's former boss at Davis Miner Barnhill & Galland; **Cullen Davis** - Democratic Black American son of Obama's former boss.

"Davis and his partners, including sons Jared and Cullen, have gotten more than one hundred million dollars in taxpayer subsidies to build and rehabilitate more than 1,500 apartments and homes, primarily for the poor. His deals include a massive redevelopment of the Chicago Housing Authority's Stateway Gardens, across the Dan Ryan Expressway from Sox Park. It is a lucrative business."[332]

The following year, Davis assembled another partnership to create a 10.7 million dollar renovation of five walk-up buildings in a gentrifying neighborhood. The project, a model of small-scale, mixed-income development, was subsidized by almost six million dollars in state loans and federal tax credits. Conditions deteriorated quickly. Chronic plumbing failures consumed the project's financial reserves while leaving undrained sewage in some of the apartments. After repeated complaints from building residents, the city government sued the owners, and a judge imposed a 5,500-dollar fine. New Evergreen/Sedgwick was managed by a company run by Cullen Davis, Allison

332   Lee Cary. "Obama's Friends and Chicago's New Slums."

Davis's son and a contributor to Obama's campaigns. Cullen Davis said the problems were rooted in the way New Evergreen/Sedgwick was financed. Like most new projects, a company created to own one building owns it. That company determined how much to spend on renovations, how much to set aside for maintenance, and how much to keep as profit. When the maintenance funds ran out, there was no other source of money.

> *"Mayor Daley's always talking about fair housing and decent housing, and he's got Allison Davis, who he appointed on the planning commission," says Smith, who heads the tenants' association that represents Evergreen/Sedgwick residents. "We still live in a slum."*
>
> —*From the article "We Still Live in a Slum," Mark Konkol, Chicago Sun-Times (June 29, 2007)*

Grove Parc Housing Complex

Valerie Jarrett: Democratic Black American President and CEO of The Habitat Company, President and CEO of Grove Parc's Management Firm, President Obama's White House Senior Advisor and Assistant to the President.

Grove Parc Plaza contained 504 apartments and sat in the district Barack Obama represented for eight years as a state senator. The federal government subsidized the apartments for people who couldn't afford to live anywhere else. The problem was that it wasn't safe to live there.

In June 2008, ninety-nine of the apartments were empty, most of them uninhabitable and dilapidated as the result of problems that were never fixed such as collapsed roofs, fire damage, and sewage backing up into kitchen sinks. Mice scamper through the halls and battered mailboxes hang open.

Grove Parc and several other prominent low-income HUD facilities were developed and managed by Obama's close friends and political supporters. They profited from the subsidies as many of Obama's poor constituents suffered. Tenants lost their homes, surrounding neighborhoods were blighted. Some of the residents of Grove Parc say they are angry that Obama did not notice their plight. The development straddles the boundary of Obama's state Senate district. Many of the tenants have been his constituents for more than a decade.

"No one should have to live like this, and no one did anything about it," said Cynthia Ashley, who had lived at Grove Parc since 1994.[333]

---

333   Globe staff. "Grim Proving Ground for Obama's Housing Policy." *The Boston Globe.* June 27, 2008, sec. Nation. archive.boston.com/news/nation/articles/2008/06/27/grim_proving_ground_for_obamas_housing_policy.

In 2006, Valerie Jarrett, former senior White House advisor and assistant to the president, was president and CEO of Grove Parc's management firm, The Habitat Company. During Habitat oversight, federal inspectors graded the condition of the complex a bottom-of-the-barrel 11 on a 100-point scale. This eventually led to its demolition.

Valerie Jarrett's Habitat Company also managed another larger housing complex, Lawndale Restoration, in West Chicago. Lawndale accrued 1,800 building violations in 2006. The city eventually foreclosed on the property.

Grove Parc has become a symbol for some in Chicago of the broader failures of giving public subsidies to private companies to build and manage affordable housing—an approach strongly backed by Barack Obama as the best replacement for public housing. As a state senator, the presumptive Democratic presidential nominee co-authored an Illinois law creating a new pool of tax credits for developers. As a U.S. senator, he pressed for increased federal subsidies. And as a presidential candidate, he campaigned on a promise to create an Affordable Housing Trust Fund that would give developers approximately five-hundred million dollars a year. However, a *Boston Globe* exposé found that thousands of apartments across Chicago built with local, state, and federal subsidies, including several hundred in Obama's former district, were so completely deteriorated they were no longer habitable.

According to the *Boston Globe*, wealthy developers like Tony Rezko and corrupt managers like Jarrett raked in millions while ignoring concerns from tenants. Obama claimed he never knew about the conditions at Grove Parc.

In one of those endless Chicago coincidences, Grove Parc Plaza Apartments—demolished because of years of neglect by Obama's developer friends—sat in the shadows of the proposed site of the city's 2016 Olympics Stadium. In 2009, President Obama traveled overseas to personally pitch the site to the International Olympic Committee. Valerie Jarrett was vice chair of Chicago's Olympics committee.

Lawndale Restoration

Valerie Jarrett: Democratic Black American President and CEO of The Habitat Company, Manager, President Obama Senior White House Advisor/Assistant; **Cecil Butler:** Democratic Black American HUD Developer/Owner, Obama friend and political contributor.

As the federal government positioned to seize control of more than one hundred apartment buildings in Chicago's Lawndale neighborhood, it signaled the demise of one of the most ambitious redevelopment projects in the city's history. Cecil Butler, general partner of Lawndale restoration and a longtime West Side business magnate, was two months and about 900,000 dollars behind in payments on a government-backed fifty-one million dollar mortgage. The appeal to the federal government was triggered when city inspectors found 1,800 code violations in housing units dilapidated to the point of being uninhabitable.

In 2000, Butler hired the Habitat Company. Valerie Jarrett was Habitat's Executive Vice President, later to become CEO. The deterioration of living conditions in the Lawndale Restoration continued during Habitat's involvement, though Habitat seems to have still been paid. In the final disposition of the dissolved Lawndale Restoration, its properties were sold back to the city of Chicago for ten dollars. The U.S. Department of Housing and Urban Development (HUD) assumed the fifty-one-million dollar debt at the foreclosure sale. Butler walked away. Twenty-three smaller profit and non-profit developers eventually assumed responsibility for the properties.[334]

Chicago's struggles with the deterioration of its subsidized private developments reached new heights in 2006, when the federal government foreclosed on Lawndale Restoration, the city's largest subsidized-housing complex. City inspectors found more than 1,800 code violations, including roof leaks, exposed wiring, and pools of sewage.

Lawndale Restoration was a collection of more than 1,200 apartments in ninety-seven buildings spread across three-hundred blocks of west Chicago. It was owned by a company controlled by Cecil Butler, a former civil rights activist, wealthy Obama friend, and political contributor, who came to be reviled as a slumlord by a younger generation of activists. President and CEO of The Habitat Company, Valerie Jarrett, managed Lawndale Restoration from 2000 until the federal government seized it in 2006.

Lawndale Restoration was created in the early 1980s, when the federal government helped Butler take control of a group of old buildings, including lending twenty-two million dollars to his company to redevelop the buildings and agreeing to subsidize tenant rents. In 1995, Butler's company obtained a fifty-one million dollar loan from the state to fund additional renovations at Lawndale Restoration.

Nonetheless, the buildings deteriorated. The problems came to public attention in a dramatic way in 2004, after a sport utility vehicle driven by a suburban woman trying to buy drugs struck one of the buildings, causing it to collapse. City inspectors arrived in the ensuing glare, finding a long list of code violations, leading city officials to urge the federal government to seize the complex.

Amid the uproar, a small group of Lawndale residents gathered to rally against the Democratic candidate for the US Senate, Barack Obama. Paul Johnson, who helped to organize the protest, said Obama must have known about the problems. "How didn't he know? Of course he knew. He just didn't care."

---

334   Lee Cary. "Obama's Friends and Chicago's New Slums."

Cottage View Terrace Apartments

Tony Rezko: Democratic Black American Developer, Manager, Obama U.S Senate Committee, Campaign Bundler, Associate, Friend; **Allison Davis**: Democratic Black American, Manager, Barack Obama's former boss at Davis Miner Barnhill & Galland.

The 14.6 million dollar Cottage View Terrace was funded entirely by city, state, and federal taxpayers. The project included 855,000 dollars in development fees for New Kenwood. In addition to the development fees, a separate Davis-owned company stood to make another 900,000 dollars through federal tax credits.[335]

The success rate of Rezko/Davis public housing ventures in the mid-to-late 1990s was not outstanding. The *Chicago Sun-Times* catalogued the disposition of fourteen redevelopment projects where Rezko and Davis engaged Davis' old law firm while Obama worked there.[336] After millions of dollars in government loans, the state foreclosed on four projects, and Rezmar Corp. walked away from ten.[337]

The *Sun-Times* comments on two of the properties contains a puzzling notation:

> *"Two buildings - 5630 S. Michigan and 6446 S. Kenwood. Rezmar [Rezko's company] and the Fund [for Community Redevelopment and Revitalization, a Davis company] closed on this deal in 1998. The city approved a $3.8 million loan for this project while Rezmar was facing foreclosure on another funded by the city. Rezmar gave up management of the buildings... [in 2006]."*

Why would the City of Chicago loan new money to a company about to default on a previous loan?

Barack Obama's associate and friend Tony Rezko organized his community development firm, Rezmar, in 1989. Its goal? To build and renovate low-income housing units for the poor. The record shows that over a nine-year period, Rezko and his partners received more than one-hundred million dollars from the city, state, and federal governments to rehabilitate thirty buildings in the city of Chicago. Of this total, Rezko personally received 6.9 million dollars to provide 1,025 housing units.

---

335   *Ibid.*
336   Tim Novak. "Obama and His Rezko Ties." *Chicago Sun-Times*. April 23, 2007, Special Report edition, sec. Investigation.
337   Lee Cary. "Obama's Friends and Chicago's New Slums."

By 2007, the investigative report by *Chicago Sun-Times'* Tim Novak revealed that, of the thirty buildings, six were boarded up, and seventeen were in foreclosure after Rezko abandoned them. Many of the apartment units in these buildings were vacant or needed extensive repairs. Eleven of these buildings were in the state senatorial district represented by Barack Obama.[338] Today, Rezko is unable to account for the millions given him by various government entities.

As a junior attorney in the law firm of Davis, Miner, Barnhill & Galland, Barack Obama did legal work for Rezmar. According to investigative reporter Tim Novak of the *Chicago Sun-Times*, Rezmar did fifteen building projects while being represented by Obama's firm, which helped the company get more than forty-three million dollars in government funding.

In 1997, Davis and Rezko formed New Kenwood, LLC and set out to build a seven-story apartment building for seniors called Cottage View Terrace. At the time, Davis was a member of the Chicago Planning Commission, having been appointed by Mayor Richard M. Daley. Several local elected officials, representing both city and state, wrote letters of support citing the need for senior citizen housing. Senator Obama's letter was dated October 28, 1998. He still worked as an attorney at Davis' former firm, renamed Miner Barnhill & Galland. The firm's clients included companies owned by Davis and Rezko.

New Kenwood, LLC hired the law firm of Daley & George, the Daley being then-Mayor Richard Daley's brother, Michael Daley. The city owned the two-acre vacant lot targeted for the proposed project. It had once been the site of a gas station and needed an environmental cleanup. Davis and Rezko bought the land for one dollar and spent 100,000 dollars for the cleanup.

In 2003, Rezko became one of the people on Obama's U.S. Senate campaign finance committee, which raised more than fourteen million dollars. Obama himself has since identified over 250,000 dollars in campaign contributions to various Obama campaigns as coming from Rezko or close associates and has claimed to have donated almost two-thirds of that amount to unspecified nonprofit groups.

Where did Rezko get the money that he donated to the Obama campaigns? According to Novak, at least fourteen-million came from taxpayers in the form of grants Rezko received to build Cottage View Terrace. Of this fourteen million, 855,000 dollars went to Rezko and Allison Davis in the form of development fees. Another 900,000 dollars went to Allison Davis in the form of federal tax credits.

The ninety-seven-unit "low income" Cottage View Terrace ultimately opened in 2002 at a cost of 144,000 dollars per unit. Novak discovered that Obama wrote letters to city and state officials in support of Rezko's project. The revelation clearly contradicted statements by Obama that he never did

---

338   Tim Novak. "Obama and His Rezko Ties."

any favors for Rezko. Moreover, the letters were written while Obama was a state senator and an employee of the law firm that represented Rezko's real estate interests, an obvious conflict of interest. Essentially, Obama stiffed his own constituents by accepting political contributions from a slumlord who allowed the projects in which many of them lived to deteriorate. During his tenure as a state senator, he did nothing to protest or call into question any of these practices, which clearly and blatantly harmed the people of his district.

Chicago Sun-Times (June 13, 2007):

> *"The 14.6 million dollar Cottage View Terrace was funded entirely by city, state, and federal taxpayers. The projected included $855,000 in development fees for New Kenwood. In addition to the development fees, a separate Davis-owned company stood to make another $900,000 through federal tax credits."[339]*

Urban Property Advisors, a Davis company run by son Cullen, took over management of the property.

In June 2008, Rezko was convicted on multiple counts of fraud and bribery stemming from these activities, including sixteen charges filed against him. Chief among these was using his clout with the Blagojevich administration to squeeze seven million dollars in kickbacks out of a contractor and seven money management firms seeking to do business with the state.

This transfer of wealth from government to connected Black elitists, under the guise of "building and renovating low income housing units for the poor" is symbolic of the parasitic relationship between the Royalty Class Black man and the poor Black masses they claim to "serve." This highlights the heart buried within of those who delight in exploiting the human misery of others for their own profit, power, and prestige. Truly, avarice lies at the heart of the Royalty Class Black Man.

Chapter postscript

Here is a must-see YouTube video on "Obama's Forgotten People": https://youtu.be/dWb3chi3EBc.[340]

---

339   Tim Novak. "Obama and His Rezko Ties."
340   Obama's Forgotten People. NoQuarterUSAnet, 2009. youtu.be/dWb3chi3EBc.

CHAPTER 17

THE STATE OF PRESIDENT OBAMA'S BLACK AMERICA

By the Numbers

"Like the rest of America, Black America, in the aggregate, is better off now than it was when I came into office," President Obama said in response to a question by Urban Radio Networks White House Correspondent April Ryan.

What planet African Americans are doing "better off" on is unknown. A look at every key stat as President Obama started his sixth year in office illustrates this.[341] The Great Recession of President Bush ended within six months of President Obama's inauguration. The next seven years at one percent GNP was the slowest growth since WWII. President Obama was the only U.S. president in history to never have a three percent growth quarter.[342]

Unemployment. The average rate of unemployment for Blacks under President Bush was 10 percent. The average under President Obama after six years was 14 percent. Black unemployment "has always been double" [that of Whites] but it hasn't always been 14 percent. The administration was silent when Black unemployment hit 16 percent, a twenty-seven-year high, in late 2011.[343]

Unemployed Black Teen Males. New stats from the Chicago Urban League find that 92 percent of young Black males in Chicago are unemployed.

---

341   Lauren Victoria Burke. "Is Black America Better Off Under Obama?" BlackPressUSA. January 5, 2015, sec. Op-ed. blackpressusa.com/is-black-america-better-off-under-obama.

342   Peter Ferrara. "The Worst Five Years Since the Great Depression." Business news. Forbes.com, February 7, 2013. forbes.com/sites/peterferrara/2013/02/07/the-worst-five-years-since-the-great-depression/#b5eeaec5e2b0.

343   Lauren Victoria Burke. "Is Black America Better Off Under Obama?"

Nationwide, the stats aren't that much better for Black male teens, with an 83 percent unemployment rate. In Illinois as a whole it is 88 percent, reports Fox 32 Chicago (via Bossip). Chicago has 600,000 fewer jobs now than the city did in 2000.[344] Black teen unemployment increased 35.3–36.8 percent.[345]

In August 2011, Congresswoman Maxine Waters called the Black unemployment rate "unconscionable." She later hammered President Obama for failing to "acknowledge the economic disaster in the African American community" while addressing his jobs agenda in the battleground state of Iowa.[346]

Labor Force Participation. The recession inherited by the Obama administration officially ended in June 2009, but the labor force participation rate continued to drop during Obama's two terms, hitting 62.4 percent in September 2015, its lowest point in thirty-eight years. [347] The decrease from 65.7 percent in January 2009 to 62.8 percent in May 2016 is a portrait of disengagement not witnessed since March 1978. For Black adults, that number slipped from 63.2 to 60.9 percent. While 29.6 percent of Blacks aged sixteen to nineteen were working when Obama took power, only 27.9 percent were employed.[348]

Poverty increased under President Obama. Overall, 14.3 percent of Americans were below the poverty line in January 2009, versus fifteen percent in 2012, according to the latest available data from the Census Bureau's Current Population Survey. Similarly, the share of Black Americans living in poverty expanded from 25.8 to 27.2 percent.[349] Currently, more than forty-five million people—one in seven Americans—live below the poverty line.

Food Stamps. America's population of food stamp recipients soared overall from 32,889,000 in 2009 to 46,022,000 in 2012, the latest Agriculture

---

344   Ann Brown. "No Openings: 92% Of Black Male Chicago Youth Are Out Of Work." Entertainment. Madame Noire (blog), January 22, 2014. madamenoire. com/342987/92-young-black-males-chicago-unemployed.

345   Deroy Murdock. "Black Americans Are Worse Off Under Obama." National Review. May 16, 2014, Online edition, sec. Politics & Policy. nationalreview. com/2014/05/black-americans-are-worse-under-obama-deroy-murdock.

346   TJ. "Black Unemployment at Lowest Level in 17 Years." Discussion, Politics. BlueWhiteIllustrated, n.d. bwi.forums.rivals.com/threads/african-american-unemployment-is-at-a-17-year-low.187330.

347   Susan Jones. "Labor Force Participation Rate Dropped to 62.8% In April: 94,044,000 Out." CNS News. May 6, 2016, sec. National. cnsnews.com/news/article/susan-jones/labor-force-participation-improves-americans-not-labor-force.

348   Lauren Victoria Burke. "Is Black America Better Off Under Obama?"

349   Deroy Murdock. "Black Americans Are Worse Off Under Obama."

Department statistics show. For Blacks, the analogous numbers are 7,393,000 when Obama arrived to 10,955,000 in 2012.[350]

Inflation-adjusted median household income fell across America, from 53,285 dollars in 2009 to 51,017 dollars in 2012, the most recent Census Bureau data indicates. Income for Black households slid too, from 34,880 dollars to 33,321 dollars, and at a much lower income level.[351]

The Housing Market Bailout. Despite 275 billion dollars in housing-market bailouts that President Obama unveiled in his first month in office, home ownership waned. In the first quarter of 2009, 67.3 percent of Americans owned homes. By 1Q 2014, that Census Bureau figure was 64.8 percent. Meanwhile, Black home ownership during this interval sagged from 46.1 to 43.3 percent.[352]

Education. The high school dropout rate improved during the Obama administration. However, forty-two percent of Black children currently attend high poverty schools, compared to only six percent of White students. The Department of Education's change to Parent PLUS loans requirements cost HBCUs more than 150 million dollars and interrupted the educations of 28,000-plus HBCU students.[353]

California DOE (2017) reported that 75 percent of Black boys failed to pass standard reading and writing tests.[354]

President Obama's first act as president was to defund a successful school voucher program for Washington, D.C. children, thus denying over two-thousand poor Black children per year access, that he gave his two daughters, to a quality

---

350 Kelsey Farson Grey, and Esa Eslami. "Characteristics of Supplemental Nutrition Assistance Program Households: Fiscal Year 2012." Study. Alexandria, VA: U.S. Department of Agriculture, Food and Nutrition Service, Office of Policy Support, February 2014. fns-prod.azureedge.net/sites/default/files/2012Characteristics.pdf.

351 Carmen DeNavas-Walt, Bernadette D. Proctor, and Jessica C. Smith. "Income, Poverty, and Health Insurance Coverage in the United States: 2012." Population. Current Population Reports. Washington D.C.: U.S. Department of Commerce, Economics and Statistics Administration, U.S. Census Bureau, September 2013. census.gov/prod/2013pubs/p60-245.pdf.

352 Robert R. Callis, and Melissa Kresin. "Residential Vacancies and Homeowner-ship in the First Quarter 2014." U.S. Department of Commerce: Social, Economic, and Housing Statistics Division, April 29, 2014. census.gov/housing/hvs/files/qtr114/q114press.pdf.

353 Lauren Victoria Burke. "Is Black America Better Off Under Obama?"

354 Matt Levin. "75% of Black California Boys Don't Meet State Reading Standards." *The Mercury News.* June 5, 2017, sec. Education. mercurynews.com/2017/06/05/75-of-black-california-boys-dont-meet-state-reading-standards.

education. A 2010 study published by Patrick Wolf of the University of Arkansas found that the scholarship recipients had graduation rates of 91 percent. The graduation rate for D.C. public schools was 56 percent, and it was 70 percent for students who entered the lottery for a voucher but didn't win. [355]

SBA Loans. In March 2014, *The Wall Street Journal* reported that only 1.7 percent of twenty-three-billion dollars in SBA loans went to Black-owned businesses in 2013, the lowest loan of SBA lending to Black businesses on record. During the Bush presidency, the percentage of SBA loans to Black businesses was 8 percent—more than four times the rate during the Obama presidency.[356]

The Wealth Gap. The wealth gap between Blacks and Whites in America is at a twenty-four-year high. A December study by PEW Research Center revealed the average White household is worth 141,900 dollars, and the average Black household is worth 11,000 dollars. From 2010 to 2013, the median income for Black households plunged 9 percent.[357]

Income inequality. "Between 2009 and 2012 the top one percent of Americans enjoyed 95 percent of all income gains, according to research from U.C. Berkeley," reported *The Atlantic*. It was the worst since 1928, as income inequality widened during President Obama's time in office.[358]

Black Conservative Deroy Murdock is a Manhattan-based Fox News contributor and a media fellow with the Hoover Institution on War, Revolution, and Peace at Stanford University. He summarized the eight years of President Obama's promise of hope and change for the Black community as follows:

> *"...these sad statistics do not capture the intangible humili-*
> *ation of watching America's first Black president expose*
> *himself as a lazy, incompetent liar. This inescapable truth*
> *is confirmed by Obama's eerily detached demeanor, his 169*
> *rounds of golf while in office, his scores of skipped intelli-*
> *gence briefings, his unforgivable absence from the Situation*
> *Room during the Benghazi massacre, and his burgeoning*
> *scandals—from Fast and Furious to the IRS's persecution*
> *of conservative groups, to the forty or more war heroes who*
> *died without medical care while languishing on secret Veter-*
> *ans Affairs wait lists."*

---

355 Daniel Doherty. "Why Is Obama Turning His Back on School Vouchers?" Townhall.Com via Salem Media Group. April 16, 2012, sec. Tipsheet. townhall.com/tipsheet/danieldoherty/2012/02/16/why-is-obama-turning-his-back-on-school-vouchers-n703863.

356 Lauren Victoria Burke. "Is Black America Better Off Under Obama?"

357 *Ibid.*

358 *Ibid*

And remember, Obama's oft-repeated "If you like your health care plan, you can keep it" promise was PolitiFact's 2013 *Lie of the Year*.[359]

Considering this dismal record, about the best Obama can say to Black Americans is, "nothing personal." President Obama's focus on resentment and redistribution, rather than robust growth, failed the entire country, not just Black folks.

Blacks Are Worse Off Under Obama
Socio-economic indicators among
black Americans on Obama's watch

		1/20/09	2012	2014
Unemployment rate (USA)	Jan. 2009 and April '14	7.8		6.3
Unemployment rate (black Americans)	"	12.7		11.6
Unemployment rate (black Americans ages 16 to 19)	"	35.3		36.8
Labor force participation rate (USA) -	Jan. 2009 and April '14	65.7		62.3
Labor force participation rate (blacks 16+ seasonally adjusted)		63.2		60.9
Labor force participation rate (blacks 16-19 seasonally adjusted)		29.6		27.9
People below poverty line (USA)		14.3	15.0	
People below poverty line (black Americans)		25.8	27.2	
Real median household income (USA)		$53,285	$51,017	
Real median household income (black Americans)		$34,880	$33,321	
Food Stamp participants (USA)		32,889,000	46,022,000	
Food Stamp participants (black Americans)		7,393,000	10,955,000	
Percent who own homes (USA - 1Q 2009 and 1Q 2014)		67.3%		64.8%
Percent who own homes (black Americans - 1Q 2009 and 1Q 2014)		46.1%		43.3%

Sources:

U.S. Bureau of Labor Statistics: Historical data; *The Employment Situation -- April 2014*
U.S. Census Bureau, Historical Poverty Tables, Table 2: Poverty Status, by Family Relationship, Race, and Hispanic Origin
U.S. Census Bureau, *Income, Poverty, and Health Insurance Coverage in the U.S.: 2012*, Table A-1 "Households by Total Money Income, Race..."
U.S. Dept. of Agriculture, *Characteristics of SNAP Households*: FY 2009 and '12: Table A-23 "...Participants by Selected Demographic"
U.S. Census Bureau, *Residential Vacancies and Home Ownership* 1Q 2013 and '14, Tables 4 and 7 "Home Ownership Rates..."

Chart: Deroy Murdock - NationalReview.com, May 16, 2014

---

359   Deroy Murdock. "Black Americans Are Worse Off Under Obama."

CHAPTER 18

THE NFL, THE FLAG, AND GLOBALISM

"The deepest betrayal begins with ultimate trust."
—Burgess Owens

The Urban Black Community

Detailed throughout this book is the *modus operandi* of the Socialist/Marxist Democratic Party, best summarized in three words: *use, abuse, and discard.* The longing for hope by those who trust them does not engage their empathy and witnessing the misery of others does not generate within their hearts a desire to act. The urban Black community has been betrayed for decades by anti-Black legislation supported by "trusted" Black politicians, all of which has resulted in chronic joblessness, illiteracy, and hopelessness. The Socialist/ Marxist Education Labor Unions in control of our nation's public schools have indoctrinated urban children to feel justified with their ever-increasing anger, White racism, and anti-American sentiments. They are encouraged to "act-out" by Leftist teachers who hide behind their safe and tenured positions and by Royalty Class Black politicians who hide behind the dependable votes of their loyal, uneducated constituents. Immersed in hopelessness, emotionally charged, encouraged to riot, loot, and demonstrate every election cycle, they are forced to deal with the consequence of their ongoing negative interactions with authority.

After decades of loyalty to the party, this community is now being replaced by illegal foreigners, who are being granted the financial resources once set aside to aid Black Americans in achieving the American Dream of education, housing, jobs, and opportunities for business ownership. Unfortunately, due to indoctrination and total trust in Socialist/Marxist politicians and entertainers, the majority of urban Black Americans fight for survival as they elect the instruments of their own demise into power.

The Black community has trusted the Democratic Left for over sixty years with election cycle predictability that has delivered a consistent voting bloc of over 90 percent. When considering its broad diversity of experiences, this accepted perception that the Black race, unlike all others, is only capable of thinking and voting by skin color alone is shameful. It has been this belief that with common skin color comes inherent loyalty, faithfulness, and honor. Only within the relationship with elected Black politicians has this knuckleheaded perception flourished. The facts are that with the exponential growth in Black Democratic politicians, there has also been an exponential rise in Black misery and failure.

From 1970 until 2012, the number of elected Black officials rose from fewer than 1,500 to more than 10,000.[360] During this period of Black political empowerment, we've had the election of a Black president, twice. Some misguided conventional wisdom points to the pathway to progress and how it can only be followed through the efforts of Black politicians. Yet facts show that with this increase in political empowerment, Black progress has been *slower* than White American progress while poor Black Americans have consistently lost ground.[361]

The only conclusion taken from the dismal Black progress since 1970 while simultaneously experiencing exponential growth of Democratic politicians is that the Socialist/Marxist ideology embraced by Black officials has harmed Black progress. Conversely, minority communities that have subscribed to assimilation and acceptance of American values such as hard work, stable families, and education have succeeded, regardless of race or culture.

To change the downward trajectory of the Black community, it is vital to review the impact of decades of voters' over this 90-percent benchmark of abject loyalty to the Democratic Party. As documented earlier, from fifty years after slavery until the late 1960s, the Black community was the most competitive of all American minority communities. By the early '50s, it led our nation in the percentage of families entering America's middle class. It led our nation in its commitment to the Christian faith, the commitment of its men to the institution of marriage, of entrepreneurs, and of men committed to higher education. With its transition to the secularized Socialist/Marxist Democratic Party, the once-Christian, entrepreneurial, patriotic community left its conservative God-centered mooring and has been drifting downstream ever since. To experience the success of preceding generations, this community *must* return to the values of service, pride, vision, and true manhood and womanhood within the Judeo-Christian ideals upon which our nation was founded.

Its trust in the Democratic Party of anti-God secularism has resulted in its displacement at the very top of our nation's misery index. Sixty years away from its competitive heights of the 1960s, it is now the community that leads

---

360   Jason Riley. "Blacks in Power Don't Empower Blacks."

361   *Ibid.*

our nation in every category of failure: unemployment, illiteracy, abortion, crime, child abandonment, incarceration, among others. Its percentage of entrepreneurs, a key barometer of a community's success in entering the middle class sector, is at 3.8 percent. What is the differential responsible for today's dismal statistics and those from an era of vibrant success? It is in the choice of ideology, one that has been trusted and adhered to for far too long, the mistake by millions to trust in a party that trusts in the anti-God secularism of Socialism/Marxism. To resurrect an era of success, the Black race must return to the Judeo-Christian values offered by an omnipotent god.

By embracing a Socialist/Marxist doctrine, the Black community has accepted its demeaning devaluation. They promote the narrative that it is expected of Black Americans to vote on skin color rather than stance. It accepts that failure is also innately predictable based the color of one's skin. Black Americans have accepted the present as "normal" when seventy-five percent of its Black boys in California, the most populist state in the union, fail in reading and writing. If this was the state of White, Asian, or even illegal immigrants a national dialogue with politicians on both sides of the aisle would demand answers. Not so with Black Americans. If framed in the proper context that education administered fairly is no respecter of race, creed, or color, it then follows that this percentage of failing children of one race must be innate.

The lack of ire among Americans regarding this targeted racism and decades-long attack on poor Black families points at the Democrats' recalibration of lowering expectations of those with darker skin and in poor financial conditions. Sadly, this subtle indoctrination has become accepted by an entire new generation of Americans and resulted in the progressive demeaning of the human body and spirit.

It was this subtle and insidious bigotry that Martin Luther King and his leadership identified as destructive, as were the Jim Crow laws and policies. It was addressed during the 1960s hot summer civil rights marches by wearing a uniform that demanded respect. MLK's leadership wore White shirts, dark ties, dress slacks, and dress shoes as a strategic visual message of contradiction to the Southern Democrats' condescending Black stereotypes. That stereotype contained such descriptive adjectives as lazy, inarticulate, sloppy (in dress and character), irresponsible breeders, emotionally vs. logically-driven, incapable of critical thinking, unintelligent, disloyal, unable to provide leadership over the White race, "*but boy do dey love to sing and dance.*" This stereotype had been prevalent and pervasive throughout America and the late 1800s south. This evil and demeaning narrative of other Americans based on skin tone has been revived within the last two decades and is now spawning in the denigrating hip hop subculture. It is a narrative of propaganda controlled by the White Socialist/Marxist owners of Black Entertainment TV (BET) and its all-White board at Viacom. All of it facilitated by Black elitists, who prioritize their profits and social standing over the welfare of their own people.

The scientific genesis of this racist stereotype was the theory of evolution offered to the world by atheist Charles Darwin. Accepted as "settled science" among the world's academic elitists, it served to justify the demeaning treatment and segregation of the Black race who, according to the evolutionist, were the first iteration from the African ape that would later "evolve" into the superior White race.

Throughout American history there have been Black Americans who have accepted and perpetuated the theory of genetic superiority/inferiority based on skin color. One of the more prominent historical Black Americans promoted within today's public school system is one of these—W.E.B. Du Bois was a eugenicist, abortionist, atheist, and anti-American Marxist/Communist who, at the end of his life, renounced his American citizenship and moved to a foreign country. He is praised as a great Black intellectual leader. It was this early 1900 Democrat elitist who perceived himself and others like him as genetically superior to uneducated, darker, poorer members of his race. This special category of Black people he called "The Talented Tenth." Du Bois prophesized that this special class of Blacks would pull the remaining "best of his race" away from the worst; the "Waste of the Masses." This negative perception of members of his own race explains why Du Bois sat proudly on the abortion board of pro-KKK, pro-Nazi, Planned Parenthood founder Margaret Sanger. It was Du Bois who facilitated Sanger's first missions into Harlem to abort poor Black babies. It is this same negative perception of members of their own race that allows Royalty Class Black elitists to support the abortionist killing fields in today's poor Black neighborhoods. It explains their vehement stance against school choice vouchers for poor Black children. It remains the goal of Socialist/Marxist Democrats to pull themselves from the *"Waste of the Masses,"* the urban poor.

It was this visionary fight for perception and respect, from within the community and out, that can be seen through the dress, articulation, discipline, and courage of Martin Luther King's leadership. It was a fight that was being won by the previous generations of Black Americans. Due to the use of deception, stealth, and indoctrination by today's entrenched but patient Socialist/Marxists, the fight for progress and freedom has taken a big hit.

Black Entertainment TV and other Democratic-owned media outlets successfully deliver a steady message of misogyny, anti-Americanism, anti-Capitalism, anti-family, anti-White indoctrination to our Black youth 24/7. These same Socialist/Marxists have burrowed their way in, like insidious ideological termites, undermining the foundation of learning in our educational institutions. As they encourage the use of Marxist tactics, we see the increase of high school and college-age students using violence, intolerance, and bullying to end free debate and silence the voices of anyone different from them.

DACA

The DACA (Deferred Action for Childhood Arrivals) community has been betrayed for the sake of political expediency by Socialist/Marxist Democrats. The unfulfilled promises to this group is not about jobs, education, or opportunity, but asylum and a pathway to American citizenship. They are promised the end of the fear of deportation. Once in control of both Houses and the Executive branch, the Democratic Party had the political power to craft and pass an immigration bill of its choosing. As this Royalty Class of politicians calculates overwhelming loyalty, support, and the vote of the Black community, it did so with the Hispanic population as well. Instead of addressing, once and for all, the immigration issue, Obama's Democratic message of "hope and change" strategically gambled their political capital on forcing through a socialized national healthcare system and transgender politics. Neither of these Democratic initiatives addressed what most Americans want.

In January of 2018, President Trump's administration offered a DACA proposal that neither Democrats nor Republicans expected. He proposed this to the chagrin of his strong anti-asylum base:

> *This proposal would include not just the roughly 700,000 "Dreamer" immigrants who have applied for DACA protection since 2012, but an additional 1.1 million illegal immigrants who could have qualified (but have not yet applied). This doubles the number of people who could take advantage of the pathway to citizenship. Democrats were hoping to come out of these negotiations with protections for about 800,000 people. Without even presenting a counteroffer, they're being offered protection for 1.8 million.*[362]

Also, the plan would allow Dreamer spouses and their minor children to come into the country to join them.[363] In return, President Trump asked for:

> *Limiting chain migration, Immediately ending the draft lottery, and Building a wall to protect our nation from drug and human trafficking—and terrorists.*

For the 1.8 million DACA recipients who are presently in America and who would have had a pathway to American citizenship, Democrats said *NO*. The use of fear and misery as a political "Get out the Vote" strategy was just too enticing. Once again this highlights the empathy-free heart and soul of the Socialist/Marxist to *use, abuse, and discard.*

---

362   Jake Novak. "Democrats Would Be Crazy to Reject Trump's DACA Deal." CNBC. January 26, 2018, Markets edition, sec. Commentary. cnbc.com/2018/01/26/trump-daca-deal-is-a-dream-come-true-for-democrats-commentary.html.

363   *Ibid.*

The Black NFL Player

> *"You can't make Socialists out of individuals. Children who know how to think for themselves spoil the harmony of the collective society, which is coming, where everyone is interdependent."*
>
> —John Dewey: Atheist, Socialist, Humanist; NAACP Board member, ACLU Union founder and father of the modern public school system

Loyal NFL fans have watched in dismay and anger over the last two NFL seasons as Black millionaire NFL players refused to stand in honor of the American Flag due to perceived social injustices brought upon them by White Americans. These young men are sincere in their beliefs, many of whom have seen firsthand the misery and hopelessness within their urban communities. They have worked hard, sacrificed, and are now living the American Dream as multi-millionaires with wealth, fame, the status of a respected profession, yet they feel no loyalty or gratitude to the flag that represents country that has granted them this opportunity. As the national anthem plays and the American flag waves, they can be seen kneeling, stretching, or remaining in the locker room, all to highlight to the rest of the country their disdain for their country, which they perceive as one of oppression and racism.

They have never been taught that the same economic system that has provided their pathway to wealth, Capitalism, can be used by them individually or collectively to provide wealth and solutions within the urban community. They have not been taught the power of American individualism highlighted by the most empowering three words in the history of mankind: "We the People." They have not been taught *true* American history of a nation-leading successful Black community, as early as fifty years after the end of slavery or the historical collaboration by a vast diversity of Americans for the cause of freedom and opportunity starting with the first shot of the Revolutionary War.

Instead, America has seen the implementation of stealth described over one hundred years ago by the founder of Marxism and author of the *Communist Manifesto*, Karl Marx, who stated: The first battlefield is the re-writing of history." Another crown jewel of Marxism thought comes from the mid-1900s avowed Socialist/Marxist, atheist, and father of the public school system, John Dewey, who claims change "...must come gradually. To force it unduly would compromise its final success by favoring violent reaction. In other words, Socialistic ideas [must] be done slowly; otherwise those who truly [care] about educating children would become angry and resist."[364]

These young Black NFL millionaires have, throughout all their years of public education, been targeted, indoctrinated, and betrayed by Socialist/

---

364   Samuel Blumenfeld. *Revolution via Education and Other Essays.* 1st ed. Vallecito, CA: Chalcedon, 2009.

Marxists who dictate the curriculum for public schools; the National Education Labor Union. Its Leftist perspective can now be seen in liberal colleges' graduation lines and standing on NFL sidelines across our country. They have been spoon-fed a dogma that is anti-American, anti-White, anti-Capitalism, anti-male, and anti-God. Consistently absent nationwide within these educational programs: pro-American history, respect for the American flag, and the acknowledgement of the Judeo-Christian influence in the founding of freedom for all Americans regardless of race, creed, or color. Some of these players who led the NFL-sanctioned anti-flag demonstrations will sacrifice their careers and millions of dollars in income for this misdirected cause.

Due to the lack of defined guidelines by the NFL commissioner, these players had no idea what type of protest actions were inappropriate in the NFL workplace or of the unexpected blowback once outside their own social justice echo-chamber. They also lack understanding of important components of Capitalism, that as employed entertainers they are all dispensable. New to the job market with a naive tendency of overestimating personal value, they never considered the consequences of an equation that all enterprise owners are keenly aware, called *the bottom line*. Once on the wrong side of this line, regardless of their position, time served, respect, or amiability, they are no longer of value. They have made themselves dispensable.

Some of the protesting players' values will be tested in the off-season; it is, after all, a game in which careers are built and come to an end based on the ability to win. The game itself will go on, although for some of the players who were misled and misused by Anti-American Socialist/Marxist advocates, this career window and financial opportunity will close, never again to open.

Urban-American Alternative

Offered by then-presidential candidate Donald Trump, came a challenge that finally broke the tether to DEM-imposed Black misery. "What the hell do you have to lose?" was asked as a solution called *The New Deal for Black Americans was offered.*

Not only did the Democratic party *not* discuss the merits of whether these initiatives would help those suffering in the urban community, their mainstream media cohorts did not acknowledge a proposal even existed. This proposal for urban renewal was *not* seen or discussed on major news channels such as CNN, MSNBC, NBC, CBS, ABC, or BET.

Donald J. Trump's New Deal For Black America With A Plan For Urban Renewal

Nobody needs to tell African-Americans in this country that the old New Deal from the Democratic Party isn't working. In election-after-election, Democratic party leaders take African-American voters for granted, and year-after-year the condition of Black America gets worse. Inner city conditions are unacceptable. Too many African-Americans have been left behind. African-Americans need a New Deal from their next president.

The following are ten promises announced by Donald Trump on October 26, 2016 in Charlotte, NC to define a New Deal for Black America:

1. **Great Education Through School Choice.** We will allow every disadvantaged child in America to attend the public, private, charter, magnet, religious, or home school of their choice. School choice is the great civil rights issue of our time, and Donald Trump will be the nation's biggest supporter for school choice in all fifty states. We will also ensure funding for Historic Black Colleges and Universities, more affordable two and four-year colleges, and support for trade and vocational education.

2. **Safe Communities.** We will make our communities safe again. Every African-American child must be able to walk down their street in peace. Safety is a civil right. We will invest in training and funding both local and federal law enforcement operations to remove gang members, drug dealers, and criminal cartels from our neighborhoods. The reduction of crime is not merely a goal, but a necessity.

3. **Equal Justice Under the Law.** We will apply the law fairly, equally, and without prejudice. There will be only one set of rules, not a two-tiered system of justice. Equal justice also means the same rules for Wall Street.

4. **Tax Reforms to Create Jobs and Lift up People and Communities.** We will lower the business tax from 35 percent to 15 percent and bring thousands of new companies to our shores. We will have a massive middle-class tax cut, tax-free childcare savings accounts, and childcare tax deductions and credits. We will also have tax holidays for inner-city investment, and new tax incentives to get foreign companies to relocate to blighted American neighborhoods. We will empower cities and states to seek a federal disaster designation for blighted communities to initiate the rebuilding of vital infrastructure, the demolition of abandoned properties, and the increased presence of law enforcement.

5. **Financial Reforms to Expand Credit to Support New Job Creation.** We will have financial reforms to make it easier for young African-Americans to get credit to pursue their dreams in business and create jobs in their communities. Dodd-Frank has been a disaster, making it harder for small businesses to get the credit they need. The policies of the Clintons brought us the financial recession, through lifting Glass-Steagall, pushing subprime lending, and blocking reforms to Fannie Mae and Freddie Mac. It's time for a 21st century Glass-Steagall and, as part of that, a priority on helping African-American businesses get the credit they need. We will also encourage small-business creation

by allowing social welfare workers to convert poverty assistance into repayable but forgivable micro-loans.

6. **Trade That Works for American Workers.** We will stop the massive, chronic trade deficits that have emptied out our jobs. We won't let our jobs be stolen anymore. We will stop the offshoring of companies to low-wage countries and raise wages at home, meaning rent and bills become more affordable. We will tell executives that if they move their factories to Mexico or other countries, we will install a 35 percent tax on their product before they ship it back to the United States.

7. **Protection from Illegal Immigration.** We will restore the civil rights of African-Americans, Hispanic-Americans, and all Americans by ending illegal immigration. No group has been more economically by decades of illegal immigration than low-income African-American workers. Hillary Clinton's pledge to enact "open borders"—made in secret to a foreign bank—would destroy the African-American middle class. We will reform visa rules to give American workers preference for jobs, and we will suspend reckless refugee admissions from terror-prone regions that cost taxpayers hundreds of billions of dollars. We will use a portion of the money saved by enforcing our laws, and suspending refugees, to re-invest in our inner cities.

8. **New Infrastructure Investment.** We will leverage public-private partnerships, and private investments through tax incentives, to spur one trillion dollars in infrastructure investment over ten years, of which the inner cities will be a major beneficiary. We will cancel all wasteful climate change spending from Obama-Clinton, including all global warming payments to the United Nations. This will save one-hundred billion dollars over eight years. We will use these funds to help rebuild the vital infrastructure, including water systems, in America's inner cities.

9. **Protect the African-American Church.** We will protect religious liberty, promote strong families, and support the African-American church.

10. **America First Foreign Policy.** We will stop trying to build democracies overseas, wasting trillions, but focus on defeating terrorists and putting America first.[365]

---

365   MTO staff. "Donald Trump REACHED OUT TO US . . . He's Offering This 'NEW DEAL' To Black Americans . . . We Have The FULL TEXT Of Pres-Elect Trump's OFFER . . . And It Sounds Interesting!! (Do You ACCEPT IT . . . Or NAH??)." News. MTO News, November 11, 2016. mtonews.com/donald-trump-speaks-offers-new-deal-black-americans-full-text-pres-elect-trumps-offer-accept-nah.

Promises Kept

Education

School Choice: Education Secretary Betsy DeVos has made one thing clear when it comes to education policy: Their priority is expanding "school choice." This is a primer about the school choice movement, which supporters say seeks to expand alternatives to traditional public schools for children who have poor educational options in their neighborhoods and to give parents a choice in their children's education.[366]

Historically Black Colleges and Universities (HBCUs): In February 2017, President Trump signed an executive order aimed at boosting his administration's support for Black colleges. He approved a measure that will move the government's program for promoting HBCUs from the Education Department to direct oversight by the White House.

"Education has the power to uplift, it has the power to transform and, perhaps most important, education has the power to create greater equality and justice in our lives," Mr. Trump said in a signing ceremony in the Oval Office with the leaders of about twenty schools.[367]

HCBU LOAN Forgiveness: The U.S. Education Department granted full forgiveness of 322 million dollars in loans to four historically Black colleges and universities that suffered damage after Hurricanes Katrina and Rita struck the Gulf Coast in 2005. In the aftermath of the storms, Dillard University, Southern University at New Orleans, Tougaloo College, and Xavier University of Louisiana collectively borrowed more than 360 million dollars through the HBCU Capital Financing Program in 2007. The money was used to renovate, refinance existing debt, and build new facilities. The schools struggled to repay the debt amid depressed enrollment, and in 2013 received a five-year reprieve on payments set to expire this spring.

"This additional disaster relief will lift a huge burden and enable the four HBCUs to continue their focus on serving their students and communities,"

---

366   Valerie Strauss. "What 'School Choice' Means in the Era of Trump and DeVos." *The Washington Post*. May 22, 2017, sec. Analysis. washingtonpost.com/news/answer-sheet/wp/2017/05/22/what-school-choice-means-in-the-era-of-trump-and-devos.

367   Dave Boyer. "Trump Signs Order Supporting Historically Black Colleges." *The Washington Times*. February 28, 2017, Online edition, sec. National News. washingtontimes.com/news/2017/feb/28/donald-trump-sign-order-supporting-historically-bl.

Education Secretary Betsy DeVos said in a statement. "This relief provides one more step toward full recovery."[368]

President Obama and HCBUs: Because of a change in the Department of Education's student loans policy in 2011, it forced an estimated 28,000 students who were enrolled in HBCUs to drop out for lack of funds, costing these one hundred and five schools about 150 million dollars in expected revenue. The administration's direct spending on HBCUs fell about 145 million dollars. William Harvey, chairman of the President's Board of Advisors on Historically Black Colleges and Universities, pointed out that in 2010, at the height of Obama's commitment to HBCUs, federal agencies only allotted 1.7 percent of their total grants for higher education to HBCUs, even though HBCUs comprise three percent of schools. Health and Human Services directed only one percent of its college and university grant funding to HBCUs. If the administration were to calculate HBCUs' fair share according to their relative wealth or the financial need of their students, it would be a lot more than 1.7 percent, and potentially more than three. "The state of Black colleges and universities could and should be better," Harvey said, but it seemed Obama wasn't listening. [369]

Employment: Black and Hispanic

In December 2017, African-American unemployment fell to 6.8 percent. That's a record low since the statistic was first calculated in 1972. The previous record low was seven percent in April 2000 and September 2017. The Hispanic unemployment rate also dropped by a full percentage point, from 5.9 percent in December 2016 to 4.9 percent in December 2017. This is close to the data point's all-time low of 4.8 percent in October and November 2017.[370]

As the mainstream media refuses to report on the improving status of the Black community, it continues to opt for the Socialist/Marxist politicians whose strategy has been effectively implemented for over sixty years.

Use, abuse, and discard.

---

368   Danielle Douglas-Gabriel. "Education Department Forgives $322 Million in Loans to Help Historically Black Colleges Recover." *The Washington Post*. March 15, 2018, sec. Local. washingtonpost.com/news/grade-point/wp/2018/03/15/education-department-forgives-322-million-in-loans-to-help-historically-black-colleges-recover-from-hurricanes.

369   Nora Caplan-Bricker. "Why Black Colleges Might Sue the Obama Administration." *The New Republic*, July 10, 2013. newrepublic.com/article/113761/why-Black-colleges-might-sue-obama-administration.

370   Louis Jacobson. "How Accurate Is Donald Trump about Black, Hispanic Unemployment?" *Politifact*. January 8, 2018. politifact.com/truth-o-meter/statements/2018/jan/08/donald-trump/how-accurate-donald-trumps-about-black-hispa.

CHAPTER 19

CORPORATE GLOBALIST: PROFITS OVER PATRIOTISM

Media Globalist - ABC

On a peaceful, cloudless morning on September 11, 2001, a terrorist attack on our homeland resulted in the deaths of over three-thousand men and women. In a display of patriotism, Americans of all political, racial, and cultural persuasions set aside their differences and began to fly the American flag. In front of homes, federal and private office buildings, car radio antennas, this window of time in American history was one of solemn unity and harmony. I would surmise that not since the surprise attack on Pearl Harbor has there been such an organic display of patriotism by the American people.

Not long after this attack on our homeland, then-president of ABC News, David Westin, chose a path that broke from this unified display. He chose a path for his national media enterprise that prior American leaders would have considered unthinkable after such an attack resulting in the death of thousands. He prioritized the acceptance and resulting profits of globalist interests versus American nationalism. Westin chose "neutrality" between America and its enemies rather than risking branding ABC as loyal to the American Way.

Westin articulated his position: "When you're reporting the news, you should be reporting the news, not taking a position." He showed his position by directing ABC anchors and journalists to not wear the American flag pin on their lapel. Years later, when asked his about his "No American Flag" stance, the unrepentant Liberal Democrat Westin was quoted: "I believe to this day that it was the right decision."

Use, abuse, and then discard.

Social Media Globalist - Facebook

During an April 10, 2018 testimony before the US Senate, Facebook billionaire Mark Zuckerberg responded to a Senate inquiry in a way that successful entrepreneurs of past generations never would have. When asked if the growth of Facebook was indicative of opportunities available in America, Zuckerberg managed to bob and weave with non-answers until a Facebook-friendly Senator interjected, "My question was meant to be an easy yes."

Consistent in the world of Socialist globalists is the need to walk the tightrope of international neutrality. As with the approach of the president of ABC after the September 11 killing of three-thousand innocents, loyalty, patriotism, and the welfare of Americans consistently take a backseat to potential revenue that can be generated from foreigner customers. In discussing the American culture of freedom versus the Russia authoritarianism, a typical American might say something like: "America is a democracy with reasonable levels of freedom and justice, and Russia is an autocracy with considerably less of those things."

Globalist Mark Zuckerberg would instead say, in his official capacity as Facebook's CEO, he doesn't choose sides in national rivalries or make value distinctions between different forms of government. If he were to choose a side, proclaiming a loyalty to his own free Capitalist country that allowed his wealth, he would risk excluding people. Facebook may be an American company beholden to U.S. laws, but its loyalty is to its two-billion users, more than three-quarters of whom live in other countries.[371] So it is that Socialist globalist Zuckerberg shares the same lack of loyalty perspective toward his American base as does the Socialist globalist and former president of ABC. This same strategy of distancing itself from its loyal American base for the sake of neutrality can be seen within the NFL, as it apparently sets its sights on the international market.

Use, abuse, and discard.

The words attributed to our Founding Father, Thomas Jefferson, highlight the symbiotic relationship between education and freedom: "If we are to guard against ignorance and remain free, it is the responsibility of every American to be informed."[372]

---

371   Jeff Bercovici. "Mark Zuckerberg Is Weirdly Quiet on Russian Election-Hacking Ads." *Inc.*, September 7, 2017. inc.com/jeff-bercovici/zuckerberg-russia-facebook.html.

372   "If We Are to Guard against Ignorance... (Spurious Quotation)." Historical. Thomas Jefferson Foundation, n.d. monticello.org/site/jefferson/if-we-are-guard-against-ignorance-spurious-quotation.

Any ideology that undermines the opportunity for education also hinders the acquisition of wisdom and knowledge and stops one from experiencing the empowerment of critical thinking. Such ideology is an enemy to freedom and our American culture. Understanding the intrinsic connection between education and freedom allows clarity in identifying the danger of the Socialist/Marxist policies facilitated by the Democratic Party. In every urban community that Democratic labor union education reigns, there you will find lack of education, wisdom, knowledge, and critical thinking skills. With this absence comes the increased inability to dream and envision. Hopelessness.

It is within the "at risk" population where, once again, can be found the Socialist globalist modus operandi to *use, abuse, and discard*. Consistently, and predictably, they prioritize the interests of the illegal foreign population. They neglect to address the high misery index of joblessness, illiteracy, crime, and the implosion of the family unit within the urban Black communities. Because of Democratic policies, they turn their energy and zeal to the promotion of open borders. With a narcissistic and unconscionable zeal, the Democratic Socialist/Marxists opt to stake their entire political future on a new set of voters, the illegal (non-American) immigrant. With the help and cover of the first Black president, Barack Obama, and secession-minded Leftist-run states, all available federal and state resources have been prioritized to ensure the successful settling, within our nation, of a new appreciative, dependent, and soon-to-be Democratic voter—illegal foreigners.

With absolutely *no shame*, the betrayal of native-born Black Americans can be seen in our country's leading sanctuary state of California:

- 2017 California's Department of Education (DOE) found that seventy-five percent of Black males were unable to pass standard reading and writing tests.[373]
- In San Francisco's predominantly Black high school, Charles R. Drew Preparatory Academy, nine out of ten of its students failed reading and math exams.
- San Francisco's poor White students outperformed their Black peers by more than thirty percentage points,[374]
- With historically low college attainment among African Americans, it was found that less than twenty-three percent of Black adults have a bachelor's degree, about half the rate of White Californians, and thirty percent have some college but no degree.

373   Matt Levin. "75% of Black California Boys Don't Meet State Reading Standards."
374   Jessica Calefati. "Why Is San Francisco the State's Worst County for Black Student Achievement?" *The Sacramento Bee*. October 28, 2017, sec. Education. sacbee. com/news/local/education/article181525146.html.

"In the Black community, there's this story that the road to freedom comes through the schoolhouse," said Ryan Smith, executive director of The Education Trust-West. "Looking at the state of Black students in California right now is a call to action."[375]

Because of the ideological leadership consistently chosen by the Black community, there will be no call to action. Instead, as FAIR (The Federation for American Immigration Reform) reports, federal and state resources will continue to flow to non-Americans. It was found that it cost taxpayers an estimated 43.9 billion dollars to educate illegal alien students in the 2015–2016 school year, and 59.2 billion dollars for programs to educate students lacking proficient English skills. FAIR estimated that it cost an average of 12,128 dollars per illegal immigrant student in the last school year and there were an estimated 3.618 million illegal immigrant students nationwide. In addition, it takes at least 1.7 billion dollars to educate 119,000 unaccompanied alien minors.[376]

The total cost at the federal, state, and local levels for undocumented immigrants is 113 billion dollars. State and local governments pay the clear majority—84 billion dollars. It has been President Trump's vision that the money spent on illegal immigration over the next ten years could provide one million at-risk students with a school voucher. At the behest of the Socialist/Marxist Public School Labor Union, the Democratic Party consistently stands vehemently against this freedom of educational choice.[377]

"Twenty-five billion dollars a year in costs associated with illegal immigration represents a fiscal crisis that affects California's ability to meet its basic obligations to citizens and legal residents," said Dan Stein, president of FAIR. While clearly the federal government bears responsibility for its failure—or *refusal*—to enforce our immigration laws, in California's case many of the burdens of illegal immigration are self-induced.

Despite overwhelming evidence that illegal immigration represents an unsustainable fiscal burden to the state, the California legislature and local governments across the state continue to provide new benefits, services, and privileges to illegal aliens, even as the state neglects the needs and concerns of

375   Alexei Koseff. "Where Have California's Black College Students Gone?" *The Sacramento Bee*. December 26, 2016, sec. Capitol Alert. sacbee.com/news/politics-government/capitol-alert/article122563984.html.

376   Alex Pfeiffer. "New Estimate Shows It Costs Nearly $44 Billion To Educate Illegal Aliens Annually." Political news. Dailycaller.com, September 14, 2016. dailycaller.com/2016/09/14/new-estimate-shows-it-costs-nearly-44-billion-to-educate-illegal-aliens-annually.

377   Miriam Valverde. "Donald Trump Says Illegal Immigration Costs $113 Billion a Year." *Politifact*. September 1, 2016. politifact.com/truth-o-meter/statements/2016/sep/01/donald-trump/donald-trump-says-illegal-immigration-costs-113-bi.

other Californians. The costs will continue to grow so long as the state continues to reward illegal immigration and impedes immigration enforcement. California taxpayers will continue to be the losers in this unhappy scenario.[378] Instead of providing the resources to help resolve this education and opportunity crisis faced by native-born Americans, the Silicon Valley tech conglomerates and elites import more than 1.5 million low-skilled foreign nationals every year. Mass immigration is responsible for native-born Americans becoming a minority in the tech hub of Silicon Valley, with seventy-one percent of high paying, high skilled, White collar jobs going to foreign-born workers.[379]

With the inability to successfully train the Black minority community to meet the most basic bar of literacy, there will be no competition for foreign-born workers from native-born Americans. Interesting was the absolute media silence, state and nationwide, and the lack of fanfare, concern, or consternation with the growing majority (75 percent) of illiterate Black boys in this state and the looming disastrous life changing consequences. The study serves as a statistical projection of a future of hopelessness and premature death for millions upon millions of Black Americans and a life sentence to poverty for multiple generations. It is the lack of a national uproar and a demand by politicians on both sides of the aisle that is most telling. Guaranteed, for example, would be a demand for a national conversation by invested interest groups if these boys betrayed by California politicians and educators were White, Asian, Hispanic, or even children of illegal immigrants. Because the only "invested interest groups" for urban Black Americans is a collection of Royalty Class Black elitists, the NAACP, the Congressional Black Caucus, and self-absorbed multi-millionaire entertainers, there has instead been a deafening silence and acceptance of these horrendous results.

One theory as to this silence is based on the perception of poor, uneducated members of minority races by Black and White elitists and eugenicist members of the Democratic party. It is a perspective first self-identified in 1900 by the Black intellectual, elitist, and self-avowed Socialist, W.E.B Du Bois, as he defined his social class of light-skinned, wavy haired intellectuals as the Talented Tenth. In Du Bois's own words: "...my panacea of earlier day was flight of class from mass through the development of the Talented Tenth." It is the view of this social class of elitists that intellectual inferiority and the resulting

---

378   "Illegal Immigration Costs California Taxpayers More Than $25 Billion a Year, Finds FAIR." Federation for American Immigration Reform (FAIR). June 19, 2014. fairus.org/press-releases/illegal-immigration-costs-california-taxpayers-more-25-billion-year-finds-fair.

379   John Binder. "Mark Zuckerberg Says Facebook Will 'Not Proactively' Work with ICE to Arrest, Deport Criminal Illegal Aliens." Breitbart, April 10, 2018. breitbart.com/big-government/2018/04/10/mark-zuckerberg-says-facebook-will-not-proactively-work-with-ice-to-arrest-deport-criminal-illegal-aliens.

inability to learn is the normal outcome for poor, dark skinned, and lower gene quality people. This was also the prevailing belief of the southern White racist and northern Socialist elitist throughout the '60s. These historical beliefs were evident in America's favorite national pastime, the NFL. Up through the mid to late '70s, Black athletes chosen to play in the NFL were considered capable of only playing skilled positions, not positions of thought, calculation, and leadership. Therefore, until the late '70s, leadership positions lacking in color were QB, center, middle linebacker, and free safety. Talented Black college QBs were, for instance, automatically transitioned to defensive backs or receivers.

A second theory has been perpetuated by Black Socialist/Marxist apologists and has taken root within the urban community. It is the belief that the Black community is failing because of slavery. In summary, "...the slavery of Black strangers by White strangers (now dead for over one hundred years) is the reason that the Black community is now at the top of our nation's 'Misery Index.'" This convoluted reasoning accepts the narrative that somehow, unlike all other races or cultures in the history of mankind, the experience of slavery for the Black race has been *forever branded* into its DNA. This excuse of blaming our present conditions on dead White strangers is one of the most illustrious examples of how to guarantee abject failure! Blame someone else, no matter how long they've been dead, for present personal actions and attitudes? If we adhere to this train of thought, we must also accept the godless Left's conclusion that there is no omnipotent god who blesses all who adhere to His will, regardless of race, creed, or color. Instead, it has been an all-powerful master White race that has dictated the progress of the Black race for over two-hundred years; therefore, it is a race that must be hated, derided, and plagued with "White Guilt" dictated by nothing more than the color of their skin. This would normally sound like the mind of the angry, illogical, and sick racist, if not for the Left's narrative that people with Black skin are inherently too weak and lacking power to be racist. The Socialist/Marxist public education system has been so effective in denying this community training for developing critical thinking skills that many Black Americans don't even know how to use common sense. They willfully accept the demeaning, degrading precept that, as members of the Black race, they are so hapless, weak, and powerless that the unjustified hate of others because of skin color is acceptable and perfectly rational.

This deluded yet pervasive perspective Black people have been indoctrinated to believe about their own ancestry is the greatest of all insults imaginable to past generations that produced the likes of Fredrick Douglas, Harriett Tubman, Booker T. Washington, and Martin Luther King. It's a vision that can only take root by deleting over two-hundred years of Black pride, success, and contribution, and replacing it with anti-American divisive Social/ Marxist propaganda. It does confirm the age-old strategy outlined by Karl Marx, that the ideological termites of Socialism and Marxism have for the last century undermined our nation's institution of learning and transformed them into centers of indoctrination. "The first battlefield," wrote Marx, "is the re-writing of history."

Our universities of indoctrination neglect to teach the factors surrounding the history of slavery. These are considered inconvenient truths to today's social justice warriors. History, for instance, informs us the very word "slave" stems from "Slav," i.e., a reference to the millions of (White) Slavish people who endured centuries of slavery at the hands of African Muslims—Europeans of various backgrounds were enslaved by African Muslims. Another obscure truth: as many as four-thousand free Black families owned Black slaves.[380]

Black Harvard scholar Henry Louis Gates discovered that free Blacks were in America before slavery. While researching the book and documentary *The African-Americans: Many Rivers to Cross*, Gates recorded that Blacks freely came to Florida as early as 1513—over one-hundred years earlier than the accepted date of 1619. A free Black man whose name is now known as Juan Garrido, was a conquistador in search of the Fountain of Youth while Juan Ponce de León lived in the antebellum South. Gates delivers a double whammy to the orthodox line on race and slavery in America when he revealed that it was "African elites" who "converted" the African masses to Christianity, and it was these same elitists—not European abductors—who sold their fellow Black Africans into slavery across the Atlantic.[381] What a stark reality check to once again see the interwoven character of the Black elitist, regardless of their African or American lineage. The act of enslaving their own for power, wealth, prestige, and class comes natural to them.

A final theory regarding the status of seventy-five percent of California's illiterate Black boys is that it has nothing to do with their skin tone. Instead, their lack of education is because of decades of anti-Black policies targeting them based on skin color and income level. Policies like the Democratic Party's No School Choice ensure the enslavement of poor Black children into failing labor union indoctrination centers. Leaving these students ill-equipped to enter the workplace or higher education, their illiteracy leads to a future of joblessness, hopelessness, and, for millions of boys and girls, an expressway to incarceration.

These American-born boys will not be equipped to compete for lucrative Silicon Valley jobs being offered by open border, globalist, social media giants. As labor union teachers continue their failure to educate, Socialist globalist media elitists continue to notice, and rather than rectify this travesty, they continue importing tens of thousands of foreigners annually. And regarding the Black community, they continue to...*use, abuse, and discard.*

---

380   Jack Kerwick. "Inconvenient Truths About Race & Slavery." *FrontPage Mag*, May 14, 2014. frontpagemag.com/fpm/225521/inconvenient-truths-about-race-slavery-jack-kerwick.

381   Henry Louis Gates, Jr. *Life Upon These Shores: Looking at African American History, 1513-2008*. Illustrated. New York: Alfred A. Knopf, 2011..

Entertainment Globalist - The NFL

During the 2016 and 2017 NFL seasons, dozens of NFL athletes were granted permission to demonstrate in a way that previous generations of NFL players would have considered unthinkable. They knelt, sat, stretched, raised their fist, or remained in the locker room while our flag, culture, and the sacrifice of countless millions of Americans from every background, creed, and color were being revered. In this setting, the NFL's commissioner, Roger Godell, made a decision that was antithetical to all past policies established to protect their brand. He chose to act as a "Mexican Matador" as his employees insulted millions of its loyal NFL fans weekly.

Emboldened by their employer's tolerance, the anti-flag protest grew to dozens as the protest peaked mid-season. With no check on the players who disrespected the flag, the players who knelt were treated as civil rights activists—heroes in our culture. Meanwhile, the point of view that the good ol' red, white, and blue as a symbol of what is best in America wasn't given a voice.[382] At no time during these seasons of protest were the voices of pro-flag players sought or welcomed. There was even a suggestion by the liberal Democrat sports writer Craig Calcaterra that the politically polarizing image of the American flag was the problem, not the players who disrespected it. As the lead baseball writer for NBC Sports, Calcaterra claimed that the image of the American flag is political. He tweeted, "Will you keep politics out of sports, please? We like sports to be politics-free."[383]

Tone-deaf as usual, the NFL and its media cohorts decided, before final team selection at the Super Bowl, they would televise any player protesting the anthem. "When you are covering a live event, you are covering what's happening," NBC Sports EP Fred Gaudelli told reporters at the Television Critics Association. "If there are players who choose to kneel, they will be shown live."

According to Fox News, "The anthem will be aired live and is scheduled to be performed by Pink. Potential protesters will have an opportunity to make a statement in front of a massive audience, as 112.2 million people watched Super Bowl LI last season, the fifth most-watched program in television history." [384]

---

382 Frank Miniter. "What If NBC and the NFL Had the Guts to Be Honest about Anthem Protests at the Super Bowl?" Fox News. January 14, 2018, sec. Opinion. foxnews.com/opinion/2018/01/14/what-if-nbc-and-nfl-had-guts-to-be-honest-about-anthem-protests-at-super-bowl.html.

383 Jon Street. "NBC Sports Writer Excoriated on Twitter after Saying American Flag Is Political." TheBlaze. April 16, 2017. theblaze.com/news/2017/04/16/nbc-sports-writer-excoriated-on-twitter-after-saying-american-flag-is-political.

384 Dylan Gwinn. "NBC Will Show Protesting NFL Players Live on Camera During the Super Bowl." Sports. Breitbart, January 10, 2018. breitbart.com/sports/2018/01/10/nbc-will-show-protesting-nfl-players-live-camera-super-bowl.

For decades, the NFL has had a no-nonsense reputation as the protector of its stellar pro-American brand. Concerns about any action that deflects from this perception, on and off the field, have resulted in actions from player fines to career-ending suspensions. Player fines vary by infraction type: from drugs, fighting, profanity, unsportsmanlike conduct, down to color of socks and cleats, extensive celebration in the end zone, and equipment alterations. Since 2007 over four million dollars in fines have been levied by the NFL on its players.[385] None of these have come close to the game-changing damage in the relationship between NFL fans and their teams resulting from the two-year tolerance by the NFL commissioner of the weekly anti-American flag protest and disrespect. Fans across the country have responded with their pocketbooks, eyeballs, and feet. The result of fan participation during the 2017 season has been:

- Thirty-three percent of the NFL fan base have stopped watching[386]
- NFL viewership down twenty percent in the last two years[387]
- The average audience per game fell 9.7 percent from 16.5 million fans in 2016 to 14.9 million in 2017[388]
- The NFL lost thirty million dollars in ad revenue[389]
- Super Bowl LII ratings for football's biggest game is lowest since 2009[390]
- Viewership down to 103.4 million people from last year's 111.3 million—the smallest audience since 2009 for TV's biggest perennial event

After two seasons of disruption, in which NFL fans by the millions shredded decades of tradition, they were rewarded at the end of the 2017 season with the

385 "Fines & Appeals: The NFL/NFLPA's Schedule of Infractions and Fines, and a Process for Appeal." Sports. NFL OPS, n.d. operations.nfl.com/football-ops/fines-appeals.

386 Darrelle Lincoln. "Poll Reveals 33% Of Fans Boycotted the NFL This Season Either in Support of Colin Kaepernick or Donald Trump." Total Pro Sports, January 8, 2018, sec. Poll. totalprosports.com/2018/01/08/poll-reveals-33-of-fans-boycotted-the-nfl-this-season-either-in-support-of-colin-kaepernick-or-donald-trump.

387 Austin Karp. "NFL Viewership Down Across The Board Again In '17; Cowboys Lead Top Telecasts." Street & Smith's Sports Business Daily. January 4, 2018. sportsbusinessdaily.com/Daily/Issues/2018/01/04/Media/NFL-TV.aspx.

388 Joe Flint. "NFL Ratings Fall at Faster Pace." *The Wall Street Journal*. January 4, 2018, sec. Articles. wsj.com/articles/nfl-ratings-fall-at-faster-pace-1515061801.

389 Warner Todd Huston. "NFL Lost $30 Million in Ad Revenue Over Cratering TV Ratings." Sports. Breitbart, January 28, 2018. breitbart.com/sports/2018/01/28/nfl-lost-30-million-ad-revenue-cratering-tv-ratings.

390 AP staff. "Super Bowl LII: Ratings for Football's Biggest Game Lowest since 2009." CBS News. February 5, 2018, sec. News. cbsnews.com/news/super-bowl-lii-tv-ratings.

opportunity to see the extent of arrogance and anti-American leaning of the NFL commissioner and the executive committee of billionaire owners. This multi-billion-dollar enterprise continues to disregard their pro-American fan base by granting a multi-million dollar, no-strings-attached donation to the Marxist social justice activists who have forever tarnished the Pro-American NFL brand. It is to this Marxist faction, supportive of and supported by the Democratic Party, NFL's leadership has unanimously chosen to transfer ninety million dollars. Negotiated within this package, 75 percent, or 67.56 million dollars, have been allocated to entities that have shown no history or interest in addressing the core needs of urban America. In the case of the reported avowed Marxist Van Jones, what is missing from his many federally-funded non-profit enterprises is any empirical data proving impact versus being nothing more than another façade of liberal executive projections, profits, and hype.

Meanwhile, throughout our country, thousands of established grassroots and experienced urban organizations can present such measurable data proving their *real* impact within the Black community. Instead of hyping the potential future of wealth for Renewable Energy Credits and green energy, they have been rolling up their sleeves, working hand-to-hand and heart-to-heart with programs that make real personal impacts via tutoring, mentoring, entrepreneurship, job training, and teaching financial, occupational, and personal life skills. Many of these non-profit organizations struggle annually and from one fundraising campaign to another, fighting to keep their doors open. The fact that the NFL chooses to give tens of millions of dollars to unproven, inexperienced social justice activists speaks to the true heart of their management. After all, the two-year protest they've allowed through sanctioned tolerance has centered on Black players' frustration of the chronic hopelessness within their depressed urban communities. If they sincerely cared about the outcome and improvement of Black lives, they would have approached this initiative as meticulously as they do when investing in a new stadium. They would have insisted on measurable algorithms from experienced applicants and a return on investment metrics proving promises made would be promises kept. If they cared, they would utilize panels of experts, not kowtow to hands-out, palms-up civil rights activists who only help acerbate the misery found in every Democratic stronghold—lack of education and jobs, disrespect for authority, the lack of entrepreneurial opportunities, record high father abandonment, and failure of the public school system.

The upside of the actions taken by the NFL to empower an anti-American ideology is that its fan base can now pull back the curtain and view the real heart and vision of NFL owners who prioritize global profits over national patriotism and their own brand. Millions will come to realize that this is not the same enterprise they grew up with and came to love and respect. It is no longer the corporation built by WWII-era entrepreneurs, coaches, and players who had an innate and extremely heartfelt love for our country reflected in its brand of traditional reverence for our National Anthem and the American flag. It was this All-American game that led our nation away from the era of

Jim Crow segregation into a sociality that saw firsthand teams and friendships come together with the strengths of diversity. It gave fans the opportunity to visualize tolerance and acceptance through its commitment to meritocracy and its "Just Win Baby" priority. It was built by America-loving men like Commissioner Pete Rosell, owners like Al Davis, coaches like Tom Landry, George Allen, Vince Lombardi, and generations of players, including mine, who would occasionally shed a tear listening to our national anthem and proudly watching the American flag wave.

Instead, for two years NFL fans have been forced to witness weekly anti-American sentiment and the unfolding of a globalist strategy that has become very common and prevalent with corporations controlled by the Liberal Left.

Use, Abuse, Discard.

DISCARD the American fan, as it's been demanded of them to tolerate the disrespect of our American flag/America way televised to millions throughout our country and around the world. Protesting the American flag has become a symbol of Black oppression embraced by young and wealthy athletes, educated and indoctrinated in Socialist/Marxist labor union public schools.

DISCARD the American fan, as NFL owners unfold a global strategy to tarnish the All-American brand with the goal to be more attractive to foreign markets and fans. This will in time is projected to replace the revenue sacrificed by the defection of NFL's once loyal pro-American fan base. This new global revenue represents a potential windfall of untold millions of international NFL fans and billions in foreign market TV revenue. Needed to attract and keep this new base of foreigners is the rebranding of the NFL, as with World Soccer, as globally neutral. This repositioning is a replication of the strategy used by the president of ABC after the September 11th attack when he banned his employees from wearing the American flag lapel pin. This is the mindset of globalists who justify minimizing American patriotism for the sake of maximizing global profits.

According to the NFL, Super Bowl XLI was broadcast to 232 countries and territories worldwide in 34 different languages. Based on data from the International Federation of American Football, there are 80 countries with organized NFL federations governing the game, from China to Germany to South Africa.[391] The top NFL foreign team countries are:

NFL International:
- China
- England
- Mexico

---

391   Kevin Seifert. "How American football is becoming a worldwide sport." ESPN, May 5, 2016. espn.com/nfl/story/_/id/15273529/how-american-football-becoming-worldwide-sport-europe-china-beyond.

- Brazil
- Japan
- Canada
- Sweden
- Germany
- France

DISCARD the urban Black community. Consistent with decades of Leftist promises and false mirages, behind the NFL curtain of the ninety-million-dollar social justice deal can be seen the old familiar "bait and switch." Instead of addressing the real needs of the Black community with opportunity, job creation, and the delivery of quality education, the NFL pieced together a proposal that in part awarded 22.5 million dollars to a former self-avowed communist, social justice incubator and Democratic Party pundit, Van Jones.

Another portion of the NFL's ninety-million-dollar payout was a fifty-million-dollar commitment to the Black community through the NFL's in-house Hopewell Fund. Though the initial demands for social justice were made by Black players and commitments of millions, for opportunities within the Black community, the decision of where it goes, how it's used, or even *if* it's used, is completely controlled by the White owners of the NFL. This strategy of using Black faces as a powerless façade for a White initiative is nothing new. It is reminiscent of the founding of the NAACP and the present status of Black Entertainment Television (BET).

The NAACP was founded in 1910 by twenty-one White, Socialist, Marxist, atheist, and eugenicist Democrats. Other than the name, the NAACP had nothing in common with the Black community during that era, who were Christian, Capitalist, patriotic, family-focused, and Republican. What should be noted is that after over one hundred years of the NAACP's influence and leadership, this is no longer the status of this once-proud and principled community. It has been transformed by this organization of Black elitists into a community that has voted in monolithic "groupthink" for Black Socialist, Marxist, atheist, and eugenicist Democrats.

The sole Black figure given a position within the NAACP infrastructure was an employed publisher of *The Crisis*, a Socialist and (later) avowed Communist, W.E.B Du Bois. As a powerless Black facade, Du Bois was required to submit all his articles to several of White NAACP Board members for overview before releasing to the Black community. He was fired in the early 1930s when he expressed views that were counter to the NAACP board members. Du Bois' controversial views came at the onset of the Depression, during a time when many of the businesses within the segregated Black community were failing. Unlike his earlier position as an unabashed integrationist, he felt during these times of hardship that Black consumers should support Black enterprises instead of White businesses. For stepping out of bounds on this "integration at all cost" position of the all-White Board of the NAACP, he was fired.

This same bait and switch strategy of using powerless Black façades to shield the agenda of White owned and controlled enterprises can be seen with the 2000 purchase of Black Entertainment TV by media giant Viacom. Though still perceived by its Black customers as a Black-owned and run enterprise this is, like the NAACP, a Black-faced façade. Though it features Black rappers, Black entertainers, and Black sports figures, has all-Black employees and a website with all-Black faces, its programming, direction, and mission is dictated by an all-White board of directors without the input of a single Black board member. When majority shareholder, Socialist/Marxist Sumner Redstone purchased BET, he understood this was an open pipeline to millions of Black urban children. This unfettered pipeline could have been used to infuse inspiring, educational, and encouraging programming. Instead, for almost two decades now, BET has represented a filthy and festering pool of Marxist indoctrination. It is through the White Viacom-owned media portal where we find the genesis of Black hate for country, White Americans, Capitalism, police, and women. It is *the* source of indoctrination for Black victimhood, the insulting and demeaning narrative of White superiority (i.e., "White Privilege"), the spewing of angry racist Black Lives Matter proponents, and where the Marxist-inspired Antifa and social justice finds 24/7 advocacy.

As seen in the stealth ingratiation of the NAACP's White Socialist/Marxist founders into the Black community in 1910, it is similar ingratiation of the Socialist/Marxist Viacom leadership into the 2000 urban Black community today. Added to the tenacious indoctrination efforts faced by the Black community, the recent NFL's 2017 ninety-million-dollar payoff to social justice (Marxist) causes will, in time prove problematic for this already-demoralized community.

It is predictable, based on past Leftist initiatives, that the real impact of these NFL dollars into the Black community will be fruitless and damaging. After the initial national PR praise for the NFL's good intentions have died down and proper tax write-offs have been deducted, the spreading of wealth from the Hopewell Fund will begin in earnest amongst their own kind. With the players lacking any control of where, how, to whom, and *if* these funds are directed, the NFL management team controlling these funds will likely bypass the experienced, established, urban-based non-profit organizations. Most assuredly, there will be funnel of funds to the same political leaning organizations who supported the anti-flag protest for two seasons finding backchannel means to connect their causes to the NFL's handout bonanza.

Once again, those within the urban community who believed in the promises of hope and change will face disappointment with the transfer of the NFL's wealth to social justice activists. They will again be forced to live with the reality of the true heart and soul of Socialism, Marxism, and atheism. Summarized?

Use, Abuse, and Discard.

Dream Corps (22.5 Million Dollars)

Dream Corps founder, Van Jones, is a self-avowed radical revolutionary Communist,[392] and presently a Democratic pundit. Dream Corps sponsored the anti-Trump "We Rise" tour and provided catchy posters for its ongoing "Anti-Fascist War." One reads: "Real Men Rep the F-Word #Feminist." Another proclaims: "No Ban. No Wall. Sanctuary for All."

In 1994, Jones formed a Socialist collective called "Standing Together to Organize a Revolutionary Movement," or STORM. In the spring of 2004, the group held "structured political education" training at every meeting "to help members develop an understanding of the basics of Marxist politics." They "trained members on Capitalism and wage exploitation, the state and revolution, imperialism, and the revolutionary party."[393]

Jones is also noted for signing a petition in 2004 from the group 911Truth. org that questioned whether Bush administration officials "may indeed have deliberately allowed 9/11 to happen, perhaps as a pretext for war."[394] It was during the Obama administration, as the Green Czar, that Jones rose in prominence with a mandate to use federal dollars and donations as a non-profit entity to create green jobs in Oakland, California. What has been most discerning about Jones as a "community leader" is his silence regarding the dismal state of education for Black children throughout his state. Understanding that the future of the Black community will be directly linked to the education of its children, why has Jones *not* been one of Black children's strongest advocates for quality education? Instead, he advocates for open borders, which creates competition for Black Americans at the lowest rung on the economic ladder and increases demand and competition for educational resources needed by Black children. He stands with his fellow Royalty Black Class elitists against school choice options that would allow poor Black children to use vouchers to access the same quality education granted to middle and upper class children. Why did the NFL choose Van Jones—whose Marxist and Communist leanings can be Googled—to receive a payout of twenty-two million dollars?

The United Negro College Fund (UNCF), also known as the United Fund, is an American philanthropic organization that funds scholarships for Black students and general scholarship funds for thirty-seven private historically

---

392   Robert Farley. "Glenn Beck Says Van Jones Is an Avowed Communist." Politifact. September 8, 2009. politifact.com/truth-o-meter/statements/2009/sep/08/ glenn-beck/glenn-beck-says-van-jones-avowed-communist.

393   *Ibid.*

394   Scott Wilson, and Garance Franke-Ruta. "White House Adviser Van Jones Resigns Amid Controversy Over Past Activism." *The Washington Post.* September 6, 2009, sec. Politics. voices.washingtonpost.com/44/2009/09/06/van_jones_resigns.html.

Black colleges and universities. UNCF was incorporated on April 25, 1944 by Frederick D. Patterson, then-president of Tuskegee University, Mary McLeod Bethune, and others. UNCF supported approximately 65,000 students at over 900 colleges and universities with approximately 113 million dollars in grants and scholarships. About sixty percent of these students are the first in their families to attend college, and sixty-two percent have annual family incomes of less than 25,000 dollars. UNCF also administers over 450 named scholarships having a direct, measurable impact on the lives of Black children leaving poverty. With a reach that supports the education of 65,000 students, why did the NFL give it the same financial priority of 22 million dollars, as that of a former communist, Socialist Justice incubator activist?

The Players Coalition was a group of about forty NFL players who negotiated with the league owners on a deal to commit at least eighty-nine *million* dollars through 2023 to local and national community efforts related to social justice reform. This *spending breaks down over seven years and involves donations of 250,000 dollars per year per owner, with an equal amount contributed by players. That's chump change, especially considering how that money might be spent. The rest of the money is to come from the league's coffers, but, according to 49ers safety Eric Reid, one of the original social justice advocates,* "the league could simply shuffle around funds that had already been allocated to charity projects or spend the money on public service announcements that essentially served as advertising for the league itself." *Reid concluded that the NFL may be doing little more than transferring dollars between charitable organizations, like Salute to Service and Breast Cancer Awareness, to social justice causes. He called the deal a "charade"*[395] *and a glorified NFL Cares.*[396] He told Slate magazine, "...it would really be no skin off the owners' backs. They would just move the money from those programs to this one," adding that he and other players were not on board with the agreement because "we weren't trying to cut other worthy programs."

Reid's understanding is that regarding the source of funding, the money would come from funds that are already allocated to Breast Cancer Awareness and Salute to Service. Reid removed himself from the Players Coalition, believing that the agreement was essentially a cop-out that would do little to affect real change, and he believed the league pushed fellow social justice activist, Eagle Safety Malcolm Jenkins, into an agreement so the announcement

---

395   Jeremy Stahl. "'It's a Charade.'" *Slate*. November 30, 2017, sec. Sports. slate. com/culture/2017/11/eric-reid-says-nfl-wants-to-use-money-from-military-programs-to-buy-off-players.html.

396   Barry Petchesky. "The NFL's Proposal To End Anthem Protests Gives The League All The Power." Deadspin, November 30, 2017, Sports edition, sec. NFL. dead-spin.com/the-nfls-proposal-to-end-anthem-protests-gives-the-nfl-1820876878.

could be made before Roger Goodell's contract was discussed at the owners' meeting. [397]

> NOTE: Allowed by the NFL league to protest as anti-flag activists, Reid and Kaepernick have effectively tarnished their individual reputations and brand. These factors not only determine the length of NFL careers, but also the financial value of their name and brand after retirement. As the 2018 season neared, neither were employed, with no team showing interest.

> Use, Abuse, and Discard.

The NFL Hopewell Fund

The NFL Hopewell Fund is part of an NFL/ Players Coalition agreement to stop the anti-flag protesting during the national anthem. It's a deal that, by design, gives the all-White NFL management team voting control over the fifty million dollars in "charitable contributions" slated for the Players Coalition.

The agreement gave twenty-five percent of the national fund, separate from the money contributed by owners and players, to the United Negro College Fund, twenty-five percent to Dream Corps, and the other fifty percent to the Players Coalition. But the Players Coalition isn't a real charity, and the report goes on to add that it has not "filed 501(c)(3) and 501(c)(4) paperwork for nonprofit status as a fiscally sponsored project." That project will then be overseen and advised by the Hopewell Fund.[398]

It's important to recognize that a fiscally-sponsored project is not a charity, it's a project that is overseen by another 501(c)(3) organization.[399] Think of it as a project housed within a charity. One of the most important distinctions is that they do not file public tax returns. They are not charities.[400] In context, it must be remembered that this league has a history of being heavy-handed with its generosity. When the NFL pledged thirty million dollars to concussion

397 Chase Crosby. "NFL, Some Players Reach $89 Million Deal That Could Still Include Protests." Forbes.com, November 30, 2017. forbes.com/sites/chase-crosby/2017/11/30/nfl-some-players-reach-89-million-deal-that-could-still-include-protests/2/#21373d8841f4.

398 Diana Moskovitz. "What The Hell Is The Hopewell Fund?" Deadspin, December 1, 2017, Sports edition, sec. NFL. deadspin.com/what-the-hell-is-the-hopewell-fund-1820881123.

399 "Fiscal Sponsorship for Nonprofits." Advocacy. National Council of Nonprofits, n.d. councilofnonprofits.org/tools-resources/fiscal-sponsorship-nonprofits.

400 Diana Moskovitz. "What The Hell Is The Hopewell Fund?"

research, it demanded final say on what research received the money—and blocked it from going to a researcher who had been critical of the league. The NFL eventually pulled out of its partnership with NIH with more than half of that thirty million unspent.[401]

As for how future money will be disbursed, the proposal creates a group of five players, five owners, and two league staffers. Do the math. NFL management carries this voting body 7-5, making it dubious how much say players will have in how the money is spent.

Let's recap. NFL owners are pledging to spend a paltry amount, not pledging that they won't just take that money from previous charitable pledges, not promising that they won't veto players' preferences on where the money should be spent, setting up a voting body specifically designed to outvote those players, and expecting that this will stop players from protesting during the national anthem. No wonder so many players from the so-called Players Coalition have walked away in disgust.[402]

Interestingly, the National Basketball Association, whose rooster makeup is eighty percent Black and share the same social justice concerns, made clear the value of its fan base. The NBA commissioner, unlike the NFL commissioner, set parameters in a preseason statement that the anti-flag protest would not be tolerated during business hours. The NFL's support of their players' anti-flag/anti-White sentiment became apparent from the beginning of its 2016 election season.

The initial kneeler, Colin Kaepernick, began his protest during the fall of the presidential election year. Always consistent with the Democratic Party's "Riot the Vote" strategy for urban Black Americans are the riots, flag-burning, anti-police, anti-American demonstrations that can be guaranteed to be employed to energize their frustrated and hopeless base. Kaepernick represents a prime example of college Marxist indoctrination training. For the four years prior, during, and after his anti-flag/anti-White oppression protest, he failed to use any of his twelve-million-dollar salary to start a business and hire even one of the eighty-three percent of Black teen males unemployed across our nation. He has been utterly mute about the status of the seventy-five percent of Black boys failing to pass standard reading and writing tests in his home state of California. To speak on this matter would take real courage since the education system is controlled by fellow Socialist/Marxists, the National Education labor union. With months of free time during his off-season, Kaepernick did not take the initiative to pull together his NFL, NBA, and multi-millionaire entertainment peers to start a MAN-UP awareness campaign, a campaign sorely needed in a community where seventy percent of

401   *Ibid.*

402   Barry Petchesky. "The NFL's Proposal To End Anthem Protests Gives The League All The Power."

Black men desert their own children. He has not traveled to Chicago, Detroit, Ferguson, or Baltimore to assess what kind of service he could perform to give a message of encouragement to the hopeless, uneducated, jobless Black boys who are killing each other by the thousands.

Instead, our young, college-indoctrinated, Marxist, after controversy erupted around him, saw the benefit of contributing some of his own money to his cause, and alerted the press of his generous offering. Predictably, Kaepernick will contribute to social justice initiatives committed to produce more Marxists like him. Totally clueless of Cuban American history, he opted to go to Miami, Florida to be interviewed wearing a T-shirt depicting the all-time oppressing Communist dictator and murderer, Fidel Castro. Taking cluelessness to another level, he then showed up at practice wearing socks depicting police pigs. Meanwhile, the team paying him twelve million dollars to take them to the Super Bowl is ranked at the bottom of their division.

With his season of missteps, Kaepernick somehow missed the memo from the Democratic Party stating the primary purpose for the "Riot to Vote" strategy and the NFL commissioner's tolerance for his anti-American protest during the presidential campaign season. His angry energy was supposed to propel him to the polls to vote Democrat. Unfortunately for the Democrats, Kaepernick and other social justice warriors like him didn't bother to vote this pivotal election year at all. This in part highlights the danger posed by Democrats. In convincing their young Marxists that their power comes only with groupthink and group bullying, they don't see the importance or power as single individuals to vote.

Due to Kaepernick's Marxist training of disdain for American culture, history, and values, he arrogantly casts a broad net accusing the White race as oppressors and the root cause for all the ills of the Black race. He lives in a country that has granted Black Americans more freedom and opportunity than any other in the history of mankind, yet his ingratitude allows him to discount the efforts of thousands of White Americans who facilitated the freedom of over one-hundred-thousand Black men, women, and children via the Underground Railroad. His mind remains stubbornly closed to the true history of the Republican party, whose sole purpose for existence was to fight against slavery. He remains totally enamored, blindly loyal, and dedicated to a party of Black and White elitist Democrats, whose policies today reflect their animus for the poor within the Black race. It has been from its beginning, as it remains today, the party of death and evil. Within their urban city-run plantations, whose overseers are elitist wealthy Black politicians, is found the exact same forces of divisiveness found throughout the 1800s antebellum south: Slavery, Segregation, Secession and Socialism. Home within this party are the policies that are the genesis of Black misery; welfare dependency, educational segregation, targeted illiteracy, infanticide, and elderly euthanasia. This is the party of states whose disloyalty led to an unconstitutional attempt for secession, and deaths of 600,000 Americans. This is the party that banned prayer from school, are attempting to rebrand the American flag as political speech, attempting to ban conservative free speech on college campuses and social media venues, attempting to ban the right to worship as a Christian, and the right to bear arms as a free American.

It is the Democratic Party that serves as home for the godless ideologies of Socialism and Marxism, leaving in its wake young pro-Cuba Marxists like Colin Kaepernick, who has animus for police authority and those of a different color than himself. He's been taught to discount the more than six hundred thousand White Civil War soldiers whose lives symbolize the atonement of a nation that put a violent end to the evils of slavery. He takes on the role of an unforgiving judge who hates White strangers that lived and died hundreds of years before he was ever born. He remains unaware of the purposeful failure of his anti-American, anti-God, Socialist/Marxist professors to teach the correct history of slavery. They have failed to inform him that slavery wasn't a White innovation. It has been in existence worldwide for over three-thousand years and among Black African Muslims for over one-thousand. It was in America that this evil was totally eradicated within seventy-nine years of the country's founding.

Kaepernick is probably also not aware that slavery and sex trafficking still exist today in third world countries and among Black African Muslims. He is likely unaware of White Americans today who seek out and free sex slaves of all nationalities throughout the world (as part of Operation Underground Railroad).[403]

Kaepernick is now free and wealthy enough to take part and support the ending of physical bondage to thousands around the world and millions of his own race in mental bondage to a godless ideology. He can now personally *act* and do more than take a knee to ensure that future generations will not judge him as little more than an empty suit.

Unfortunately, for those who remain in bondage beyond the sound-bites of Marxist social justice rhetoric, there will assuredly be no help from our wealthy millionaire Marxists like Colin Kaepernick. Black misery has been present in every urban community in our country, and yet none of it is being discussed or addressed by Leftists in the Democratic Party.

- Seventy-five percent of Black boys in the state of California failed to pass standard reading and writing test[404]
- Eighty-two percent of Black teen males in Chicago are unemployed...83 percent nationally[405]

---

403   "Operation Underground Railroad (O.U.R.): Paving the Way for Permanent Eradi-cation of Child Sex Trafficking." Operation Underground Railroad, 2018, 2017. ourrescue.org.

404   Grace Carr. "Report: 75% Of Black California Boys Fail To Meet Reading And Writing Standards."

405   Ann Brown. "No Openings: 92% Of Black Male Chicago Youth Are Out Of Work."

- Seventy-two percent of Black children are deserted by their fathers[406]
- Forty-one percent increase in welfare under President Obama[407]
- Twenty-million babies, or forty percent of the present population of Black Americans, have been killed by White Democratic abortionists since 1973
- 3.8 percent participation of Black Americans as entrepreneurs, a race low[408]

The consistent motive operandi of the Marxist elitist, outside of leading demonstrations and headlining with racially divisive speeches, is they do not engage in any of the "personal" heavy lifting; of rolling up their sleeves and giving hand-to-hand, heart-to-heart service. Such efforts are beneath them.

NFL: Profits over Patriotism

For those who understand the power of Capitalism, it is easy to calculate motivation, good or bad, by following the money. NFL Commissioner Roger Godell's leadership over the last several years has led to a precipitous decline in ratings, fan support, attendance, and ad revenue. There is a probability that the stellar All-American NFL brand that was built over many decades will never recover to its former days of glory. As will be discussed in this chapter, that may be by design.

For allowing the disruptive and destructive nature of partisan politics to be introduced to the NFL for two seasons, Godell was rewarded with an extension of his position as commissioner. His five-year, 200 million-dollar-plus corporate jet perks comes as a surprise to those who have traditionally connected large executive contracts offerings with substantial corporate growth Interestingly, the NFL has experienced a substantial decline in viewership and ratings as follows:

Factors in the 2016 NFL: A Rating Decline of roughly 12 percent:
- Players not standing
- Viewers distracted by the presidential campaign
- NFL's handling of domestic violence cases involving players
- Games on too many days (oversaturation)

---

406   NewsOne staff. "72 Percent Of Black Kids Raised By Single Parent, 25% Overall In U.S." NewsOne, April 27, 2011, sec. Nation. newsone.com/1195075/children-single-parents-u-s-american.

407   S. Noble. "Welfare Increased 41% Under Obama." Independent Sentinel, April 22, 2012, sec. US news. independentsentinel.com/welfare-increased-41-under-obama.

408   "Black Owned Businesses." Metrics. Black Demographics, 2012. blackdemo-graphics.com/economics/Black-owned-businesses.

- Market increased interest in postseason baseball
- Ongoing controversy over head injuries in the NFL
- A decline in quality of play on the field[409]

In 2017, NFL ratings declined an additional nine percent during the regular season and six percent during the playoffs.[410]

Looking at some of the details of a 200-million-dollar contract released to the public might shed some light as to the commissioner's growth strategy. Of the forty million dollars/year contract, ninety percent of it is based on growth in incentives, with only 4 million dollars/year guaranteed.[411]

From a traditional ROI perspective, having overseen consecutive years of a softening American market with no end in sight, it would appear a bit curious that the NFL commissioner would stake ninety percent of his fifty million dollars/year contract on growth incentives. With the most precipitous decline over two years of anti-flag protesting ending with the doubling down by the NFL management paying tens of millions of dollars to Marxist social justice activists, the question arises for any reasonable investor: Where is this NFL growth coming from that would justify an additional 180 million dollars in salary over a five-year period? Is it possible that it has already been calculated that the American fan base will continue to trend negatively, so it is no longer the marketing priority? Is it possible that tarnishing the once-stellar All-American NFL brand was purposeful and not a result of gross marketing ineptitude? Is it possible that the two-year tolerance and promotion of anti-flag, Anti-American, "White oppression" Marxist propaganda was designed to rebrand a more neutral perception of the NFL? Strategically this would improve the NFL's global acceptance and image for its new foreign fans much akin to soccer's. World Cup attraction and billions in global TV revenue. This has, after all, been the priority of other US elitist globalists—"profits and power over patriotism."

It is this "profits and power" equation that Americans witnessed after 9/11 when ABC banned the American flag lapel pin for the sake of global

---

409 Ryan Wilson. "Poll: Main Reason for NFL Ratings Drop Due to Players Kneeling during Anthem." CBS News. October 27, 2016, sec. News. cbssports.com/nfl/news/poll-main-reason-for-nfl-ratings-drop-due-to-players-kneeling-during-anthem.

410 Peter Kafka. "NFL Ratings Were down All Season, and There's No Reason to Think They'll Get Better next Year." Technology news. Recode, February 4, 2017. recode.net/2017/2/4/14508632/nfl-tv-ratings-down-moffettnathanson.

411 Dylan Gwinn. "NFL Commissioner Goodell Signs New Contract Worth Up To $200 Million." Sports. Breitbart, December 6, 2017. breitbart.com/sports/2017/12/06/nfl-commissioner-goodell-signs-new-contract-worth-200-million.

neutrality. It is what Black residents in California see as Silicon Valley's Democratic elitists import thousands of foreign laborers while failing to invest in or *demand* a quality education that would prepare millions of failing Black American children to compete.

Americans witnessed this equation recently as elite globalist and CEO of Facebook, Mark Zuckerberg, during his Congressional testimony when he refused to answer in the affirmative whether his business represented opportunities indicative of the America way. Power over patriotism can be seen in today's Democratic party of Socialist/Marxists who are obsessed with allowing unfettered open border access. They somehow justify protecting the most despicable and heinous illegal felons and putting at risk every American who cannot afford to live in armed, gated communities. Black Americans are especially hit hard by the empathy-free policy of open borders, as they chronically suffer in misery at the bottom at the economic rung. The Democratic Party's vision is of millions of illegal foreigners flooding into our country and eventually obtaining the right to vote through unconstitutional laws passed by a Democrat-dominated House of Representatives. These laws would be upheld by a series of Socialist/Marxist-dominated courts all the way to the Supreme Court. They encourage the invasion of foreigners from every anti-American third world nation around the world, many of whom have no desire to assimilate into the American culture. Some enter the land of the free un-vetted and with a strong anti-American animus. These are the new inhabitants welcomed unabashedly by the Socialist/Marxist Leftists in the Democratic Party.

> *Transformation: "to make a thorough or dramatic change in the form, appearance, or character of."*

> *"We are five days away from fundamentally transforming the United States of America."*
>
> —*Barack Obama, October 30, 2008*[412]

> *"We are going to have to change our conversation; we're going to have to change our traditions, our history; we're going to have to move into a different place as a nation."*
>
> —*Michelle Obama, May 14, 2008*[413]

---

412   Victor Davis Hanson. "Obama: Transforming America." National Review. October 1, 2013, Online edition, sec. Politics & Policy. nationalreview.com/2013/10/obama-transforming-america-victor-davis-hanson.

413   *Ibid.*

Born out of these Socialist/Marxists' transformed society would be the extension and growth of an unlimited dependent class that supplants the Black community. This would be a community of diverse illegal foreigners granted through the courts full voting rights as American citizens without the requirement of love for and appreciation of the American citizenry. Due to the potential political power of this new group of dependents, they will be granted priority for jobs, education, business opportunities, and the like. As they have in the sanctuary cities and states, they will compete for and take away these opportunities from Black American men, women, and teens. This is the way of the Socialist/Marxist and elitist globalist of the Democratic Party.

Use, Abuse, and Discard.

The Global Stats: Profits vs Patriotism

- NFL's US Market Status
- NFL fans who intentionally stopped watching: 33 percent
- Viewership down 18 percent
- Loss of thirty million dollars in ad revenue
- Super Bowl ratings plummet to an eight-year low

NFL's Global Market: Status

According to the International Federation of American Football (IFAF), there are eighty countries with organized federations governing the game, from China to Germany to South Africa. Overall, IFAF's best estimate is that there are thousands of leagues and hundreds of thousands of boys, girls, men, and women playing at levels ranging from high school to soccer-like club leagues powered by player dues and local sponsors. China's leagues received a boost when the NFL acknowledged plans to stage a game there in 2018. The country also will host the under-19 world championship in the summer of 2018 at Harbin University of Commerce in the Heilongjiang province of northeast China.

In America, the NFL's annual revenues have reached thirteen billion dollars. The league is attempting to grow that number to twenty-five billion by 2027, and China's vast resources and population offer an obvious market. The league has staffed a marketing office in China for a decade and is hopeful of drawing 10,000 people for this summer's under-19 championships. It's a small number for a country so large, and most games in China draw no more than 5,000 fans, but the sport's five-year growth from almost nothing is notable, and a new television-friendly arena league is scheduled to debut in the fall of 2018.

Ultimately, the endgame of staging Chinese football leagues could be to enhance curiosity about the NFL. Consider that two countries with long histories of American football, the United Kingdom and Mexico, drew more than 350,000 to four NFL regular-season games they hosted in 2016.

England

Games in the United Kingdom are broadcast by the BBC and Sky Sports, either live on BBC2 or online via the BBC Sports website and interactive TV, and on Sky Sports Action. The games have been popular, with tickets for the two games per season selling out in two days, nine months in advance. According to the NFL, only three percent of those attending the London games are Americans or American expatriates, while twenty-two percent are from London and sixty percent from elsewhere in Britain. Ticket prices are from thirty-five British pounds for end zone seats to a hundred pounds for lower sideline seats. A team that plays a home game in London sells a cheaper season ticket package for its own stadium with seven regular season games rather than the usual eight. Each designated home team receives one million US dollars for giving up the home game.[414]

The United Kingdom has surpassed all other countries along a timeframe roughly parallel to the NFL's increased regular-season presence there. NFL teams played three games in London in 2016: two at Wembley Stadium and one at Twickenham Stadium. Internal NFL numbers count thirteen-million NFL/American football fans in the U.K., and four million U.K. residents tuned in to watch Super Bowl 50, according to the NFL's U.K. office. Registered players in the U.K. doubled to 50,000 between 2011 and 2014.[415]

- NFL is already talking about a Super Bowl in London
- A permanent NFL team in London
- Tickets are twice as expensive in London
- Jaguars have a multiyear contract; the price for media rights has doubled since 2007

London Mayor Sadiq Khan told *Talksport* that he's eager to see the NFL expand its presence in his city, and he believes there could be a franchise based in London full-time, and a Super Bowl in London. "I've been saying since the first day I became Mayor my ambition is to have *more American football games in London* and ultimately for there to be a franchise there and, dare I say it, even the Super Bowl," Khan said. "I met recently one of the owners of the Jacksonville Jaguars, Shahid Khan. I've met the NFL commissioner on a

---

414   Omar Kelly. "Dolphins Will Host New York Jets in London in 2015." Sun Sentinel. November 6, 2014, sec. Sports. sun-sentinel.com/sports/miami-dolphins/sfl-dolphins-will-host-new-york-jets-in-london-in-2015-20141106-story.html.

415   Kevin Seifert. "How American Football Is Becoming a Worldwide Sport." Sports news. ESPN, May 5, 2016. espn.com/nfl/story/_/id/15273529/how-american-football-becoming-worldwide-sport-europe-china-beyond.

number of occasions, most recently at the game at Twickenham this year and my team is working very closely with the NFL."[416]

Mexico

Mexico, whose long history with American football dates to 1896,[417] fields competitive national teams and is one of two countries besides the U.S., the other Canada, with a true professional league that pays players enough to make it a full-time job during the season.[418] The NFL will host Estadio Azteca for Monday Night Football in November 2018 when the Raiders face the Texans.[419]

Germany

There are roughly 35,000 registered players in Germany.[420] The emergence of German wide receiver Moritz Boehringer, the first player to be drafted into the NFL directly from a European league (sixth round, Minnesota Vikings), brings a new level of attention. But for the moment at least, international football is a world of football-industrial diplomacy where long-term health concerns and NFL-related cynicism have not yet descended.[421]

Ireland

In 2012 League officials visited Dublin's Croke Park and found the venue "very attractive." The home of the Gaelic games and more than a few U2 concerts, Croke has a capacity of 82,500.[422]

Brazil

Teams in Brazil, another country the NFL has targeted for a possible game, record wild fan interest. In some cases, they're challenging established club soccer teams with 15,000 fans per game. The Corinthian Steamrollers,

---

416   Michael David Smith. "Mayor Angling for an NFL Franchise and a Super Bowl in London." Sports news. NBC Sports, March 27, 2018. profootballtalk.nbcsports.com/2018/03/27/mayor-angling-for-an-nfl-franchise-and-a-super-bowl-in-london.

417   Pablo Viruega. "Mexico's Long Love Affair with Football, American-Style." Sports news. ESPN, October 1, 2008. espn.com/espn/hispanicheritage2008/news/story?id=3620057.

418   http://www.espn.com/nfl/story/_/id/15273529/how-american-football-becoming-worldwide-sport-europe-china-beyond.

419   Kevin Seifert. "How American Football Is Becoming a Worldwide Sport."

420   *Ibid.*

421   *Ibid.*

422   Dan Hanzus. "NFL Considering Ireland for Regular-Season Game." Sports news. NFL, June 20, 2012. nfl.com/news/story/09000d5d82a0040a/article/nfl-considering-ireland-for-regularseason-game.

founded in 2004 and based in Sao Paulo, boasts more than 1.4 million likes on their Facebook page.

Japan
Japan, meanwhile, has a competitive corporate entity known as the X League, made up of teams of players from the companies where they work. Japan's national team has advanced to the finals of the quadrennial IFAF World Championship in four of the past five tournaments. (The 2015 title went to the U.S., which has won each of the three times it has competed.)

Canada
Has a true professional league that pays players enough to make it a full-time job during the season.

Sweden
Belgrade SBB Vukovi players played in 2015 European Champions League final. The Serbian squad lost to Sweden's Carlstad Crusaders in the title game.

"In terms of the NFL, players are one thing, but in terms of fan base, as more football happens here, and more fans become educated, you'll see it grow more from an entertainment standpoint than maybe as a player pool," said Zach Brown, American Football League of China co-founder.[423] In the early days, before he spoke Chinese and with little clue where it would lead, Brown printed up a business card. Translated from Chinese, it read: "I play American football. You look like a dude who could play. Contact us here."

Brown, now 29, was a former Division I player working in the international business world. He loved football and wanted to keep playing while based in Shanghai, but he also understood the potential for growth in the world's most populated nation. Brown and another former college player, Chris McLaurin, formed the American Football League of China and began recruiting players, handing out Chinese business cards to one big dude at a time.

Today, the AFLC includes about one-thousand players on sixteen teams throughout China, the most significant football league in a country that now counts about five thousand men and women playing some level of tackle football. While it is a small number relative to China's population of 1.4 billion, it has grown in the past five years and is part of a large global movement endorsed by the NFL but unknown to most Americans, to spread what is perceived to be a uniquely American game around the globe.[424]

---

423   Kevin Seifert. "How American Football Is Becoming a Worldwide Sport."
424   *Ibid.*

South Africa

In South Africa, organizers held a training camp to gauge interest and skill level for a proposed new league. They have received calls from interested parties in Zimbabwe, Uganda, and Nairobi, all asking for advice on how to start a tackle football league. Regions wanting to promote American football but lacking in expertise have imported coaches for training and clinics.

CHAPTER 20

THE SOLUTION: "WE THE PEOPLE"

"I've spoken of the Shining City all my political life. In my mind it was a tall, proud city built on rocks stronger than oceans, windswept, God-blessed, and teeming with people of all kinds living in harmony and peace; a city with free ports that hummed with commerce and creativity. And if there had to be city walls, the walls had doors and the doors were open to anyone with the will and the heart to get here. That's how I saw it and see it still."

—*Ronald Reagan's farewell address to the nation*

*W*e *the People*. The most empowering combination of three words ever inspired of God to man. In a nation unique in its unselfish approach to addressing the problems of its people, these first three words of our Constitution highlight the framers' intent to encourage inclusion, fairness, and opportunity for all. In the history of mankind, there have never been three more powerful words that conceptualize the vision of a freedom seeking people.

"We the People."

This signifies the confidence of a Heavenly Father who confirms that within a collection of unified individuals are the answers to our most inspired dreams and solutions to our most daunting problems. By searching within, *we* can overcome our obstacles, *we* can mend our differences and forgive, *we* can choose our pathway, support, defend, and provide for our own families, *we* can receive Heavenly guidance and be led in keeping our nation free. These three words of self-empowerment capture the mission of a country that continues to improve to find its better self. *We* have done better than any other society in the history of mankind due to our innate ability to see beyond our many differences to instead embrace our commonality...*being Americans.*

I have written this book, in fact, to educate and empower *all* Americans.

"We the People."

With an understanding of the pitfalls experienced over the last sixty years by millions within our minority population, we can establish warning buoys that will prevent our country from traveling into that same destructive territory.

There are lessons to be learned from the Black communities' journey over this last century. Some are based on God's spiritual truths that define happiness for all of humankind. Others show the benefits of political empowerment of the individual, transferring power away from the powerful and influential. All solutions center on the concept of accountability and point to the precept of the Golden Rule—treating others as we ourselves would like to be treated. Acceptance of this creed should not only be expected as part of an individual's demeanor but should be demanded of those paid to serve in the public square.

The Golden Rule should be the standard by which we hold *all* educators accountable as they teach our children. There should be no employment protection, tenure, or labor union-contrived job security for those who provide inferior and inept services to others because of their race, color, creed, religion, or zip code. The legacy of our nation is predicated on this notion, the foundation of empathy and the genesis of charity and compassion. At no other time in the history of mankind has there been a better implementation of the Golden Rule than in America. It has generated an attraction and sense of endearment that has drawn billions from around the world to its shores. It is this inherent attraction that can be best defined as "a shining city on a hill."

For centuries, our forefathers sacrificed so that we might be the recipients of the blessings of freedom. Should we not be willing to pass those same freedoms on to future generations? How do we?

We are First and Foremost AMERICANS

> *"We must be righteous. Our Constitution was made only for a moral and religious people. It is wholly inadequate to the government of any other."*
>
> —*John Adams*[425]

---

425 "Message from John Adams to the Officers of the First Brigade." BeliefNet.com, n.d. beliefnet.com/faiths/faith-tools/the-founding-faith-archive/john-adams/message-from-john-adams-to-the-officers-of-the-first-brigade-1p.aspx.

"If a nation expects to be ignorant and free, it expects what never was and never will be."

—*Thomas Jefferson* [426]

We owe a debt to those who have paid the price for freedom to understand the cause for which they sacrificed. "If we forget what we did we don't know who we are."[427]

The Magna Carta, Mayflower Compact, Federalist papers, Declaration of Independence, and the Constitution represent visions of freedom over the centuries that were fought for, enhanced, built upon, and passed on. The 1439 Gutenberg Printing Press opened the doorway to mass education, inspiration, and to a new dawn of thought and reason. It is ironic and fitting that the first book printed was the Gutenberg Bible. This event marked the end of the Dark Ages and the beginning of an enlightened Renaissance. This invention empowered individuals with an opportunity for independent thought, to ask questions, and to debate a plethora of ideas. It allowed for the blueprint of a nation, still centuries away, whose environment empowers individuals "to think and reason beyond all previous boundaries." It was indeed a historical paradigm shift that would lead to the concept of freedom, a time during which the connection of the individual to a Big God empowered them to dream big. This empowerment to dream allowed an envisioned future free of control by kings, popes, and landlords.

As we equip ourselves to hold on to these gifted freedoms, it is imperative that as Americans we remain educated and engaged. The documents that define our nation's values, principles, and priorities were inspired and written to be a guide for an educated, thoughtful, independent, and engaged "We the People." We must become involved in civic affairs to ensure that we are properly represented.[428]

It is the obligation of a free people to roll up their sleeves, lift their voices, to serve each other, and then cast their ballots to hold their representatives accountable. In a free society our elected officials reflect who we are. If we are a good, wise, and honest people we will in turn elect those who are good, wise, and honest legislators. If our representatives become debased, with lack of character, it is a direct reflection of who we collectively have become. We must therefore be personally accountable to higher laws that demand that

---

426　"Thomas Jefferson Quotes." BrainyQuote, n.d. brainyquote.com/quotes/thomas_jefferson_136269.

427　"Ronald Reagan: 'Farewell Address to the Nation.'" The American Presidency Project, January 11, 1989. presidency.ucsb.edu/ws/?pid=29650.

428　""A More Perfect Union"." Resources. LDSFamilyFun.com, n.d. ldsfamilyfun.com/fhe/lessons/fhe_moreperfectunion.htm.

we seek our "righteous" desires. Holding others accountable to the same is therefore possible. We must make our influence felt by our votes, our letters, our teaching, and our advice.[429]

In a country founded on the premise of individual freedom, religion, speech, thought and expression, the press, association, and the pursuit of life, liberty, and happiness, our vote reflects the individual's innermost thoughts, intents and desires. Collectively it is a vote for or against God, the author of all freedom. It is therefore up to "We the People" to vote wisely. This act is a precious gift, paid for by the blood, sweat, and tears of generations and experienced by only a handful in the perspective of time. The collective power of "We the People" should not be frivolously taken for granted or abused. It is our responsibility to vote wisely, vote as an educated citizen, vote for the welfare of our nation, vote for the blessing of our God, and vote often.

An Eternal Truth: A Marxist is a Marxist is a Marxist

> One winter a farmer found a snake stiff and frozen with cold. He had compassion and, taking it up, placed it in his bosom. The warmth quickly revived the snake, and resuming its natural instincts, it bit its benefactor, inflicting on him a mortal wound. 'Oh!' cried the farmer with his last breath, 'I am rightly served for pitying a scoundrel.'

The farmer in this fable failed to understand the immutable nature of the snake. It simply did what it was instinctively designed to do. The Royalty Class Black Man is to the Black community what the snake is to the farmer. They, by nature, innately seek wealth, power, and fame to the detriment of the community that trusts them. They appear harmless and feign advocacy until warmed by the opportunity of self-interest. This is when the empathy-free and heartless ways of the liberal Socialist are revealed.

How best to explain the heartless-soul of a Socialist/Marxist Royalty Class Black politician than by defining the heart and soul of a narcissist. They are, at their core, one and the same. The focus and endgame for both will always be *self*. A narcissist will pretend to be operating from high standards, but the reality is that they are only critical of others while the standards for their own behavior are non-existent. This results in them being flaky hypocrites who pander to the public image while something much darker lurks under the surface. They frequently make promises that they have no intention of keeping and spend a lot of their energy seeking people who will adore them (i.e., illegal

---

429   IDSConservative. A Message of Warning & Hope - Ezra Taft Benson Society, 2010. youtu.be/MgNZ0aTKQAo.

immigrants) or who they can vent their aggression on either by provoking fights or spreading gossip and lies.

Narcissists often follow a pattern of seducing and then abandoning lovers and friends, as well as other people they have conned into admiring them. Their lack of empathy and excessive self-interest mixed with an ability to manipulate and charm others make them highly abusive to live with. It doesn't bother them to exploit their partners. They will hinder any attempt by their partner to regain self-esteem and will seek to keep them servile and, in effect, a kind of slave (i.e., the poor, urban Black community).

The reality is that a narcissist is like a selfish child; they find it hard to share anything, especially attention. They have a driving need to be the center of attention and will go to lengths to be the focus of everyone in their environment. Often, they will fabricate stories to make them seem more important than they are, and they will consistently blame others for any wrongdoings they commit. This behavior flourishes in those that are charming and attractive because this gives them an advantage and allows them to get away with this behavior more often. They pretend to be humble and very likeable in public and choose a less socially-competent partner to be their foil and will mercilessly exploit them to get whatever they have chosen as their goal. Narcissists usually sulk or get angry if they are seen to be in the wrong or make mistakes, they will rage or throw tantrums and often insist on rewriting history to cover their mistakes (i.e., the Socialist/Marxist Congressional Black Congress).

Works Defines and Refines a Man

The Minimum Wage

The number of employed high school students has hit its lowest level in more than twenty years, according to new figures from the National Center for Education Statistics. In 1990, thirty-two percent of high school students held jobs versus just sixteen percent now.[430]

These unemployment statistics have an even more profound impact when gauging the amount of Black teenage males across our nation who are not participating in the work force. In a segment in which seventy percent are fatherless, forty percent are dropping out of high school and college, and an increasing number are being drawn to gang violence, the opportunity to learn life skills through work is imperative. A 2014 national study found that ninety-two percent of Black male teens are unemployed in Chicago and eighty-three

---

430 Ben Wolfgang. "Number of High-School Students with Jobs Hits 20-Year Low." *The Washington Times.* May 24, 2012, Online edition, sec. Politics. washington-times.com/news/2012/may/24/number-of-high-school-students-with-jobs-hits-20-y.

percent are unemployed nationally.[431] What is numbing about this report of non-working youth, unemployed now, soon to be unemployable, is the lack of outcry from politicians who mandate anti-Black policies like the minimum wage law. These same politicians are educated enough to understand that they are also sentencing another generation to hopeless misery.

In a *Wall Street Journal* article, "The Young and the Jobless," the minimum wage hike has driven the wages of teen employees down to $0.00. Economist David Neumark of the University of California, Irvine, wrote that the seventy-cents-an-hour increase in the minimum wage would cost some 300,000 jobs. The teen unemployment rate in September of 2009 was 25.9 percent, the highest rate since World War II, up from 23.8 percent. Some 330,000 teen jobs have vanished in two months. Hardest hit of all: Black male teens. Congress began raising the minimum wage from 5.15 dollars an hour in July 2007, and there are now 691,000 fewer teens working.[432]

There is a reason that labor unions favor the perpetual increasing of minimum wage. With each increase, it gives employers justification to hire "skilled workers" (union labor) versus unskilled entry-level teenage workers trying to get work experience. Within months of being inaugurated, President Obama suggested raising the minimum wage from 7.90 to 9.50 dollars per hour, this time tied to rate of inflation.[433] This is a gift from a grateful Black politician to Socialist/Marxist White labor unions that have never been a friend to the Black community.

The New Frontier of Civil Rights Education

It is imperative for America's future that our children's education becomes our number one priority and at the forefront of our nation's dialogue. Regardless of the community, "We the People" must garner the same passion that was once present during the civil rights era. This is the new civil rights issue of our era. It impacts millions of Americans and plays a vital role in providing a gateway to the American Dream. Quality education also provides protection from the progressive stealth of Socialism/Marxism. As stated by Karl Marx and

431   Staff. "92% of Black Male Teens Unemployed in Chicago, 83% Nationally." Black Youth Project. January 21, 2014, sec. News. blackyouthproject.com/92-of-black-male-teens-unemployed-in-chicago-83-nationally.

432   WSJ staff. "The Young and the Jobless." *The Wall Street Journal*. October 3, 2009, sec. Review & Outlook (U.S.). wsj.com/articles/SB10001424052970203440104574402820278669840.

433   Annie Lowrey. "Raising Minimum Wage Would Ease Income Gap but Carries Political Risks." *The New York Times*. February 13, 2013, Online edition, sec. Politics. nytimes.com/2013/02/13/us/politics/obama-pushes-for-increase-in-federal-minimum-wage.html.

John Dewey, the goal of this anti-American ideology is to indoctrinate trusting minds to become part of its collective. *"The first battlefield is the re-writing of history."*

> *"You can't make Socialists out of individuals. Children who know how to think for themselves spoil the harmony of the collective society, which is coming, where everyone is interdependent."*[434]
>
> —John Dewy: Socialist, Humanist, atheist and Father of Progressive Education

Solutions

- Immediately revive the successful Washington, D.C. voucher program, which impacted over 2,000 poor inner city children per year and 16,000 over the two terms of President Obama.
- Develop a nationwide plan that grants students who receive federal education assistance the opportunity to take their federal voucher to the public and charter school of their choosing. Push decisions to states to offer enough options so that the choice would be meaningful.
- Streamline teacher-quality programs at the federal level and award them to states based on how well they promote good teachers. Demand better transparency from schools, such as a more useful grading of public schools' performance, which lets parents make better choices.
- Give parents more choices in schools to push reforms in troubled school systems.
- Remember God.

> *"Truth is scarcely found. But integrity and truth are hardly found within the Black population as a whole, at least not where it involves Black people. Most Blacks have pledged allegiance to their Blackness, not truth, not to America, not even to God as many profess. Integrity and truth has to go out the window if it somehow poses a threat to the 'positive' image of Blackness."*
>
> —Anonymous

---

434   Dave Thomer. "Dewey Watch: Thinking for Themselves." Pop culture, public affairs. This Is Not News (blog), January 3, 2006. notnews.org/philosophy/dewey-think-for-themselves.

The greatest influential institution within the Black community as early as 1758 has been the Black church. Religion offered a means of catharsis, as Africans retained their faith in God and found refuge in their churches. They have long been the centers of communities, serving as school sites in the early years after the Civil War, taking up social welfare functions such as providing for the indigent, and establishing schools, orphanages, and prison ministries. As a result, Black churches have fostered strong community organizations and provided spiritual and political leadership, especially during the civil rights movement.[435]

The church of my youth in the early '60s segregated town of Tallahassee was Bethel Baptist. It represented the community's gathering place for civil rights updates, strategies, and demonstration planning. The Black church today continues to have an influence. A book published in 1990 by researchers Lincoln and Mamiya titled *The Black Church in American Experiences* surveyed 1,900 ministers and 2,100 churches to find that around 71 percent were engaged in some aspect of community service or outreach program. This included day care centers, job search assistance, substance abuse prevention, and food and clothing distribution. Churches in Harlem have undertaken real estate ventures and renovated burnt-out and abandoned brownstones to create new housing for residents. They have fought for the right to operate their own schools in place of the often inadequate public schools found in many Black neighborhoods.

Here lies an interesting paradox. As a community, Black Americans are far too religious and involved in the church to be experiencing so many social problems. The destruction of the Black family, Black mothers accepting the degraded value placed by others on the life of their own unborn children, and the gross abandonment of Black men as responsible husbands and fathers highlights that there is something peculiar about this reality. It reflects a detachment of the head from the body, a kind of cultural and spiritual decapitation. The church is the primary institution among Blacks, but it is obvious, considering our societal challenges, that the head is not properly communicating with the body.[436]

The influence of liberal secularism has embedded itself deeply within every sector of American society, including the "Christian" pulpits. The challenge to the Black ministry, who, in the past, represented an oasis for hope and progress, is whether they still envision their godly calling to guide their flock to promised blessing available only through adherence to God's laws.

In today's "groupthink" popularity culture, guiding will take an absolute faith in the cornerstone of the Christian faith, the Lord Jesus Christ. It would

---

435   "Black Church." Wikipedia. Wikimedia Foundation, Inc., July 14, 2018.
       en.wikipedia.org/wiki/Black_church.

436   *Ibid.*

take courage to take a stand against pride, popularity, and profit. It would take God-fearing leadership to call out those who consider themselves Christian Ministers yet fall in line in support, marching arm-in-arm in advocacy for anti-God Socialists, Marxists, and atheists. What has become crystal clear is that far too many Black Christian ministers today do not have enough of either faith or courage.

CHAPTER 21

THE SOLUTION: CHIVALRY

"Anyone who knows anything of history knows that great so-cial changes are impossible without feminine upheaval."

—Atheist, Socialist Founder Karl Marx [437]

The sacred nature of womanhood is taught universally, but nowhere has it been held with such high esteem as within the Judeo-Christian ideals of the American culture. It is through dedicated mothers that mankind witnesses its closest experience of the pure, unconditional love of Christ. It is motherhood that gives birth, shapes souls, and forms the character of our nation. It is through her teachings, example, and spiritual intuitiveness that our daughters are taught to fight the worldly message that encourages the lowering of their moral standards.

Simultaneously, through a connection that is divinely unique, motherhood encourages sons to raise their standards. It is by its very nature a sacred trust of the highest order. Men can only stand aside in wonderment and admiration viewing the sacrifice, dedication, courage, and patience that accompanies the mother phase of womanhood. It is the nature of mothers and wives that encourages a self-sufficient and self-confident man to search further within, to find his better self. It is for approval and respect of women men find a deeper commitment for courage, a stronger clarity of vision, a deeper willingness to risk, and the desire to start again if he fails.[438]

437   Ellis Washington. "On Karl Marx and the First Principles of Evil." Ideo-logical. Ellis Washington Report (blog), May 4, 2015. elliswashingtonreport.com/2015/05/04/on-karl-marx-and-the-first-principles-of-evil.

438   Burgess Owens. *Liberalism or How to Turn Good Men into Whiners, Weenies and Wimps*. Brentwood, TN: Post Hill Press, 2016. Ch. 16.

This chapter on chivalry is taken from my book *Liberalism or How to turn Good Men into Whiners, Weenies and Wimps*. Without embracing the understanding of manhood, our nation can never return to its principled mooring. Our young ladies must be trained to identify manhood and imparted with the self-esteem to never accept anything less. Our young males must be trained to accept the responsibility to Man-Up and Stand Up regardless of their challenges. The courage to respect and honor womanhood must be accepted at his very core as his most sacred duty. Only with this understanding can a man call himself a real man.

Manhood's divine nature and role is founded upon distinct characteristics and attributes. Among these are integrity, empathy, charity, commitment, loyalty, honesty, principles, faithfulness, and vision. The very keystone of his nature, though, is courage. Without this, he is naught. A man of principle has the courage to stand, regardless of the price asked of him—even if he must do so alone. Before his test begins, he believes that because his cause is just, he must endure to the end, regardless of where that end might take him.

The most important deployment of courage for manhood is for the protection and care of womanhood. Throughout the history of mankind, the most attractive and admired trait of manhood is his innate courage to pay any price, including his own life, for the well-being, safety, and honor of women. Chivalry, as an ideal, has been in the crosshairs of the Socialist for decades. It has done its best to blur the line between genders, thus facilitating and encouraging the demeaning of both.

It is here where the ideology of liberalism has prevailed in its greatest damage to the Black community. For where there are no men available to protect, defend, and honor the sacred role of womanhood, there are no men. When Black males accept the role of silence and collusion, White liberal racists disrespect Black women in the vilest and most reprehensible ways.

The Socialist's most hated and feared minority within the American populace is the successful, independent, and articulate Black woman. It is with this minority segment of the Black community, in their attempts to intimidate and silence, where the despicable and ugly face of liberal White bigotry erupts. Predictably, it is also here, in the shadows, where the cowardly and compliant Royalty Class Black man is found. Even though his community's youth desperately crave positive male and female role models, the Royalty Class Black man is willing to sacrifice his race's best and finest upon the altar of his chosen political doctrine.

This minority's message of overcoming all odds, of embracing universal success ethics, of pride in race accomplishments, and of the availability of opportunities throughout the American free enterprise system is a threat to the Socialist. It is therefore a threat to the symbiotic relationship with the Royalty Class Black man as he submissively colludes with liberal White racists.

As women of his race who hold independent political views are verbally abused and depicted in racist caricatures, he remains silent. As the liberal White man propagates the myth that success for the Black race is only possible through the benevolence of liberalism and its demeaning "Black specific" policies, he remains silent. And as Black Americans speak independently of alternative solutions, the racist liberal White has no fear of condemnation or reprisal. As seen with the racist treatment of one of the Black community's most respected women, Condoleezza Rice, the Royalty Class Black man performs his duty well as he acquiesces to his fellow Socialist and remains silent.

Condoleezza Rice was born in the Deep South, segregated Birmingham, Alabama in 1954. She graduated from the University of Denver at the age of sixteen and eventually became a professor of political science at Stanford University, earning many other honors while at the university. During her tenure there she served on the National Security Council as the Soviet and Eastern Europe Affairs Advisor to President George H.W. Bush during the dissolution of the Soviet Union and German reunification. She was the distinguished director of Stanford University's Global Center for Business and the Economy, Senior Fellow of the Institute for International Studies, Senior Fellow of the Hoover Institution, and founder of the Center for New Generation, an afterschool program created to raise high school graduation numbers. She was also a spokesperson advocating leadership roles for girls. She became Secretary of State for George W. Bush, the first Black female to serve in such a capacity.[439] As such, she came under attack from the liberal left.

White liberal radio hosts Gregg "Opie" Hughes and Anthony Cumia laughed as a guest they called "Homeless Charlie" talked about wanting to rape Secretary Rice. Cumia gleefully said, "I just imagine the horror in Condoleezza Rice's face...as you were just like holding her down."[440] The program director and morning host John Sylvester called Rice, then the nation's first female national security advisor, "Aunt Jemima." When asked by his critics to apologize, Sylvester said he was planning a giveaway on Friday's show of Aunt Jemima pancake mix and syrup. "I will apologize to Aunt Jemima."[441]

Comic writer Garry Trudeau called Secretary Rice "Brown Sugar" in *Doonesbury,* and Aaron McGruder suggested a boyfriend might stop her from being "hell-bent to destroy" the world in the now-defunct *The Boondocks.* Ted Rall suggested she is a "house nigga" who needs "racial re-education."[442] On the editorial pages, Jeff Danziger and Pat Oliphant drew her with accentuated

439   "Condoleezza Rice." Wikipedia. Wikimedia Foundation, Inc., July 8, 2018. en.wikipedia.org/wiki/Condoleezza_Rice.

440   David Almasi. "Hold Your Tongue, Unless You're Criticizing A Conservative." Project 21 Black Leadership Network, May 1, 2007. nationalcenter.org/project21/2007/05/01/hold-your-tongue-unless-youre-criticizing-a-conservative.

441   Tom Held. "Radio Talk Show Host Refuses to Back off Remark about Rice." News/Current Events. Free Republic, November 21, 2004. freerepublic.com/focus/f-news/1285542/posts.

442   David Almasi. "Hold Your Tongue, Unless You're Criticizing A Conservative."

features and mimicked her, using poor diction as these blatant and inexcusable racist comments were presented to nationwide audiences. Danziger drew a cartoon that was critical of Rice where he used racial stereotypes concerning the look and speech of African Americans. He was criticized by the National Black Republican Association, who stated that Danziger depicted Doctor Rice as an ignorant, barefoot "mammy," reminiscent of the stereotyped Black woman in the movie *Gone with the Wind* who remarked, "I don't know nothin' 'bout birthin' no babies."[443]

What should be noted with the demeaning comments and racist depictions of Condoleezza Rice is the common bond shared between Gregg "Opie" Hughes and Anthony Cumia, Jeff Danziger, Pat Oliphant, Garry Trudeau, and John Sylvester. They are *all* White liberal Democrats. They *all* take comfort in portraying a successful Black woman in the most despicable and racist stereotypical manner. Their Ebonics speaking, big-lipped, ignorant, Black mammy caricature is reminiscent of the portrayal of Black Americans during the southern White Democratic era of the KKK. With the arrogance of cowards who hide under White hoods, behind Black masks, or in the shadows of free speech, these White Socialist elitists expose who they really are: racist bullies and cowards. As they demean the best and brightest women within the Black community, they again steal models of Black American exceptionalism from the urban Black youth.

With the silence from the Left of assaults on conservative women is exposure of the true heart of the Democratic Party. It is a party of Black and White elitist bullies and cowards. It is a party of White liberal males who feel safe and sheltered behind their big company prestige, who bully and attack more successful Black Americans.

We also see, within the Democratic Party, Black elitists remaining silent as the respect for their race and self-image of their youth is undermined with century-old racist stereotypes. This example of success, America's first Black female National Security Advisor and first Black female Secretary of State, would, for any other culture, be a time for celebration. Not so with the Royalty Class Black man. He is indeed the quintessential cowardly man who takes this opportunity to show his priority of choosing class over race.

The Independent Women's Forum was one of the few national women's organizations to take issue with this apparent collaborative attack on a successful, Black women. In a November 2004 article entitled "IWF Denounces Racist Depictions of Dr. Condoleezza Rice in Popular Editorial Cartoons," they stated the following:

---

443   cwalls. "Simple Sambo." CNN IReport, August 20, 2008. ireport.cnn.com/docs/ DOC-63232.

"The Independent Women's Forum today denounced as blatantly racist several editorial cartoons featuring Doctor Condoleezza Rice, National Security Advisor and President Bush's nominee for Secretary of State. These cartoons clearly draw upon centuries of deep-rooted, wicked, and indefensible portrayal of Black women.

"'The depiction of Doctor Condoleezza Rice by Jeff Danziger, Pat Oliphant, and Garry Trudeau as an Ebonics speaking, big-lipped, Black mammy who just loves her 'massa' is a disturbing trend in editorial cartoons,' said Michelle D. Bernard, senior vice president of the Independent Women's Forum. 'These cartoons take the racism of the liberals who profess respect and adoration for Black Americans to a new level. It is revolting.'"

Danziger, Oliphant, and Trudeau, whose editorial cartoons are very popular in the United States, are also renowned all over the world.

444 "Calling Susan Rice Incompetent Is Racist. Smearing Condi Rice, 'House Nigga?' Okay!" Freedom Is Knowledge (blog), January 22, 2013. freedomisknowledge. com/emails/2013/01222013.html.

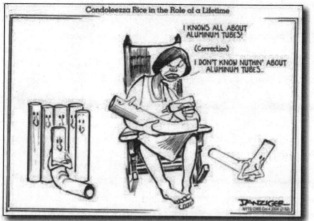

Jeff Danziger, Los Angeles Times

445

"*The most powerful woman in the United States is young, gifted, and Black. Given our nation's history of race-based slavery, the ensuing civil rights movement, and our continual battle against race/sex based discrimination, every citizen in our nation should take pride in Doctor Rice's accomplishments,*" said Bernard. "*She is a representation of America's past and future all at once. One must ask where is the outrage of the nation's civil rights leadership, feminist organizations, and the so-called liberals who only seem to embrace Black America in election years?*

"*Condoleezza Rice was the first woman ever appointed as National Security Advisor. After Secretary of State Colin Powell, Doctor Rice will be the second African American to hold both posts. These cartoons are decidedly unfunny.*"[446]

Once again, these degrading images of Black women reveal the true heart of the racist White liberal/Socialist, as it also highlights the spineless backbone of the Royalty Class Black man. This diatribe of Uncle Tom-ery drew

445 *Ibid.*

446 Louise Filkins. "IWF Denounces Racist Depictions of Dr. Condoleezza Rice in Popular Editorial Cartoons." Independent Women's Forum, November 17, 2004. iwf.org/media/2434659/IWF-Denounces-Racist-Depictions-of-Dr-Condoleezza-Rice-in-Popular-Editorial-Cartoons.

the predictable response from the complicit Royal Black Class, the NAACP, John Lewis, Elijah Cummings, Congressional Black Caucus, Al Sharpton, Jesse Jackson, Maxine Waters, Royalty Black academia, entertainers, and MSNBC Black talking heads—silence! In the new PC age, in which saying Merry Christmas during the Christmas holidays might be taken as offensive, these comments were met with no outrage, no condemnation, no outcry of racism, no feminist outcry of misogyny, and no dialogue regarding the negative message given to Black youth, as another successful Black role model is denigrated.

More importantly, the Royal Black Class has delivered their subtle message to all: Racist White liberals will be given carte blanche authority to besmirch your name, reputation, and financial future if you dare act as an independent Black woman. Note the difference in the Man-Up potential of the Royal Black Class man if we were to substitute the name of the *first* Black female Secretary of State, *first* Black female advisor, and *first* Black female selected to the National Security Council with that of the wife of the *first* Black president, Michelle Obama.

It is guaranteed the Royal Black Class man would respond like real men and demand that heads roll. Guaranteed would be the loud voices of protest, demonstration, threats of boycotts, lawsuits, and demands for multiple levels of media firing. For with the Royal Black Class man, it is not the verbal insults of successful members of his race that generates his most passionate ire, nor is it the disrespect given by racist White men to prominent Black women, role models of his own community. Instead, the Royalty Class Black man saves his courage, his ideals of chivalry, to defend his most precious ideology. Class over race.

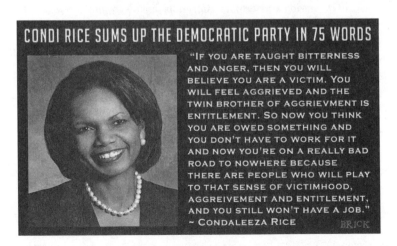

The fickle status of wealth is reported almost daily in our reality TV culture. Outside the arena of sports and entertainment, the stories of Black Americans obtaining long lasting, real success through the utilization of traditional success principles are very rare. Those who have done so through the free market/ Capitalism remain unheralded. It is not beneficial to the ideology of liberalism to celebrate Black Americans who have, through their own ingenuity, tenacity, and willpower, proven that the American Way works. The idea that poverty is a *choice* and not a permanent condition is a contradiction to the ideology of liberalism. It is a dagger that strikes at its very core when an individual recognizes that government dependency is akin to mental, emotional, and spiritual slavery. Like a malignant cancer this form of dependency eats away the essence and value of the soul. It is worse than physical slavery because it enslaves the human will, necessary to fight for and achieve freedom.

Therefore, it is imperative for the survival of the ideology of liberalism that the successful voices of conservative Black Americans are ignored or silenced. If they become too vocal and too visible they are, with collaboration of the Royalty Black Class and the White liberal elitists, demeaned, discredited, and destroyed if possible. Understood by the ideology of liberalism is the threat that these independent thinking Americans pose to their dependent base of urban Black Americans. The message that escape is possible from the sweet enticement of government dependency and its Siamese twin, poverty, could inspire others to also seek self-sufficiency.

Such is the case of conservative Black American, Star Parker. Star was a single welfare mother in Los Angeles, California. After accepting Jesus Christ in her life, she returned to college, earned a BS degree in marketing, and launched an urban Christian magazine. The 1992 Los Angeles riots destroyed her business, and yet served as a springboard for her focus on faith-based and free market alternatives to empower the poor. As a social policy consultant, Star gives regular testimony before the United States Congress, and is a national expert on major television and radio shows across the country. Currently, Star is a regular commentator on CNN, MSNBC, and FOX News. She has debated Jesse Jackson on BET, fought for school choice on Larry King Live, and defended welfare reform on the *Oprah Winfrey Show*.[447]

Star has written three books: *Pimps, Whores and Welfare Brats* (1996), *Uncle Sam's Plantation* (2003), and *White Ghetto* (2006). In 1995, she founded the Center for Urban Renewal and Education (CURE),[448] which works with Black religious and community groups on social policy issues like school choice.[449] She is also a syndicated columnist for Scripps Howard News Service, offering weekly op-eds to more than four hundred newspapers worldwide.[450]

---

447   "Star Parker Biography." All American Speakers Bureau, n.d. allamericanspeakers.com/celebritytalentbios/Star-Parker#sthash.a7DfvJmP.dpuf.

448   "Cure: Center for Urban Renewal and Education." Awareness. Urban Cure, n.d. urbancure. org.

449   "Star Parker." Wikipedia. Wikimedia Foundation, Inc., July 26, 2018. en.wikipedia.org/wiki/Star_Parker.

450   "Star Parker Biography." All American Speakers Bureau.

Star represents the possibilities, the rags to riches and middle class American Dream, for millions of near hopeless Black Americans. She is independent, smart, articulate, courageous, accomplished, and proof that poverty in America is a choice. It does not have to be permanent. She is a great example, a role model, and a voice in the wilderness for millions of young Black girls in a community sorely lacking in hopeful messaging.

What has been the response of the pro-welfare ideology of liberalism to this successful Black American woman who has successfully broken the chains of welfare? There is no better example of the condescending, misogynistic, and racist-based spirit of the ideology of liberalism than the comments of blogger, Gaius Publius. Typical of a liberal White racist, he accepts the premise that he is an expert on the acceptable degrees of Blackness. From his exalted perspective he sees his role as a judge capable of defining for Americans those who are truly worthy of being called Black. Consistent with White liberal racists is the liberty and comfort he takes in disrespecting Black women.

As America's smallest minority segment, with the audacity to step out of place, the independent Black woman is granted the highest degree of disdain from White liberal racists. As Publius verbally assaults and demeans another successful Black role model, he is also confident of the praise forthcoming from his fellow backslapping PC collaborators. He will travel home to his integrated community of liberals, expecting the wink and nod from the ever-predictable Royalty Black Class.

This gang-bullying cowardice is typical of liberal White racism. Though it is not politically correct to call a Black American who has stepped out of their place "a nigger," this group gleefully uses such terms as "Uncle Tom," "Oreo," and "porch monkey" to accommodate their racist disdain. They will, after all, have the blessings and cover of their good Black people, the Royalty Black Class.

Imagine the racist, misogynistic, and disrespectful comments made of another Black woman of our day, First Lady Michele Obama. There are both Black and White Americans who will never see this correlation, because they have unfortunately accepted the basic premise of the ideology of liberalism. This premise states that the sacred nature of the liberal ideology requires loyalty that is much deeper than that required for the honor and respect of Black women. Where has this liberal premise found its most secure home? With the whiners, weenies, and wimps, also known as the Royalty Class Black men.

Gaius Publius, representative of White liberal racism, defines for Americans "a good Black" versus "a self-loathing bad Black" or, what he calls Uncle Toms. The following are his comments about national leader, successful, vocal Christian, and Black role model, Star Parker:

An African American unemployed single mother who got abortions the way normal people use tissues and who was arrested multiple times on multiple charges.

A right wing huckster pedaling Republican nonsense-for-pay.

Her specialty is phony moralizing and African American self-loathing, as in her pathetic autobiography.

She pimps full-time for the GOP.

Widely considered one of the most prominent Uncle Toms of the GOP.

The Republican Party cleaned her up nicely before they sent her out to talk trash about poor people and tell everyone that they should read the Bible and hope for a better life in Heaven.[451]

I believe in the resiliency of the Black race. Though its manhood has been under attack for over sixty years, there are still millions of *real* Black men, alive and well throughout our nation. These are men who are proud of their race, their heritage, their women, and who are willing to defend them. It will be these men who demand—not beg, plead, or negotiate—for the end of the disgraceful and degrading attacks on Black American women. Whether our women have reached successful pinnacles of national visibility or not, it is time for this debasement to end.

It is time we call out every Black *and* White elitist, who chooses to disrespect Black women because they believe their racist misogamy is funny and in vogue. The age of covering for obnoxious White liberal racism is over. As the ideology of liberalism attacks and demeans Black women it shines an insightful light on its view of Black men, who are also viewed with disrespect. From the perspective of the 1900s Black community and my proud 1960s segregated community of Tallahassee, Florida, we ask: What kind of man "remains in his place" as our women are being verbally abused and assaulted? The answer from every other proud generation of men: *Whiners, Weenies, and Wimps.*

NOTICE: *For the White Socialist/Marxist racists who have taken solace in the predictable cover granted to you by the Royalty Class Black man while you, with smug confidence and no thought of consequence, denigrate our Black women, those days are over. The resurrection of the Black community will have within men who will ensure the light of exposure and free market consequences.*

As with Condi Rice, the depth of vitriol from the ideology of liberalism/Socialism has no concern for PC backlash or self-reflecting shame, because within this ideology there is no shame. As the Royal Black Class is invited into the

---

451   DownWithTyranny. "Palin Picks Another Loser: Star Parker." Down with Tyranny! (blog), June 18, 2010. downwithtyranny.blogspot.com/2010/06/palin-picks-another-loser-star-parker.html#sthash.ManNUKP7.dpuf.

free forum of debates, their lack of critical thinking becomes apparent, as does their limited vocabulary. In frustration, the Royalty Class Black man reverts to his condescending and judgmental words such as ignorant, Uncle Tom, turncoat, Oreo, and a full list of others listed in Kevin Jackson's book *Race Pimping*.[452]

It is consistently the ideology of liberalism/Socialism, not conservatism, that thrives on disrespecting Black women. It is the liberal manifested rap culture funneled through liberal White owned MTV and BET that depict misogyny as funny, cool, and in vogue. Here lies the Royalty Class Black man's disconnect with manhood. For where there is a lack of respect and a heightened degree of cowardice in defending women, there is in like kind a lack of manhood presence. To those who wonder where all the good, courageous, and thoughtful men have gone, the answer is, "Liberalism's got 'em."

In kowtowing to the demands of the ideology of liberalism/Socialism, the liberal Black man has lost the belief in the potential of his race and most important, the courage to fight for the sanctity of womanhood within. Nowhere in America has the lack of respect for its women and children been more prevalent and damaging than in the Black community. As the Royal Black Class man acquiesced to the attraction of power, wealth, and fame, he opted out as the protector of his race. As a facilitator, he aided in the ingratiation of the ideology of liberalism's degraded view of manhood. He served as the trusted messenger of its subversive, filth-laden, women degrading sub-culture through music and video that has ravished the minds and souls of today's Black youth. He opted to remain silent or, in the case of the academic Royalty Class Black man, encouraged young Black sons to accept as normal referencing our Black daughters in the most degrading terms. Their silence and lack of condemnation encouraged our Black daughters to accept such denigrating labels as "baby mamas," defined by Webster's dictionary as "the mother of one or more of a man's children, especially one who is not his wife or current partner."[453]

No longer is there an expectation of respect for the urban Black woman to be referenced as "mother" or "wife," but instead "partners" to several, passing through, non-committal, sorry Black males. After decades of leadership from the Royalty Class Black man, this has come to define liberalism's degraded version of manhood; an increasing number of Black boys who are totally clueless about commitment, respect, loyalty, and their responsibility to Man-Up.

---

452   Jackson, K. Race Pimping: The Multi-Trillion Dollar Business of Liberalism. Fast-Pencil, Incorporated, 2014.

453   "Baby Mama." Wikipedia. Wikimedia Foundation, Inc., June 18, 2018. en.wikipedia.org/wiki/Baby_mama.

CHAPTER 22

THE SOLUTION: MAN-UP/ STAND-UP

"This is the test of your manhood: How much is there left in you after you have lost everything outside of yourself?"

—Orison Sweet Marden

Advice to Young Black Boys from Black Male Conservatives

MAN-UP. First and foremost, show the respect that you have for yourself and others: pull up your pants! Learn to speak fluent English; it is what is expected if you are communicating to others or on their behalf. The clothes you wear and the markings on your body are a direct message to others of what you think of yourself. Unlike the sports and hip-hop heroes, you will have to make a living in the real world. Your success will depend on your ability to show up to work daily, work hard, be reliable, be respectful, and be consistent.

Reality Check: Tattoos on your neck, face, hands, and arms will limit your career options and the lifetime of income you will generate.

Reality Check: People will hire you *only* if you bring them value. Your value is not in *your* presence but in the effort you exhibit while in *their* presence. Yep...when you're working for someone, it's all about *them*. If you don't impress *them*, you will not be offered *their* job. It is essential that *they* feel comfortable around you, not vice versa. Acting, looking, and dressing like a gangster will guarantee you a lifetime of either low-skill or no employment.

MAN-UP. Learn to respect authority, control your emotions, and understand that your feelings have nothing to do with it. There is power in submission to authority. People will like and respect you more if you first show respect to them. With respect for their authority will come the potential of advocacy by them for you, due to their respect for you. "Give respect to get respect". Discipline yourself and know that you will get in life what you give in life. You are guaranteed to go nowhere by being an insolent, obnoxious victim whose hurt feelings control all actions.

MAN-UP. Work harder than anyone around you. If that bar is set too low, work harder than everyone *not* around you. Learn to dream outside of your boundaries, and if there are no examples or mentors around you, pick up a book. Read about the many others who have overcome greater obstacles than yours. There are many, many others whose lives would be inspirational to you, because they have experienced much worse, *and overcome much more.*

You live in a country that allows you as many do-overs as you have the vision and tenacity to take. Learn from your failures. Each is specifically designed and customized to get you closer to success.

Choose your associates and advisors very, very carefully. Who you spend time with and communicate with reflects how you see yourself now and where you project yourself in the future. You will become whom you associate with and what you read, both good and bad. Every relationship you enter, whether business or personal, must be a win/win if success is your goal. Work to ensure that you always bring value to your relationships.

Recognize that you have a great heritage and come from a great stock. Research your own personal bloodline, heritage, and discover those of your ancestry who have endured and overcome tough times and succeeded. We *all* have family members from our past who can inspire us. Find them, *appreciate* them, and *learn* from them.

Always pay close attention to your emotions and spirit regarding your sources of information and input. If you're watching a channel, reading literature, or associating with people that leave you feeling less hopeful, less appreciative, less grateful and angry...*change the channel*. It will be your choice to pick the colors and tones that will paint your future, *dark or bright*. It is your choice alone!

MAN-UP. Find ways to be of value by servicing others. It is possible to *serve* your way out of poverty, hopelessness, a loveless environment, and through all the other rough patches of life. Serve, and when you think you're done, find an opportunity to serve some more. There are eternal laws in place that influence our happiness. They are perfectly fair, equal to all, and they are totally agnostic.

We are all familiar with the physical laws of gravity and inertia. We understand them and faithfully rely upon them in every segment of our lives. The process of picking up the book you're now reading began with the application of the physical law of gravity that you take for granted daily. There are also spiritual laws that, though invisible to the naked eye, are just as real and predictable. The spiritual law of Seed and Harvest, for example, is also fair, equal to all, and totally agnostic. It mandates that every seed planted, given the needed nutrients and cultivation, will predictably grow in its own season to produce its own kind. Apple seeds will only grow into apple trees. All that is asked of the gardener is to prepare and cultivate the soil to ensure an environment conducive for growth. Patience is then required for the anticipated blossoming.

This same spiritual Law of Harvest mandates that good acts, deeds, thoughts, and actions are spiritual seeds that blossom into the good fruit of blessings. As predictable, bad seeds produce only bad fruit. As we are the gardeners of our lives, it is imperative that we choose daily the seeds we plant to ensure our harvest. We will indeed *reap what we sow.* Work daily to serve and sow good seeds.

MAN-UP. Respect and honor *all* women, old and young, irrespective of race or color. As a man, this will represent the most important set of thoughts, actions, and habits in your life. If embraced, it will reward you with a lifetime of love, respect, admiration, and self-esteem. You'll need to reject the narcissistic messaging of the godless Socialist/Marxist ideology hidden within the seductive lyrics of hip-hop and rap. Women are not objects to be used at your pleasure. Inversely, the respect and protection of womanhood represents an opportunity to find the real man within and to become your very best self.

If we are to resurrect our communities and country, this message must resonate. We cannot depend any longer on the Royalty Class Black man to do what he has proven incapable of doing. Chivalry is at the very heart and soul of all real manhood and it is evident that the Royalty Class Black man's loyalty to ideology will not allow him to recognize its importance. As Socialism/Marxism continues to blur the line that distinguishes the difference between the genders, they successfully degrade both. Protecting, providing for, defending, and respecting our mothers, sisters, and daughters is at the core of manhood, and the failure to do so is an automatic degradation of it.

The phrase "Man-Up" has become an increasingly popular message of encouragement to our young Black men, however, it will take more than a phrase to understand how this transformation must occur. We do know with certainty that the resurrection of our once-vibrant and successful communities can no longer be left to the leadership of the Royalty Black Class. It's time for our community's real men to Man-Up. A community of Weenies, Whiners, and Wimps simply can't be trusted to do it.

CHAPTER 23

THE SOLUTION: COURAGE

"Our people look for a cause to believe in. Is it a third party we need, or is it a new and revitalized second party, raising a banner of no pale pastels, but bold colors, which make it unmistakably clear where we stand on all of the issues troubling the people?"

—*Ronald Reagan*

I'm thankful to those who built this great nation and who did not turn to pale pastels in their passion for freedom. Growing up in the '60s Deep South and living through the bigotry of that era, I remember as a teenager voicing what I thought distinguished the spirit of a northern and southern racist. The southern racist was bold, in your face, and predictable. There was a degree of respect for him as an adversary, because we knew who he was and what he was capable of. The northern elitist version was different, a person of subtlety. He can give you a warm smile, wrapping his arms around your shoulders and whispering words of endearment. These actions, though, did not correctly reflect his nature, for he was still a racist. At the most inopportune time and with unexpected stealth, he would stab you in the back to destroy you.

Since the turn of the 19th century, the Black community has been embraced, sung sweet lullabies to, and repeatedly stabbed in the back by Black and White liberals of the Democratic Party. The spirit of this destructive ideology has resulted in hopelessness that now influences every aspect of a Black American's life:

> *Its web touches every chapter of a Black child's life, from his/ her life expectancy in the womb to their hopes and dreams as adults.*

It has been a factor in the high illiteracy rate of school age children, high unemployment, and chronic intergenerational poverty.

It has redefined the composition of the nuclear family, traditionally comprised of a husband, wife, and children.

It has significantly lowered expectations of its Black men as loyal and responsible fathers and husbands.

It has introduced into the Black church a code of immorality that skews the message and spirit of Christianity, muting principled voices while spiritual laws are ignored or disregarded for the sake of profit, power, and fame.

It has resulted in the Black community embracing White Liberal abortionists who target its mothers and their unborn babies.

Accepted as normal is the abnormally high percentage of uneducated young Black men incarcerated, the high percentage of Black on Black crime, and the thousands upon thousands of innocent women and children left defenseless against a growing number of evil predators.

What is needed now are bold, vibrant colors of vision and courage. Only bold voices and actions can stand against the wily winds of the status quo that has demoralized our communities over the last sixty years. The fight being waged now is no longer against institutional racism. I no longer, as I did as a child, choose my NFL team based on the two or three Black running backs, receivers, or defensive backs. Over seventy percent of NFL and eighty percent of NBA athletes come from the Black community.

Wealthy Black business entrepreneurs, corporate leaders, career politicians, and entertainers receive acknowledgement and respect today that could not have been dreamed of in previous generations. From Black city mayors, county sheriffs, statewide political leaders, to elected and appointed judges, *We the People* have proven that our nation's original vision is indeed achievable, a vision articulated by Martin Luther King, Jr. in his iconic speech:

"I have a dream that my four little children will one day live in a nation where they will not be judged by the color of their skin, but by the content of their character."

In this new millennium, a major battlefront in the fight for our country's future will be for the spirits, hearts, and minds of men and women within the Black community. My dad's generation of WWII soldiers traveled to foreign lands to defend the freedom of their fellow Americans at home. It was a sense of selflessness and deep patriotism that drove *This Greatest Generation*.

That sense of selflessness is once more required to win the battle against the tide of hopelessness prevalent within the urban Black community. It will be incumbent on those who have tasted the American Dream to share with others the secrets of what can be accomplished with the combination of an optimistic mind, a willing, hardworking body, and a moral spirit. It will once again be the Black middle class embracing a bold and courageous vision, putting aside the passive pastels of apathy, compromise, and complacency. These Americans will once again prove that "dreaming big" is a unique gift in a unique setting that should not be squandered.

From the time that my ancestors began their journey from the ruins of slavery, to embracing the promises of the American Dream, the obligation to succeed for family and race was a priority. This attitude is evidenced with the successful matriculation from Black colleges during the late 1800s, the presence of Black-owned banks, and the proliferation of Black-owned businesses and farms. Success in these endeavors created a connected and empathetic Black middle class. The visibility and accessibility of this class within the segregated community granted an invaluable source of mentorship and encouragement to those who dreamed of one day earning their way to join them.

My parents' generation prepared us to succeed through the tumultuous transition of the '60s and '70s. We were taught to welcome head-to-head competition in every arena as opportunities were becoming available with the dismantling of institutional racism. Their generation was bolstered by a sense of mission to improve our country, raise their own status, and the stature of their children. They proved that regardless of the obstacles, it was impossible to close the doorway to the American Dream if you arrive prepared with a vision, tenacity, and the will to fight. These components represent the combination that opens the door for all. Generationally, every race and culture, over the last two hundred years that have applied this combination left their children with more hope, more opportunities, and better prepared to succeed than they were.

As we enter a new millennium, it is important to compare the strides the coming generation is making compared to all previous ones. This progress is best measured by our latest generation's ability to envision their pathway to success and their preparation to work and fight for its achievement.

If this is indeed the measurement baseline, the conclusion by any honest observer is that the bright torch of hope and gratitude passed to previous generations has not been dutifully passed to the present. The children of the millennial generation, unlike those in the past, have not been taught the vision, courage, and faith-based history of our own Judeo-Christian country. They have not been taught about our own economic system of free enterprise, a system founded on maximized freedom for the individual, driven by faith, dreams, risk, overcoming, and unlimited reward. Most importantly, they have not been taught to appreciate the meaning of the American Way worldwide and the sacrifice by millions to make it so. Built with the blood, sweat, and tears of individuals of every color, creed, religion, and background, this American Way is defined in the first three words of our Constitution—*We the People*.

The failure to teach to our children the essence of our American Way has allowed a crack for the insidious seed of Socialism/Marxism to take root. This seed of hopelessness has blossomed for over sixty years in the urban community. It has left millions of Black Americans rudderless and its "at risk" communities stranded, isolated, and dispirited. An analogy that best highlights the nature of the Socialist/Marxist ideology is that of the crab grass weed. The germination of this destructive weed begins with the blossoming of a deceptively attractive yellow flower. It is a plant that has an allelopathic effect, releasing a toxin that suppresses the growth of other plants. The dense mat that crabgrass forms can also smother nearby grass plants. This weed's infestation doesn't happen overnight, as is also the case in getting rid of it. It grows all season, spring through fall, with new plant growth, developing seed heads, and mature seeds present on a plant throughout the warm seasons. Mowing it won't stop it or slow it down. It will grow flatter, rather than upright and will continue to produce seeds, week after week, until you kill it or cold weather arrives. Getting rid of the plant after it dies is just as important as killing the weed. Timely removal may allow your lawn to recover.[454]

Following through with this analogy, to uproot and end the spreading of the evil weed of Socialism/Marxism, it will be imperative to identify it by its deceptively attractive flower. The herbicide that will end its spreading is granting Americans the freedom to shop elsewhere. The institutions that have been infiltrated and are now being used to attack our freedoms are education and entertainment. As seen with the rejection of the NFL during the 2017 season by a previously loyal fan base, "We The People" will respond appropriately once we realize we're under attack.

The NFL leadership's decision to side with Anti-American/Anti-flag demonstrations signaled that we are indeed under attack. As millions of Americans know they have the option to shop elsewhere for their entertainment, millions of parents should have that same freedom to shop for their children's education. Freedom of choice in a free market is at the core of our America way. Choosing to support our valued God, family, and freedom will signal the end of mandates from the Leftist Socialist/Marxists.

Ironically, as we've failed to teach our own children our American Way of life, there are millions around the world who have an appreciation for our

---

454   "Getting Rid of Crab Grass." The Garden Counselor, n.d. garden-counselor-lawn-care.com/getting-rid-of-crab-grass.html.

light of freedom that many within our own country do not. Though many new legal American immigrants have difficulty conversing in their new English language, they can easily translate the pride within their hearts for the blessing of acceptance as an American.

It was courage that once cleared the pathway for great pioneers like Booker T. Washington, Jackie Robinson, James Meredith, and Martin Luther King, Jr. It will once again be courage that will bring the necessary change to the Black community. There will continue to be the status quo misery profiteers. These are those of the Royalty Black Class who will continue to seek wealth, power, and prestige in the glow of status quo. Change is difficult and will take courage, dictating a willingness to stand alone when necessary, exhibiting boldness when challenged, humbly seeking enlightenment and wisdom when needed, and using common sense to defeat the ideological enemy.

Freedom and Critical Thinking

On the national level, Democrats typically get around ninety percent of the Black vote, even when a Black man isn't running for president as a Democrat. Al Gore got ninety-two percent of the Black vote in 2000; John Kerry got eighty-eight percent in 2004.[455]

In an era of technology that allows for unlimited, unfettered, 24/7 access to information, it can only be deemed as an egregious insult to all past generations that a race comprised of forty million individuals will allow themselves to be trained to be a predictable and thoughtless monolithic voting body. With its vast diversity of experiences and backgrounds, educational and financial status, entrepreneurial and entertainment success, corporate and government experiences, genders, ages, religious preferences, and social ideologies, how can this broad and diverse community be reduced to a body that predictably thinks and votes with their skin color? Capitalist and Communist, Christians and atheists, Pro-Life and Pro-Death, Black American Patriots and Black Lives Matter Socialists all voting for the exact same representation?

There is a question that must be posed to Black Americans who still deem "respect" as an important component of relationships. How does negating all core principals and any pretense of an independent, critical thinking mindset to vote as a predictable ninety percent "I don't care about policy" bloc...get you there?

This predictable voting activity that jettisons all pretense of accountability has resulted in over decades of rule over poor urban communities by Democratic Royalty Class Black elitists. They have ruled, with no shame, diametrically

---

455   Peter Kirsanow. "Blacks, Democrats, and Republicans." National Review. March 15, 2011, Online edition, sec. The Corner. nationalreview.com/blog/corner/Blacks-democrats-and-republicans-peter-kirsanow.

opposed to the core values and principles held by most Americans, Black and White. The acceptance of this "Black groupthink" approach to supporting professional politicians has prevented the poor urban Michigan community, overseen by Black Congressional Elitist John Conyers, from experiencing new thoughts, fresh ideas, and creative approaches for *fifty-four years!* A fifty-four year continuity of empathy-free Black Democratic leadership that, like a wealthy and powerful plantation overseer, has seen three generations of poor Black Americans live, suffer, and die in urban sprawl and misery. The career of the Royalty Class Black politician is represented by the one word that describes the longevity of this eighty-eight-year-old Socialist and alleged sexual predator, John Conyers...*forever!* For many in this elitist Black Congressional group, the only obstacle preventing them from also retiring at ninety years old are charges before the Congressional Ethics Committee or felony sentencing for greed, fraud, or sexual impropriety. Unfortunately, being voted out of office is not one of them.

Imagine if members of the Royalty Congressional Black Congress would put together a proclamation expressing their most sincere thoughts of the poor, uneducated, unemployed, and hopeless who predictably trust in them. It would read like this:

Why Work, Why Solve, and Why Oh Why Keep My Word?

Why work hard to find solutions for urban poor people when I can work easy, not find solutions, focus on popularity, and still get re-elected? Imagine, if you can, decades and decades of "easy," and having all the free time in the world to enjoy my awesome lifestyle and get into mischief. Imagine, if you can, a six-figure salary for simply giving angry speeches, voting in one-hundred percent compliance with my fellow caucus members, and proving to the rest of America that Black people do indeed think and vote with their skin. We are living proof. We are asked, as elections near, to be "on call" in case there is a need by our White Democratic leaders or big donors Planned Parenthood, to call any White American Racist and Black American Uncle Toms. Again, that is easy, since we've been on call for years.

We should note for the official record that we never knew just how beneficial our relationship with the public school unions would be in clinching our awesome lifestyle. By keeping our trusting community of poor Black folks uneducated and emotionally charged, they either won't take the time to read or can't read about our consistent votes against them. YES, as a unified bloc will vote (100 percent of the time) against Black jobs, Black education, Black entrepreneurship, and the lives of innocent Black babies.

Should there be any wonder why, during the 2018 State of the Union address, our faces showed anger, disappointment, and rage as President Donald Trump announced that Black unemployment had hit an historical all time low? How dare that White Republican negate a hopeful promise we've made and broken for decades?

Though it has been rough for millions of poor Black Americans, in the end it has all been worth it. We have, after all, been given a job worth keeping for our lifetime, and who knows, if our son or daughter has been named after us, maybe even for their lifetime.

Thank you, my poor peeps, for a wonderful, wonderful ride.

—This has been a "what if" proclamation on behalf of John Conyers, Elijah Cummings, John Lewis, Maxine Waters, and the remainder of the Democratic Congressional Black Caucus.

Remember the Socialist/Marxists' Mantra: "It All about Team... My Team (Not Yours)"

I continue to reflect occasionally on a 1981 Raiders-Browns playoff game when a nameless, shirtless Cleveland Browns Fan in sub-zero temperatures showed his commitment to pay the price of extreme discomfort for "the team." The team to whom his fanatical support was targeted took no notice and paid him no homage. Its focus and obligation that day and every other weekend would remain on the financial benefit of its players, coaches, team employees, and ultimately the team owners. Regardless of his enthusiasm and loyalty, this shirtless fan would remain a nameless statistic who, along with thousands of others, paid admission to encourage, prop-up, and to be the props for the performing well-paid professional athletes.

The question facing the Black community in this new millennium is how much more discomfort is it willing to endure for the sake of "the team"? Is it willing to continue its 90 percent blind allegiance to a failed game plan (Socialism/Marxism) by clueless and inept coaches (Congressional Black Caucus) who work for powerful, greedy, and self-centered owners (Democratic Party)? The results of this combination of characters are chronicled in every urban city throughout our nation. Statistics consistently show that where this strategy, coaches, and owners are, so is the misery of its population. It is at the cost of its own demise that the Black community continues to ignore the overwhelming data of this destructive team of ideologues. Because it is easier, less controversial, less confrontational, and assured to ruffle fewer feathers that it continues to accept misery that should not be justified.

At stake now is more than tradition, friendship, acceptance, job promotions, and business profits. We are once again at the crossroads similar to the founding of the NAACP in 1910. Awareness and actions now will ultimately determine the success and freedom of our race and country. Unfortunately, there will always be those within our community, the Royalty Class Black man, whose loyalty will be to their dark ideology, their elitist class, and to themselves. Thankfully, having survived a century long and steady assault by the Left, a vast majority of Black Americans still subscribe to their Judeo-Christian values. These values drive their priority for the freedom of *all* children to have access to a quality education, for the health and wellbeing of their babies, both unborn and newborn, and for policies that support the success of the God defined nuclear family...*One man and one woman in marriage, an equal partnership faithfully committed to the care and nurturing of their children.*

There is an overwhelming majority within the Black community who desire to recapture the ideals of a traditional nuclear family, where moms and dads commit to each other and to their children through the eternal bonds of marriage. It is in this environment where dreams and goals are fostered and where work ethic and dedication to achieve them are taught. It is here where fathers find their greatest opportunity to teach service to his family as their provider and protector. He gives his wife and children a sense of security through his leadership and vision. This is also the environment where mothers place their imprint on our nation as they nurture ideals for future generations. As partners and helpmates, this team gives to our children the best examples of imperfect people doing their best to be better. It is within this family unit where the eternal law of Seed and Harvest is cultivated and blossoms into our greatest legacies. It is the greatest legacy that is now under attack within the Black community...the love, respect, and honor of womanhood. It is the commitment to this one legacy, which is taught within the home by a loving, loyal, and committed father, that will clear the pathway for the resurrection of the Black community.

> *"...a nation will rise no higher than the strength of its homes. If you want to reform a nation, you begin with families, with parents who teach their children principles and values that are positive and affirmative and will lead them to worthwhile endeavors. That is the basic failure that has taken place in America...parents have no greater responsibility in this world than the bringing up of their children in the right way...."*
>
> —President Gordon B. Hinckley, The Church of Jesus Christ of Latter Day Saints

For this path to be taken, it will be necessary for courageous action and bold voices. The Black community must refuse to continue to be props for the Royalty Class Black man and the party that they are ultimately more loyal to. It must once again commit, as it did during early 1900s, to fight the demeaning racist stereotypes of that day. Those same stereotypes are being streamed electronically by wealthy White Democrats, owners of the façade called (BET) Black Entertainment Television.

A Good Friend Called Failure

These are the times for the Black community to reflect. Time to reflect on our purpose, goals, dreams, and the future of our families. Time to reflect, respect, and emulate the success of other races and cultures now experiencing the American Dream and who exemplify communities where the concept of "high tides raise all ships" is real. Time to reflect on an eternal truth that "high tides" does not singularly denote financial success, but also represents a benchmark for the building of men and women with vision and families with character.

Most important, it is time to reflect on the many lessons learned through failure; for it is failure that is a source of future insight and wisdom. It is also failure that could potentially be our best friend if, once formally introduced, we don't quit.

> *"The credit belongs to the man who is actually in the arena: whose face is marred by dust and sweat and blood: who strives valiantly: who errs and comes short again and again: who knows the great enthusiasms, the great devotions, and spends himself in a worthy cause; who at the best knows in the end the triumph of high achievement; and who at the worst, if he fails, at least fails while daring greatly."*
>
> —*Theodore Roosevelt*

Don't Ever Quit

- Patience, diligence, tenacity, and faith are all learned through failure.
- Lessons learned climbing out of our deepest valleys bring clarity and gratitude as we gaze from a much wiser mountaintop perspective.
- Lessons learned cumulatively as individuals can multiply to the benefit of an entire community, an entire race, and an entire country.
- The road is tough, and the path is steep, but with guidance, protection, and encouragement from a loving Heavenly Father, all things are possible.
- The Black community's greatest enemy is the gullibility and cowardice of groupthink. It is through critical thinking and making individual decision—not just based on skin color—that we find our common courage.
- Embrace the courage to commit to the nuclear family and to moral, principled actions that take a stand against status quo.
- Have the courage and awareness to strengthen our vision so that we may see through life's occasional dark obstacles.
- Embody the courage to faithfully open a different playbook, choose new coaches, and don the colors and logo of a different team.

CHAPTER 24

BLACK AMERICAN CONSERVATIVES: AMERICA'S FREEDOM SENTINELS

Why I Stand: From Freedom to the Killing Field of Socialism highlights the period during which the Black community stood at the same crossroad as our nation does today. Due to the path chosen during the early 1900s, the Black American community has paid dearly in loss of lives, souls, hopes, and dreams. Its century-long sacrifice can only be deemed worthwhile if our nation learns from its journey and chooses not to duplicate its mistake.

Allowing the planting of the seeds of Socialism/Marxism within its once proud, entrepreneurial, and Christian community in 1910 was a game changer. The consequence of this parasitic ideology can now be seen within every community where it resides. The urban communities of Detroit, Oakland, Philadelphia, Ferguson, and others stand as a warning beacon to our nation. Coming from within those same communities are Freedom Sentinels, willing to do battle for the hearts and minds of all freedom-loving Americans. These Black American conservatives understand that our nation cannot afford to lose more ground. They have also proven that above popularity and acceptance, they love freedom more.

The pioneer Black conservatives listed below, and many others throughout our country, deserve our thanks and our free market vote. We do so as we read and promote their books, listen to their shows, buy from their businesses and advertisers, and support their efforts to spread the message of conservatism. They are political free agents who are issue-driven, diverse, and fiercely independent in their views, solutions, and political preferences. As individuals, they are driven by diverse and independent thought, yet there is a guaranteed consensus among them—their love and appreciation for America and the liberty it embodies.

From its visionary beginning...

"It has been the American Way that maintains that freedom is a birthright. It is a nation that represents a perpetual source of hope for every seeking soul...those within its free borders, and those around the world dreaming to be."

Give Them Your Support

Deneen Borelli	Website: deneenborelli.com Book: *Blacklash: How Obama and the Left Are Driving Americans to the Government Plantation*
Curtis Bennett	Website: theoriginalradicals.org Books: *The Spartan Directive* and *The Conservative Prodigy*
Jennifer Carroll	Website: JenniferCarroll.com Social Media: @MrsJSCarroll Book information: *When You Get There* (autobiography) -Former Lieutenant Governor for the State of Florida
Larry Elder	Website: larryelder.com Book: *Dear Father, Dear Son: Two Lives...Eight Hours*
Harris Faulkner	Website: harrisfaulkner.com/publicity.html Book: *Breaking News: God Has a Plan: An Anchorwoman's Journey Through Faith*
Alveda King	Website: alvedakingministries.com Book: *King Rules: Ten Truths for You, Your Family, and Our Nation to Prosper*
C.L Bryant	Website: theclbryantshow.com Documentary: Run Away Slave - runawayslavemovie.com Book: A Race for Freedom
Kevin Jackson	Website: theblacksphere.net/radio/ Facebook: @TheBlackSphereRadioShow Book: Race Pimping: The Multi-Trillion Dollar Business of Liberalism
Rev. Jesse Lee Peterson	Book: The Antidote: Healing America from the Poison of Hate, Blame and Victimhood

Star Parker	Website: urbancure.org Book: White Ghetto: How Middle Class America Reflects Inner City Decay
Lonnie Poindexter	Website: urbanfamilytalk.com/radio-programs/lion-chasers-with-lonnie-poindexter
Jason Riley	Website: jasonrileyonline.com Book: Please Stop Helping Us: How Liberals Make It Harder for Blacks to Succeed Book: Let Them In: The Case for Open Borders
Dr. Carol Swain	Website: carolmswain.net/about/ Book: Abduction: How Liberalism Steals Our Children's Hearts and Minds. Be the People: A Call to Reclaim America's Faith and Promise
David Webb	Website: http://davidwebbshow.com/
Allen West	Website: allenbwest.com Book: Guardian of the Republic: An American Ronin 's Journey to Faith, Family and Freedom
Armstrong Williams	Website: armstrongwilliams.com Book: Reawakening Virtues: Restoring What Makes America Great

CONCLUSION

"The foundation of our national policy will be laid in the pure and immutable principles of private morality...the propitious smiles of Heaven can never be expected from a nation that disregards the eternal rules of order and right which Heaven itself has ordained."

—George Washington, First Inaugural Speech (April 30, 1789)

It is my prayer that America, with clarity, embraces the courage necessary to choose the right path at this critical time in history. Our journey as a nation thus far has allowed us to blend our diverse cultures into a united America. Ours is a culture that has improved every generation in its ability to view everyone the way God does...from inside out, not outside in. Ours is the country whose vision embodies the ideals of freedom, allowing the individual to pursue his or her own happiness, dreaming outside the barriers of past or present obstacles. Ours is the country that stands unique among all the world's societies because it was not founded on We the Blacks, We the Whites, We the Christians, We the Jews, We the Muslims, We the Buddhists, We the old, We the young, We the rich, or We the poor...but inspired of a game-breaking concept of We the People. Though diverse and different, through the power of unity and adherence to concrete core beliefs, we have found the common thread that defines the American Way.

A unified We the People will fulfill America's calling to be the proverbial shining city upon a hill whose beacon light guides freedom-loving people everywhere.[456] As we continue to fight as unified individuals, families, and communities to incorporate the principles that insulate us from the soul-destructive ideologies discussed throughout this book, we will experience

---

456 "America Is a Shining City upon a Hill." SourceWatch. The Center for Media and Democracy, December 6, 2013. sourcewatch.org/index.php/America_is_a_shining_city_upon_a_hill.

the vision once spoken by Martin Luther King, Jr. It was a vision that saw the promises of our founding fathers fulfilled...

"Free at last, free at last! Thank God Almighty, we're free at last!"

Addendum Page: The Congressional Black Caucus

Senate		
Senator	Party	State
Cory Booker	Democratic	New Jersey
Kamala Harris	Democratic	California

House Representative	Party	State – Congressional District
Alma Adams	Democratic	North Carolina – 12th
Karen Bass	Democratic	California – 37th
Joyce Beatty	Democratic	Ohio – 3rd
Sanford Bishop	Democratic	Georgia – 2nd
Lisa Blunt Rochester	Democratic	Delaware – At-large
Anthony Brown	Democratic	Maryland – 4th
G. K. Butterfield	Democratic	North Carolina – 1st
André Carson	Democratic	Indiana – 7th
Yvette Clarke	Democratic	New York – 9th
William Lacy Clay Jr.	Democratic	Missouri – 1st
Emanuel Cleaver	Democratic	Missouri – 5th
Jim Clyburn	Democratic	South Carolina – 6th
*John Conyers – *Dean*	Democratic	Michigan – 13th
Elijah Cummings	Democratic	Maryland – 7th
Danny Davis	Democratic	Illinois – 7th
Val Demings	Democratic	Florida – 10th
Keith Ellison	Democratic	Minnesota – 5th
Dwight Evans	Democratic	Pennsylvania – 2nd
Marcia Fudge	Democratic	Ohio – 11th
Al Green	Democratic	Texas – 9th
*Alcee Hastings	Democratic	Florida – 20th
Hakeem Jeffries	Democratic	New York – 8th
Eddie Bernice Johnson	Democratic	Texas – 30th
Hank Johnson	Democratic	Georgia – 4th

Robin Kelly	Democratic	Illinois – 2nd
Brenda Lawrence	Democratic	Michigan – 14th
Al Lawson	Democratic	Florida – 5th
Barbara Lee	Democratic	California – 13th
Sheila Jackson Lee	Democratic	Texas – 18th
John Lewis	Democratic	Georgia – 5th
Mia Love	Republican	Utah – 4th
Donald McEachin	Democratic	Virginia – 4th
*Gregory Meeks	Democratic	New York – 5th
*Gwen Moore	Democratic	Wisconsin – 4th
Eleanor Norton	Democratic	District of Columbia – At-large
Donald Payne Jr.	Democratic	New Jersey – 10th
Stacey Plaskett	Democratic	U.S. Virgin Islands – At-large
Cedric Richmond	Democratic	Louisiana – 2nd
Bobby Rush	Democratic	Illinois – 1st
Bobby Scott	Democratic	Virginia – 3rd
David Scott	Democratic	Georgia – 13th
Terri Sewell	Democratic	Alabama – 7th
Bennie Thompson	Democratic	Mississippi – 2nd
Marc Veasey	Democratic	Texas – 33rd
*Maxine Waters	Democratic	California – 43rd
Bonnie Coleman	Democratic	New Jersey – 12th
Frederica Wilson	Democratic	Florida – 24th

ACKNOWLEDGMENTS

Never have I been prouder to be an American than I am today. I'm blessed with a perspective that comes with time and a pride in country that comes with knowing our history. From the arrival to America of my great, great grandfather, Silas Burgess in the belly of a slave ship, to my upbringing in the deep segregated south, I have an acknowledgment of a proud ancestry that fought, struggled, overcame, succeeded, and with visionary diligence passed on the lessons they learned and the confidence they gained through that process.

In my formative years playing football, I experienced one of the more memorable moments while on the sideline looking anxiously at my coach with hopes of playing. I experienced my first nod. That "nod" came after years of preparation. It came after countless day-to-day decisions that I had made to not quit while pushing through pain and previous limits. It was a special nod, because it was a confirmation that it was finally my turn to join my teammates on the field of action...that they needed me, and that someone whom I respected had confidence that I could deliver.

We are blessed as Americans to be living during a time in world history when our country needs us, and our Heavenly Father has given us the Nod. It's a confirmation that our life lessons have been on purpose and personally designed, that our teammates need us, and more importantly that He has confidence that "We the People" can deliver. Regardless of our background, history, struggles, defeats, or self-doubts, we collectively have what it takes to pull His great nation back from the evil, dark abyss of Socialism and Marxism. We simply need to be willing to give our all. To serve more, give more, defend more, educate more, encourage more, and stand more boldly for all that is good.

As Americans we each add in our own special way to the beautiful tapestry of our nation. Some in bold, bright colors/patterns, others with almost indistinguishable threads that, just as valuable, connect and bind. The classic song, God Bless the USA by Lee Greenwood is a stroke of bold colors and patterns. It demands the attention of every American, regardless of our role, to take time to count his/her blessings. It's an acknowledgment that God is capable of touching each of our hearts in a special and uniquely personal way. All that is asked of us is two simple works Thank You. Let us stand with gratitude, appreciation, and a willingness to work, sacrifice, and serve each other. That is, after all, The American Way.

ABOUT THE AUTHOR

Burgess Owens spent his childhood growing up in the Deep South during a time when the barriers of segregation were being torn down. He was the third black American to be offered a football scholarship to the University of Miami. He earned a Bachelor of Science degree in biology/chemistry and simultaneously gained national recognition as a first team football All-American. During his college career, Burgess was named to Who's Who Among Students in American Universities & Colleges. He was inducted into the Hall of Fame of Outstanding College Athletes of America and later into the University of Miami's Hall of Fame and the Orange Bowl Ring of Honor. Following college, the New York Jets picked Burgess in the NFL first round as the draft's first defensive back, the 13th pick. Later that year he was selected as the Jets Rookie of the Year and to the NFL's All-Rookie team. He played with the New York Jets for seven years and was selected as the defensive team captain his last three seasons. After being traded to the Oakland Raiders, Burgess led the Raiders defensive squad in tackles during their championship season and in the 1981 Super Bowl XV game. In his final season in 1982, he led the Raider's team in interceptions and was selected as a first alternate to the NFL Pro Bowl. Since retiring from the NFL, Burgess has been involved in the corporate and entrepreneurial arenas. Over the last decade he has traveled throughout the country speaking of the intrinsic principles of freedom that underlie the foundation of our American way of life.

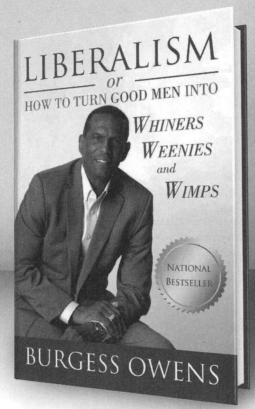